A Beginner's Guide

to

Secondhand Bookdealing

ACKNOWLEDGEMENTS

I would like to thank Gina Dolan of the PBFA, Peter Miller of Ken Spelman (York), Peter Moore of the PBFA and Cambridge, and Barry Shaw of the *Bookdealer*, for extensive reading of the text and for many helpful suggestions and corrections; Rupert Powell of Bloomsbury Book Auctions for help with chapter 3; Reg Peplow of Buckden, for help with chapter 7 and for plate 4; Mark Vera of Barclay's Bank for help with part II; Tony Cox of Claude Cox (Ipswich) for help with chapter 8; Eric Morten of Morten Books (Congleton), for writing the preface, much encouragement and for lending the originals of the frontispiece and plates 1 and 5, and Shirley Pryce for transporting the originals.

For part III I am particularly indebted to Michael Cole of the British Internet Bookdealers Centre (York), for allowing me to use much of his material, for reading the text, and for many valuable suggestions; also to Allan Edwards of Oxygen Limited for considerable help and guidance; and to Glyn Cheesman of CMX Computers Limited for allowing the use of material in their *Client Communiques*.

Thanks also to Tony Swann of Wheldon and Wesley Limited, for permission to use material on their website; to Professor Kraig Adler of Cornell University, USA, for text-figure 1; to Bill Goodall of Great Totham, for text-figure 2; to the Essex Chronicle for permission to reproduce plate 3; to Dover Publications Inc. for permission to reproduce the chapter 9 tailpiece; to the Open University as authors and publishers of the *1999/2000 Guide to Courses Book*, for permission to quote from this in chapter 18; to Ivan Rush, formerly of the University of East London, for many stimulating discussions over the years and for permission to use material from our joint *Business Planning Guide;* to Tony Fothergill of Ken Spelman (York), manager of the PBFA September Book-fair in York, for allowing the book launch there, and to Janette Ray of Janette Ray Rare Books (York) for help with publicity.

Finally I would like to thank my wife Pam for encouragement and support during the eight months of evenings and weekends it has taken to write and prepare this for the printers, and for her tolerance in letting me get away with doing no gardening or household jobs for this period.

Frontispiece. *Anatomy of an Antiquarian Bookseller.*
Copyright © Ronald Searle 1976

A Beginner's Guide

to

Secondhand Bookdealing

by

Stuart A Baldwin BSc(Open), FGS, FLS

September 1999

Also by the same author and publisher:

Dinosaurs and their Relatives Project Pack for Schools. 1983

The Cardioceratidae, with John Callomon. 1985

John Ray (1627-1705) Essex Naturalist. 1986

Dinosaur Stamps of the World, with Beverly Halstead. 1991

First published in Great Britain in September, 1999 by Stuart Baldwin
Fossil Hall, Boars Tye Road, Silver End, Witham, Essex, CM8 3QA
Tel: +44 01376 583502 Fax: +44 01376 585960
http://www.secondhandsciencebooks.com
E-mail: sbaldwin@fossilbooks.co.uk

First impression
1,000 copies

British Library Cataloguing in Publication Data:
A catalogue record for this book is available from the British Library

ISBN 0 9508063 5 8

1 3 5 7 9 10 8 6 4 2

Printed in Great Britain by
The Book Company, Ipswich, Suffolk, IP4 1DD

CONTENTS

LIST OF ILLUSTRATIONS

PREFACE

This is probably the hardest preface anyone in the trade could ever write. First the title gave me a scare and so did the idea of tailpieces, but as I read on I began to mellow - Stuart Baldwin has done a marvellous job writing on this vast subject.

The author has analysed, diluted and redefined section after section: buying, selling, the internet, book-fairs, book-stalls, book-running - and a multiplicity of places to offer your wares. Ideas have flown from his mind, catalogues, lists and private quotes come into his methodology for the trading of the book.

Money is no small feature of this work - get to know your bank manager, build up his faith in you, and never run away from a letter (it could contain a cheque), bank managers look on evasion as a sign of fright. Business plans, on which the author places much emphasis, help you along the unlevel path; it's all in here.

Remember, (yes you have to have a good memory) that intuition, intuition, and intuition, are three of the main points, along with bibliography, that turn the key to success, and success into money.

Aspiring booksellers will enjoy this book even if they only realise that bookselling is very hard work and needs undivided attention and concentration; but then so do castles on the beach, so enjoy your bookselling - it can become a lifetime's holiday. Read the book and become successful.

Eric J Morten

FOREWORD

This work is intended for a wide range of people extending from complete beginners through to experienced bookdealers. Beginners may find the depth of detail rather daunting at first, particularly if they are new to computing and the internet, whilst those with experience should still find much of interest. It is hoped that this will be looked upon as a manual or text book, to be dipped into as required according to your needs and aspirations.

Whether you are just going to dabble in books by working from home as a part-time occupation, combined with selling at the occasional book-fair, or you are seriously aiming to become a whole-time high flyer and make your mark in the world of books, there is guidance for you in here. If your exact needs are not catered for, then many pointers are given to other sources of help and information.

What ever else you do, if you are going into business, you must learn, remember, and act upon the single most important message in this book: **you must carry out cashflow forecasting and budgetary control to ensure liquidity and financial survival,** as explained in part II. Businesses that do not carry out these simple operations are far less likely to survive than those that do.

Most of the writing is based upon experiences within the UK; however, because of the nature of the secondhand book trade, and the universal principles underlying business success, it is estimated that over 90% of the material will apply wherever English is read and spoken, from Australia to the United States of America.

The world of bookdealing is very friendly and hugely enjoyable; it differs significantly from many other businesses as you will see later; welcome to it, and may it change your life for the better as it has done mine.

INTRODUCTION

Over the years there have been a large number of books written and published for lovers and collectors of books, from the *Philobiblon* of Richard de Bury completed in 1344, to the delightful writings of Percy H Muir 600 years later, such as his *Book-Collecting as a Hobby*, 1944, and beyond. There is much that can be learned about books from these and other works, but in some 63 years of book collecting and 30 years of dealing in secondhand and antiquarian books I have found very little of a practical nature on the detail of how to start and run a successful business dealing in such books. This work is an attempt to redress the imbalance.

How then did I get into bookdealing? At the relatively late starting age of 27 I discovered that collecting fossils was fun. Over a ten-year period I built up a private collection of over 100,000 specimens from the cliffs, quarries and road cuttings of southern England. (Next time you go to the Natural History Museum in London, look at the dinosaur galleries and you might spot a dinosaur skull - *Iguanodon*, I collected in those days). I joined various societies connected with geology and palaeontology and soon became known as a keen amateur collector. In 1969 I received an invitation that was to change my life - I was asked to exhibit fossils at a meeting of Teachers of Geology at Keele University. I was naturally flattered and delighted to be asked, loaded up my car with several hundredweight of my best specimens and trundled up the motorway to the meeting. When I arrived I was given a large table for my display, and after setting up with everything beautifully labelled, the table had a distinct dip in the middle under the weight of specimens.

The teachers then started to arrive and I soon discovered to my horror that they were short of good teaching material and wanted to buy my specimens. I had not been briefed on this point and didn't want to part with my fossils which had cost much blood and sweat (no tears), to collect. However one particular exhibit showing an evolutionary sequence of the Cretaceous sea-urchin *Micraster* attracted more attention than all the rest put together. (*Micraster* was famous as an example of gradualism in evolution). Something in the little grey cells stirred, inspiration struck and I asked the teachers if they would like a set of replicas showing the evolution of *Micraster*. Many answered 'yes,' placed orders and put their names and addresses on a piece of paper which I very kindly provided for them.

Two years of spare-time research and development followed, resulting in a small one-page catalogue of replicas being produced in 1971.

Success was instantaneous, orders poured in, the garden shed was no longer big enough and a larger house was needed and moved to. More products were added and the new house was soon full. An extension was needed. Planning permission was obtained for a large granny-flat attached to the house. The cost in those days was £10,000 (About £50,000 in today's money), and the problem was how to finance it. I approached my bank and they were prepared to lend me half. I looked at my library and after much soul searching decided that certain parts of it could go. I listed the books, sent a notice to the various societies I belonged to and within a few weeks I had sold enough. Part-time working (whilst doing a full-time job during the day), continued for a few years until the volume of orders was such that I resigned from my day job in 1981 to concentrate on my hobby.

Though the fossil replica business went on expanding and ultimately became the world's largest in a specialist field with over 2,000 products - it would need another book to give the full story. This then was my introduction to selling secondhand books and it didn't take long for me to realise that I could also buy books for resale. The book business and the fossil business developed in parallel for the next 25 years when the fossil business, and associated museum, were sold as a going concern to my major customer - The Open University. (About a million replicas were produced during that time).

I have been able to devote the last few years entirely to dealing in books, mainly to be able to add to my own collection which started with the first Rupert annual in 1936. Though still a great Rupert fan, where my interests lie can be deduced from my shop name: Fossil Hall, my house name: *Fossilis* and my car registration number: FOS 51L. As this seems to be a personal statement perhaps I should mention that hopefully my epitaph will read: *He devoted his life to fossils and is now doing his best to become one.*

The major aims of this book are to make money for the author-publisher (so he can buy even more books for his library); to show you how to do the same through buying and selling secondhand and antiquarian books, and to pass on some business experience accumulated in over 50 years.

It is aimed at:

▸ The many thousands who, over the years have asked questions such as: 'How do I get into secondhand and antiquarian bookdealing?' and 'Where do I get stock from?' (From here on the word antiquarian will mainly be taken as read to save repetition).

▸ Those who have always liked books, are probably collectors, currently have a full or part-time job, would like to get out of the rat-race, and would like to run a spare-time book business during their evenings and weekends, with a possible ultimate objective of making it a full-time source of income, i.e. converting a hobby into a business.

▸ Those who have been or are about to be made redundant or have taken or been offered a chance of early retirement, and would like to put their nest egg to profitable use to maintain or improve their standard of living, and to give them an additional interest in life, or to avoid stagnation.

▸ Those, such as the currently unemployed, who would like to learn how to conduct a business that is easy to get into, can be built up gradually without significant risk, is fun to run, need not involve too much initial outlay of capital, and would like to learn how to present a case to a bank or other lender, for finance.

▸ Those already dealing in secondhand books who would like to know more about the possible effects of computers and the internet on their business and future. e.g. E-mail, websites, and world wide book databases.

▸ Managerial staff of large bookshops who wish to train staff or run induction courses for them in secondhand bookdealing.

▸ Those who have only recently started in secondhand bookdealing, are still on a learning curve and would like to accelerate the process.

▸ Those already dealing in new books, e.g. in a shop, who would like to expand into the secondhand market but lack the necessary expertise or know-how.

▸ Book collectors and others, e.g. students and staff of business schools, who wish to know how the secondhand book trade operates, as much information here has never previously been published.

▸ Anyone wishing to start a small business, as many of the general principles involved are covered, especially business planning.

The specific objectives of this book are:

▸ To provide you with the necessary information enabling you to start and run a potentially profitable secondhand book business.

▸ To outline and comment on the various options open to you as a secondhand bookdealer. (Chapter 1).

▸ To ensure that you understand the marketing implications of the business that you will be in. (Chapter 2).

- To indicate some of the main sources of stock. (Chapter 3).
- To explain the principles and practice of pricing books. (Chapter. 4).
- To provide detail on selling at book-fairs. (Chapter 5).
- To provide detail on catalogue bookselling. (Chapter 6).
- To indicate some of the ways in which you can publicise yourself and your business. (Chapter 7).
- To provide data on some trade organisations, publications, periodicals and reference works. (Chapter 8).
- To show how to carry out very simple book repairs. (Chapter 9).
- To show you how to prepare, use, and update a business plan as the most important document in your business life. (Part II).
- To show you how to present a case for finance to bank managers and other sources of loans. (Chapter 11).
- To outline the significance, importance, and use of computers and the internet, to secondhand book businesses. (Part III).
- To provide you with information on sources of help and information. (Appendix).
- To provide you with a unique stock item that should generate significant cashflow and profit for you. (This book).
- Hopefully to amuse and entertain you and to provide a document of possible future historical interest in that it records one person's views at the end of the second millennium.

TAILPIECE

With the fossil replica business, I farmed out most of the production to a small army of local housewives as out-workers. They would be supplied with silicone rubber moulds, the necessary equipment and various plaster mixes. The replicas would be made in their kitchens and then dried in their airing cupboards before packing for me to collect.

In one of my early encounters with the media, the BBC Radio programme 'Woman's Hour' got to hear of this and sent a lady reporter to investigate. I explained the set up to the reporter and into her tape recorder, and then took her to see Mrs Ruth Fisher - my star out-worker. Recording all the time, she was taken through the manufacturing and drying process by Ruth. The reporter then asked if there were ever any problems. Ruth replied: 'Well occasionally we do get airing cupboard mix-ups and my husband complains of *trilobites in his underpants.*'

If I ever write the history of that business, there is a ready-made title.

Stuart A Baldwin, Witham, September 1999

PART I

SECONDHAND

AND

ANTIQUARIAN

BOOKDEALING

CHAPTER 1

BUSINESS OPTIONS

INTRODUCTION

In looking at the options available to you as a bookdealer there are three main considerations: What **premises** you are planning to use - which is strongly linked to the **type of operation** you have in mind; and what kinds of **stock** you intend to deal in. There are no hard and fast rules here, it is up to you to choose the combinations best suited to you and your circumstances. e.g. My type of operation includes six of the first seven categories below, and my book stock, all categories except modern first editions, miniature books and private press.

There is a fourth element in starting - the **timescale.** Though you may be currently employed, or redundant, one of the advantages of dealing in secondhand books is that it is very easy to enter the business gradually on a part-time basis by working during evenings and/or weekends without much risk. From your present income, redundancy payment or golden handshake you can gradually purchase stock for those week-end book-fairs, your first catalogue or for the internet. Once you have tested the water you will then have some of the necessary experience needed to make a decision either to continue on a part-time basis, or to go whole-time. Having done just this from home while working for IBM during the day I can assure you that it is a very viable option.

PREMISES / TYPE OF OPERATION
Working from Home.

Many start by working from home, often on a part-time or evening basis whilst they are building up stock, knowledge and a customer base, and perhaps whilst doing a full or part-time job concurrently.

This has the advantage that it enables you to get your toe in the water without too much risk or chancing getting your fingers badly burnt. You have the advantage of low overheads, legitimate expenses such as the use of rooms as an office or for stock, which you can offset against tax; zero time and expenses for travelling to work and the ability to claim the business proportion of your rates, electricity, telephone, heating and other expenses. It is also easy to start from a small beginning and build up gradually.

The disadvantages are that you may be breaking a covenant on your house not to use it for business purposes, and you technically need planning permission, though many do not apply and as long as there are not a flood of visitors or delivery vehicles which may cause a nuisance to neighbours you could well keep out of trouble. A few discreet enquiries in advance from your local planning office, Enterprise Agency, or Business Shop, could give you some guidance. One of the major disadvantages is that you do not have a showcase for your stock or passing trade as you would have with a shop. You therefore have to consider some of the other options as well.

From the insurance point of view, if you are operating from a house owned or rented by yourself, it is vital to inform your insurance company of your circumstances, your stock value and the expected number of visitors, etc. If you do not do this and are involved in a claim either on your business or on your house then the insurance company may invalidate any claim. If your house is being used for business purposes, you may have to consider the possibilities of being charged business rates.

In addition, if you operate from home on a long-term basis and you claim a considerable proportion of the use of your house on the business, then if you come to sell your house later, you could be liable to capital gains tax if the house has appreciated considerably in value in the meantime. This is something to discuss with an accountant at the planning stage.

With this type of operation and indeed with all, it is important to publicise yourself by getting your details into the appropriate directories and local bookdealer lists as described later in chapter 7 on 'Publicity'.

Book-fairs and Specialist Exhibitions

A separate chapter is devoted to these as they are one of the easier options to combine with working from home. (Chapter 5).

Catalogue Bookselling

As this is one of the major methods used by many bookdealers, a long, detailed separate chapter has been devoted to the detail of this modus operandi. (Chapter 6).

The Internet

As you will see in part III, the advent of the internet is having a particularly significant effect on the whole of the book trade both for new and secondhand books. Book collectors and dealers are able to look at some 12 to 15 million books on a relatively few major databases such as Antiquarian Book Exchange, Bibliocity, Amazon.com, etc., and on many thousands of websites throughout the world. Whether you operate from home or other premises or a combination of these, it is relatively easy to set up a cataloguing database on a computer, enter your books and get them put on to one of the major databases without the need to meet or speak to customers. Despite this, I feel that book-fairs, catalogue bookselling, and shops, are likely to continue for a long time to come.

Renting Space

i. Permanent shelving as a showcase in premises elsewhere.

It is possible to rent one or more bays of shelves in a wide variety of locations ranging from a local antique centre to specialist book arcades in the centre of a major town. These should be looked at very carefully before committing yourself and this is one of the occasions where I would strongly recommend the services of a solicitor or lawyer, or your trade association, to check out any agreement beforehand. You need to check its suitability for your type of stock by a personal visit and its legal implications. In addition, speak to as many dealers using the service as you can to get their experiences which will enable you to modify or form your own opinions.

ii. Storage space.

As you become more successful in your purchasing, the time may come when you can no longer pile up books in passages, your back rooms are full, the garage is overflowing, the toilet has a large extra supply of paper (for use only in emergency of course), you can't move in the shop and you have to take action to avoid grinding to a halt. That big opportunity to purchase a large library has just arrived and you need more space. Even if you don't need extra space now, it is prudent planning to do a little research so that when the time does come you can act more quickly.

To find what is available locally check out your local papers for advertisements, and see one or more local estate agents who specialise in commercial properties. Alternatively see what local friends e.g. farmers, have to offer. Rates per square metre or square foot will differ widely in different parts of the country and in different parts of any one locality. It is up to you to research the market before taking the plunge. Your main requirements are likely to be proximity, dryness, accessibility, load-bearing floors, a power and light supply and hopefully shelving.

You may finish up with possibilities ranging from a disused church, the canteen from a local defunct factory, a barn, that spare room in an elderly relation's house, to a small purpose-built warehouse facility. Try to obtain a renewable lease sufficiently long to enable you sell the stock, yet not too short so that you will be faced with the problem of moving again. Your solicitor or lawyer will advise you here. You also have one other action to take - as you will see in part II, you have to add the monthly or quarterly rental to your cashflow forecast, plus rates and insurance.

Shop

In the right position a shop can have the advantage of good public visibility and an excellent passing trade. i.e. People passing and tourists who did not know you were there, may look in. The greatest advantage of a shop however is purchasing power based on trust. As you are in a fixed geographical position and are unable to run away, you have a built in guarantee of trust from the public compared with an anonymous advert in the local paper for someone wanting to buy books. Because of this you are likely to be offered far more books to buy by the general public than if you operated from home.

Once the word gets around that you pay good prices for books (and this doesn't just apply to a shop) then you will be offered an ever-increasing volume of material in a snowball effect. You will often be able to 'cherry-pick' those choice items of interest. This can of course lead to some disappointed members of the public as you will inevitably be offered items that you do not want and which you will have to decline. You can also take positive marketing actions to encourage visitors to a far greater extent than if you were working from home, e.g. advertising - locally and in professional journals related to your speciality, brochures in your local Tourist Information Centre, promotions, etc.

As most shops are away from the proprietor's residence, there is a slight advantage in that going home at the end of the day can enable you to get away from it all. This does not always follow however, as when you are self-employed there can often be homework in the form of daily and monthly accounts, completing your monthly cashflow forecast and comparing it with budgeted figures, that quarterly VAT return or simply data entry on your computer for that next catalogue. There is a social aspect to running a shop that is absent or partly absent from some other forms of operation. The advantage is that you come face to face with your customers, you can have conversations on a wide range of topics, you have a great opportunity of selling items related to their interests and you can learn a lot.

One of the main principles of good salesmanship is to know your subject and your stock and to be able to put this over to a customer in a helpful and friendly way. A good opener is to smile broadly and to offer a 'good morning' or 'good afternoon' in as bright and cheerful a manner as you can muster. This does work. As a young man I worked part-time in my father's pharmacy whilst at college and I never forgot what a lady said one day: *'It's so nice coming in here - you get such a friendly reception.'* I commend this to your attention. The next time you go to a book shop or book-fair try a small experiment: See how you feel when someone smiles and greets you like this and compare it with the impression given by someone who looks bored and doesn't even bother to look in your direction.

In general your overheads will be relatively high and consequently the break-even point before you start making a profit will be higher than with other methods of operation. A shop however can give you the extra turnover needed to cover this and more. All this should of course have been considered beforehand in the preparation of your business plan.

Hint. Whether you are operating from home or other premises it is likely that you will encourage people to come and look at your stock. One nice little touch that can make it more interesting for customers is to keep a visitors book. I have kept one since 1974 and ask special visitors, such as academics from overseas, to sign it and if possible to do a little sketch. This forms a valuable record of who has been, their address, the date, and their interests. Visitors like looking through to see if they know any of the other signatories and to scan the sketches. In June 1999 a professor and his wife from the USA who were interested in herpetology came for the first time and spent the whole day pulling items off the shelves. They then signed the book and produced the following delightful little sketch:

Text-figure 1   **Scale x 1**
Visitor's Book illustration by a herpetology customer.

Their only complaint on leaving was that they wished they had been before.

On the down side, a shop can be the most expensive way to start, with high initial set-up costs, with rent, and rates, staff to pay to be there during opening hours when you are not there and greater opportunities for theft than with some other types of operation. Insurance for staff and for public liability is mandatory. If you are on your own you are tied to the shop unless, as I do, you shut the shop when you are not there and encourage visitors to phone first to see when you are in.

A word of warning: before taking on a shop get your solicitor to check local plans for changing parking arrangements or roads near your intended premises. Visitors may be able to park now but are double yellow lines, a new bus lane, or 'no waiting' signs planned for the foreseeable future? These can be the death knell for the small high street shop. I know of one such I have been visiting for over 60 years and at my last visit I heard the sad news that because of new parking restrictions they were having to close.

In general it is recommended that you only take on a shop once you have had at least a year or two of experience of trading.

Remainder dealer

This does not exactly come under the remit of secondhand bookdealing *per se* but is included here as many secondhand dealers do stock and sell remainders as well, which are technically speaking new books.

Details of remainder wholesalers may be found in the appropriate editions of Sheppard's Directories for your country. There are about twelve in the UK. Contact them to go on their mailing lists or to ask their representatives to call, and you will receive periodical lists of the remainder books they have for sale. You will normally get dealer's discount off the quoted prices but may have to order a minimum value to get the best terms.

By this method many publishers sell off their remaindered stock very cheaply which means that you can sell new copies at far less that the original published price. If you are going to be a general dealer then you will have a very wide range of titles to choose from. If you are going to specialise then the choice will be narrower but it does give you an opportunity to stock up on particular titles.

Remainder exhibitions are held quite often where wholesalers will display forthcoming titles and take orders for them. If you are on their mailing lists you will be notified of such events, and they are also advertised in the trade press.

Antique Fairs

The organisation of antique fairs parallels that of book-fairs. Though the range of material available at antique fairs is extremely wide, it is fairly common to find one or more bookstalls at such events. Visitors to such fairs do not necessarily have books in their uppermost thoughts, but because of their frequency and accessibility this is an option to be considered. Details of fairs and their organisers may be found in trade publications such as the weekly *Antiques Trade Gazette* and *The Antique Dealer Newspaper* which is issued monthly.

Street Markets.

Almost every weekly town market has at least one stall selling secondhand and/or remaindered books. All you need is some stock and an appropriate stall that can be removed or dismantled easily. Stall spaces are mostly rented from the local authority and as market day is usually a hive of activity you have a guaranteed audience. Markets are associated with bargains so these type of book stall are more likely to stock books priced at the low end of the market.

In the Farringdon Road in east central London the famous barrows operated almost daily for many years until recently. (I remember visiting them first in the late 1940s). These were one of the highlights of any collector's visits to London as there was an eclectic range of both books and prices. Crowds would often form before opening time and when the tarpaulins were removed a horde of eager buyers would descend to search for bargains. I am not sure whether it was bureaucracy or proprietor decline that put an end to this. If it was the latter then here could be a golden opportunity for some entrepreneur to cash in on this long tradition.

Search Service and Running

There are a large number of firms who offer a service by searching for rare and out of print books. A search fee may be charged whether or not a book is found, though many firms do not charge. Major firms may issue regular wants bulletins to specialist dealers and often advertise in trade publications such as the *Bookdealer*. The market for search services is already fairly full, it needs extensive knowledge of the book world, involves a considerable amount of paperwork and is not an option that is recommended for an absolute beginner.

Running is an easier option as it only involves spotting low-priced books for sale in one location, notifying a relevant dealer of the details with a runner's mark up, and then buying them for him if the dealer is interested. If obvious bargains are seen at boot-fairs, fetes, local auctions, etc., then a runner can afford to purchase for subsequent profitable sale to the trade.

STOCK OPTIONS

If secondhand retail book and related businesses are classified by the kind of stock they hold then they can be conveniently divided into five main categories:

General Secondhand
Specialist Secondhand with some New
Specialist with some General Stock or vice versa
Secondhand with some Remainders

New Books plus Remainders with some Secondhand.

Hint. A bank manager commented to me once that he had had a lot of recent small business failures due to businesses having all their eggs in one basket. If you are going to be an ultimate specialist and concentrate on one type of book only e.g. cricket, or a particular author or time period, then be very sure that there is an adequate market. To begin with it is much better to spread yourself a little more widely by having several specialities combined with some general stock. This not only hedges your bets but provides a more viable proposition.

Alternatively stock can be divided in other ways:

Books

Antiquarian
Secondhand
Remainders
New
Review copies
Out-of-print
Fine Bindings
Modern First Editions
Special subjects
General
Hardbacks
Paperbacks
Ex-library
Miniature
Private Press

Other

Maps, prints, plates
Manuscripts & ephemera
Product or auction catalogues

It is up to you to decide which of these options you go for depending on your interests, specialities, and the amount of capital you have available.

RELATED SUPPLIES & SERVICES FOR THE TRADE

In addition to the above options you should be aware that there are suppliers of materials, equipment, and services to the book trade offering transparent film for books and dust jackets, leather cream and polish, book-cloth cleaner, book-fair shelving, repair and binding services, internet services, etc. These are often combined with one or more of the above options.

SUMMARY

Whatever options you select, there are a number of factors that are common to all: you must know your specialist subjects and be familiar with your stock; you have to have the stock to deal in - a topic that is covered in the next chapter, and you must be prepared to work long and hard. In addition it is recommended that in the early years you take as little from the business as possible and plough as much money back as you can.

TAILPIECE

As mentioned earlier, it has often been said that the first principle of salesmanship is to know your subject and your stock. Before you can get to this stage of applying this principle, there is another item that you have to sell first - yourself.

As an aid to doing this, a smile and a welcoming, friendly attitude are two of the most powerful marketing tools available to you. They cost absolutely nothing, yet are priceless assets. Whenever Louis Armstrong, the famous American jazz musician and singer entered a room, his smile lit up the whole place, and he will always be remembered for the song - *When you're smiling the whole world smiles with you.* This was probably the inspiration behind the writer of a poem which recently appeared on the internet and is shown overleaf.

16

SMILE

Smiling is infectious,
you catch it like the flu.
When someone smiled at me today,
I started smiling too.

I passed around the corner,
and someone saw my grin -
When he smiled I realized,
I'd passed it on to him.

I thought about that smile,
then I realized its worth,
a single smile, just like mine,
could travel round the earth.

So, if you feel a smile begin,
don't leave it undetected -
Let's start an epidemic quick
and get the world infected.

Anon.

:-) :-)

This page is intentionally left blank.*

*If you would like further clarification on this point, please go to the reference section of your local library and ask for the current edition of *The Care and Use of Blank Pages* edited by A. Non and E. T. Al. ISBN 0 0000000 0 X.

Plate 1   **The Second-hand Book Dealer. Phil May, Pen and Ink, 1933**

CHAPTER 2

WHAT BUSINESS ARE YOU IN?

INTRODUCTION

Before reading any further, write down your answer to the question heading this chapter, or to the alternative question - what business are you proposing to be in? If you ask any secondhand bookdealer what business they are in then their answer is likely to be on the lines of:

'I'm in the secondhand book business' or 'I deal in antiquarian books', or just 'I'm a bookseller.' Was your answer similar?

There is nothing wrong with these answers except that they are incomplete. In this short chapter I want to attempt to change your thinking towards a more marketing orientated approach. One definition of marketing by the way is: Identifying customer needs and satisfying them profitably. The main points that I want to make can be illustrated by an event that took place in south east London in 1979.

A ONE-DAY SMALL BUSINESS CONFERENCE

In 1979 I had been working for IBM for some 15 years marketing computers, and since 1969 I had been running a small spare-time business. IBM were aware of this but as there was no conflict of interest I was allowed to continue. In order to capitalise on my experience of starting and running a small business, IBM seconded me (initially for two years) to the newly-established London Enterprise Agency as the Small Firms Adviser. (As one of my colleagues pointed out, this abbreviates to SFA).

My brief there was to organise, and run, various types of courses to help educate those wanting to learn how to start and run a small business and to fill these planned courses. The first of these was a one-day event at Lewisham, where various other professionals such as bank managers and accountants were recruited to assist. There was an audience of about 500 and my job was to compere, act as link man and to do some of the speaking on marketing. When my turn came I turned to various people in the audience and asked them the question at the head of this chapter. Replies included a sandwich bar, secretarial agency, gardening services and ladies hairdressing.

I then turned to several ladies in the audience and asked them if they went to a hairdressers, and if so why? Their replies included:

▸   My hair gets dirty and needs washing.

- It makes me feel better.
- It makes me feel more beautiful.
- It saves me time.
- It gives me a feeling of well-being.
- It enables me to catch up on gossip.
- It makes me feel more self-assured and confident.
- It's something I couldn't do for myself.
- I like the feeling of being pampered.
- I like a man touching me.
- I can unwind and relax.

I then turned to the prospective ladies hairdresser and said 'You are not in Ladies Hairdressing but in the business of providing these perceived benefits to ladies.' The whole point of marketing and of selling in particular, is that you are in the business of providing benefits to your customers. Remember that customers always look at a situation for what is in it for them.

Now it's your turn - please take a piece of paper and write down the benefits that you think your customers will obtain from you and your books. This is the whole crux of your business and you should make the list as long as possible.

After you have spent a while doing this don't worry if your list is not too long, for many this is a new way of thinking and does take some getting used to. It can always be added to - at any time when you are suffering forced inactivity, such as on a train journey, or stuck in a traffic jam. Put yourself in the position of a customer and try to think what is in it for you when you buy books to add to your collection. Later on you will be shown how to use this list in your publicity campaigns and publicity material. It should always be uppermost in your mind when talking to prospective customers. If you can't think of any then perhaps you should be rethinking whether or not to go into business.

The following is a list of some that apply to my specific business. Your business will be different from mine and therefore you should be able to add some benefits unique to you and your business such as the proximity of your business to local customers.

- Obtaining that out-of-print book, map, or scientific paper to satisfy a wants need.
- Meeting a collector's need in a specialist field. Only a collector can appreciate the enormous satisfaction in obtaining a book after many years of searching. One very happy customer recently commented

'I had been looking for that for so long I had given up all hope of ever finding it.' I now have another friend for life.

▸ Supplying a review copy of a work just published. *'I couldn't afford the full price but this is ideal.'*

▸ As a known specialist, customers will come to you for their needs in the knowledge that if you can't supply immediately, you will either record their wants and/or pass them on to other dealers who may be able to help; or from your detailed knowledge recommend possible alternatives.

▸ Your specialist knowledge can help customers look for items they *didn't even know existed.*

▸ Providing that mint copy for the must-be-perfect collector, or that fine binding or a plates volume with those superb hand-coloured illustrations.

▸ Obtaining an inexpensive copy of a textbook required for study by an impoverished student.

▸ Finding a reading or working copy for the customer interested in contents only and low price.

▸ Visitors to your shop, book-fair stand, or website, can enjoy the thrill and excitement of browsing in the hope of finding a bargain, that rare item they have been looking for for years, or joy of joys - that book they didn't know they wanted until they saw it.

▸ Finding the ideal present for birthdays, Christmas, leaving a job, or other special occasions. (I frequently get phoned by companies or geological organisations looking for a suitable leaving/retiring present for a senior executive).

▸ Supplying a suitable 'prop' for that TV or Film Company who need a book of the right vintage for that 'period piece' they are shooting.

▸ Satisfying a nostalgic need by finding and supplying a book e.g. an annual or science primer, dating from the customer's childhood or student days, or a work signed by and from the library of one of their former lecturers or professors. Nostalgia is indeed big business as is evidenced by the number of thriving specialists in childrens' books.

▸ Helping customers by referring them to other sources of supply where you cannot help directly. e.g. Visitors to my website (http://www.fossilbooks.co.uk and click on links), will find details of 40 other UK dealers who overlap with my interests as alternative sources of supply. There is also a great selling opportunity here as if a visitor wants to know where they can find a bookshop specialising in xyz, I show them the relevant entries in the current PBFA Directory, (or Cole's or Sheppard's etc.), and even if I haven't got what they came in for they often go out clutching a directory I've sold them and thanking me for my help.

▸ Helping customers by giving details of other local bookdealers.

▸ Providing stock to other dealers (who can be major customers), by pricing books at a lower-than-market-price by intent or often by ignorance of the market. We can't all be experts in all fields.

▸ Providing that odd volume for the collector who has the rest of the set.

▸ Bidding on behalf of a customer (commission bid), at an auction the customer is unable to attend.

Hopefully you can add many more to this list.

TAILPIECE

You are not only in the business of providing benefits to customers, you are also in the business of helping them. If you go into shop and ask for a book you sometimes get a curt 'No we haven't got it.' or ' we don't stock that as there's no demand for it - you're the 6th person to ask for that this week.' That sadly is all to often the end of the story.

How different if the answer was- 'No I haven't got that but I know who might have a copy and here are their details,' or 'have a look at this directory - in it you will find 30 other dealers in the UK who specialise in that subject and who could be able to help you.' As I see it you should go out of your way to be helpful to others without thought of personal gain or cost. This is good for the trade as a whole. People are grateful for this service, it costs nothing, creates the right impression and helps your colleagues.

On one occasion a gentleman rang my shop for a particular book. I didn't have one in stock but I was able to point him towards another dealer who was able to help him. The customer subsequently made a detour to visit my shop to thank me personally as he was so pleased to get his book. While he was in my shop he looked round and bought a £20 book from me. The result: two happy dealers and a new very satisfied customer whose opinion of the book trade was greatly enhanced. I leave the thought with you.

CHAPTER 3

SOURCES OF STOCK

INTRODUCTION

Where do I get stock from? is probably the most frequently asked question by anyone wanting to start their own business in secondhand or antiquarian bookdealing. Some of the possibilities are covered below.

1.   AUCTIONS

Book auctions fall into four major categories:

Book Auction Houses.

These deal entirely with books and/or related items such as maps, prints and ephemera. e.g. In the UK: *Bloomsbury Book Auctions* of London; *Dominic Winter Book Auctions* of Swindon; and *Y Gelli Auctions* of Hay-on-Wye. Auction frequency is of the order of fortnightly to six-weekly.

Major Auction Houses.

These have a department specialising in books - with main offices in London and usually with branches throughout the UK and major countries around the world. e.g. *Bonhams, Christie's, Phillips, and Sotheby's.* Their catalogues are often profusely illustrated in colour and for important sales become collectors' items in their own right. Their book auctions are normally scheduled up to a few times a year or may be on an ad hoc basis. These auction houses tend to concentrate on smaller quantities, fine books and the higher-priced end of the market, though there are no hard and fast rules here.

Regular Auctions

These may be anywhere in the UK but in auction premises usually in towns, where books may form anything from one to a large number of lots in a weekly, fortnightly or monthly sale of household or antique items or bankrupt stock. Some auction houses have special bi-monthly book sales. e.g. The Aylsham Salerooms near Norwich in Norfolk.

Occasional Auctions.

These are usually at country houses or other estates where the contents and sometimes the premises as well are sold in situ, a marquee often being erected in the grounds for the days of the preview and the sale.

INTERNET AUCTIONS

During 1999 in the United Kingdom and elsewhere a number of major auction houses announced a new type of book auction on the internet.

Little information is available at present, but what there is, has been included at the end of chapter 16 on 'Websites'.

FINDING OUT ABOUT AUCTIONS

For most auctions, catalogues are published in advance - the time ranging from a few days to a few weeks. Many auction houses, particularly those in the first two categories above, will also publish an annual or quarterly schedule in advance, enabling dates to be slotted into your diary.

Catalogues may be obtained by annual subscription or by individual purchase for a particular sale - it is up to you to notify the auctioneers of your particular interests, then even if you don't have an annual subscription you may be notified of relevant sales. Some auction houses e.g. *Bloomsbury Book Auctions*, have a special Wants List Service which caters for the needs of customers in this area. e.g. You notify them of your subject areas of interest and you will then always be informed when your particular subject(s) appear in their catalogues.

Most major auction houses now have websites in which they give details of forthcoming auctions so if you have access to the web it is well worth while paying them a visit. If you take the trouble to advertise your interests e.g. by putting your details in the relevant directories of secondhand bookdealers, then auction houses who are on the ball may contact you out of the blue. e.g. Many years ago when I had not heard of *Dominic Winter Book Auctions* of Swindon, a catalogue of theirs arrived on my desk containing a particularly important geology library. I managed to buy most of this on the day and most of the few items I missed I ultimately managed to get from the other dealers who had bought them. This was great initiative on the part of Dominic Winter and we have had a great business relationship ever since.

There are of course occasional one-off sales that you might miss, as it is not practical or economic to be in constant touch with all auction houses throughout the country. Fortunately such sales are normally advertised in the weekly *Bookdealer* and other trade publications such as the *Antiquarian Book Monthly* and *Antiques Trade Gazette* and it is important to scan your copy the moment it arrives to look for such sales. e.g. *Mallams* of Oxford had just such a sale a few years ago - selling the house and contents of a recently-deceased, well-known historian of science who had a very large library. It it also worth looking at your local weekly newspaper for such auctions. The trade press usually also contains detailed adverts for the main regular book auctions, giving dates and highlighting significant lots.

Some directories of book dealers e.g. *Sheppard's*, list some of the major book auction houses in the U.K. whilst local auctioneers can be found in *Yellow Pages* or other area directories such as *Thomson's*.

PROCEDURE AT AUCTIONS
i. Viewing.

It is standard practice for auction houses to allow viewing of the lots before the auction. This may be on the day of the sale, for one, two, or three days prior to the sale, or a combination of both. Details of viewing days and times are usually published in the catalogue. If you are unable to attend any of the official views, you may be allowed to look at other times by special arrangement but this cannot always be counted upon. For some auctions viewers are allowed to look at lots during the auction but for others this is not allowed. It is up to you to establish what is allowed in advance.

It is strongly recommended that you do not bid for any lots without first having inspected them. Catalogues give for each lot, a number, a description and usually an estimate of the expected auction price. Whilst it is not always mandatory to buy a catalogue to view or bid at a particular sale it is an essential tool for the job as it is unpractical to view without your own catalogue available in which you can make appropriate notes. For some sales you will not be allowed in without first buying a catalogue. To save time on the day, inspect your catalogue in advance, make notes of the lots you are interested in, and the price limit you would go to for each. When viewing you can then first quickly look at your lots of interest, decide whether or not they are still of interest and of any revisions to the prices you are prepared to go to. When this has been done you can then look at the other lots to see if there is anything else of interest that had escaped your attention in the catalogue. If you have trouble finding the location of any particular lots, staff will be on hand to show you where they are - a large lot may be on a different floor, or a rare item locked in a bookcase.

Price estimates given in auction catalogues may be a single figure or an upper and lower limit. For any particular lot the vendor has the right to ask for a reserve price which has to be agreed with the auctioneer beforehand. Such reserves are not published and if a lot does not reach its reserve then it will either be withdrawn by the auctioneer or 'bought in' under an auctioneer's name coined for the purpose, which basically means the same thing.

You should be aware that some lots may be withdrawn on the day of the sale, despite being in the catalogue, and that there may be last minute alterations to descriptions. Such alterations are normally posted up on the day of the sale in the auction room, and also given by the auctioneer immediately prior to the sale of the lot concerned.

Viewing can be great fun and an enjoyable experience as you will often meet colleagues in the trade and have a chance to catch up on news.

ii. Registering.

Whether you are attending the auction in person or are proposing to leave bids or to telephone bids for particular lots during the auction, the auction house will require details from you, particularly if you are a newcomer and are unknown to the auctioneers. At the very least you will need to supply your name, address, and a bank reference if you are proposing to pay by cheque. If you become a regular purchaser some auction houses will issue you with a client or customer identification plastic card with your name and a unique number embossed and your full details on a magnetic stripe. This greatly speeds up the registration process. When registering in person on the day of the sale, it is possible that you will be given a numbered paddle or a large card with a unique number. Most auction houses will require you to register before the sale though some will only ask for registration details during the sale and then only ask for details if you have become a successful bidder. If you are planning to become a regular visitor to any auction it is prudent (and required by the auction house) to establish a credit reference beforehand, e.g. from your bank, unless you always intend to pay by cash. Credit limits are sometimes negotiated.

iii. Bidding.

Before bidding it is worth bearing in mind the legal implications of what you are about to do. Although most auction catalogues include detailed pages of conditions of sale with much legalese, you must realise that if you become a successful bidder, on the fall of the hammer you are entering into a legally binding contract with the auctioneer to pay the hammer price (plus premium where applicable) within a certain length of time.

This is not a 'gentleman's agreement' or a 'deal' but a contract as deemed by English Law. (NB English Law differs from Scottish Law in many respects.) If you are in any doubt as to auction procedure it is best simply to ask the auctioneer or a member of staff before you commit yourself. Having said all this, bidding at auction can be rewarding, exciting and great fun.

In Person

If attending in person, sit or stand where the auctioneer can see you and bid by holding your paddle, or card, or catalogue in the air (or wave it about) to catch the auctioneer's attention. Once your interest has been registered the auctioneer will come back to you until you indicate you are finished. If you are new to this just watch what goes on and you will soon get the idea. If you have a firm upper limit for a particular lot then stick to it, as once you go over your limit it is all too easy to get carried away and pay far more for an item than you had intended. In calculating the amount you actually pay, a premium e.g. 15%, will be added to the final bid or hammer price, plus in some cases VAT at the appropriate rate on the premium. Full details of such charges are given in their catalogues by each auctioneer. Rates of premium vary from auctioneer to auctioneer and tend to be lower in provincial towns and higher in London.

Handed In or Posted.

If you are unable to or don't wish to attend the auction, then when you have viewed, you can make out a bidding slip giving for each lot of interest to you - the lot numbers, descriptions, and the maximum hammer price you are prepared to pay, plus obviously your personal details. Hand this to a member of staff or post it to the auction house. During the auction your bids will be taken into account by the auctioneer. If there are many such bids for a particular lot then the starting bid is likely to be much higher than if yours was the only bid.

You might wonder why anyone might not wish to attend an auction in person. The reason is that many dealers are well-known for particular subjects and the psychological logic used by some, is that if they appear at an auction then by definition the lots they are bidding for must be good. Therefore others may bid where they might not have done without this knowledge, thereby pushing the hammer price up.

Beforehand by Telephone, Fax, or E-mail.

This is basically the same as handing in or posting a bidding slip but bids are only accepted at the sender's risk and should always be confirmed by post in writing. Auctioneers invariably specify a latest time by which such bids must be received by them.

During the Sale by Telephone.

This has to be arranged beforehand with the auctioneers. When your lot or lots come up you will be telephoned just prior to your first lot by a member of staff who will convey your bids to the auctioneer and overbids (which may be on another phone line or in the auction room), back to you. The auction house will give you an estimate of the number of lots expected per hour (usually between 90 and 150) to enable you to be near your phone at the appropriate time(s).

By another person on your behalf.

If you are unable to attend an auction it is perfectly acceptable for someone to bid on your behalf. Dealers often do this for partners or colleagues in the trade. Customers who are unable to attend may place commissions with dealers to bid up to a certain value on their behalf - there is normally a small percentage charge by the dealer to the customer for this service. It is quite common at auctions to hear one person giving different names for different successful bids.

Beware Overbidding.

It is all to easy to get carried away at an auction and pay far more for an item than you intended or it is normally worth, especially if it is something you are desperate to get. You must set an upper limit and stick to it as far as possible. There is nothing worse having secured a lot at a high price, than to hear a *sotto voce* comment from a nearby dealer 'I could have sold him one of those at half the price.'

Vendor Details.

Auction houses do not normally disclose vendor details except when dealing with a large well-known library, the estates of the deceased, or with bankrupt stock. On the other hand the hammer price is normally disclosed in printed form at some time after the auction and with some auction houses the name of the purchaser is given as well. If you are bidding at an auction or have left bids and become the underbidder i.e. someone just topped your bid, it is worth noting who the successful bidder is, as it often happens that lots contain more than one item (even up to several hundred items) and that the successful bidder was after one part of the lot whilst you were after a different part. If you don't know the person, their details can sometimes subsequently be obtained from the auctioneer. If it was a trade buyer, you will be informed immediately. If it was a private buyer, auctioneers will not disclose their address or phone number but will forward a letter from you on request. You can then approach them to invite a private sale to you. Others may of course approach you for parts of your successful lots.

iv. Paying For and Clearing Lots

If you attend an auction and buy one or more lots, you can pay for these and take them away the same day. Credit cards are not normally accepted. You should verify beforehand with the relevant accounts department what methods of payment will be acceptable in the event of your being a successful bidder. Staff will collect your lots from the shelves or bins for you and deliver them to you. If however you left the auction before the end without paying or had left bids, you will be sent an invoice for your successful lots and be asked to pay this and collect your lots by a specified time. Auctioneer's terms and conditions printed in the catalogue or elsewhere, clearly indicate what will happen if you don't pay on time. Because of space shortages, if you do not clear your lots by the specified time you may incur storage charges. If you are unable to collect in person the auction house will either ship your lots for you (e.g. *Dominic Winter Book Auctions*), or put you in touch with a shipper if they or you do not have your own carrier.

AUCTION PRICES

The estimates of prices given in a catalogue will be based upon the auction house's previous experience and on published prices from earlier auctions going back many years. There are two main English language sources of published prices: *Book Auction Records* (BAR) and *American Book Prices Current*, (ABPC) which are published annually in book form. ABPC is also available on a CD-ROM. Please see chapter 8 on 'Trade Publications' for further details. If you have the details of a work e.g. author, title, and edition, issue or date, you can look it up to see what it last fetched and when. This can give a guide, but only a guide, to what it may fetch now and to its rarity. The actual hammer price will depend on a number of factors:

▸ How well the auction has been advertised and how many dealers and other bidders are there on the day. A well advertised auction can attract a large number particularly if there are some choice lots coming up. This naturally will drive the price up and bargains are likely to be few on the ground.

▸ Whether just dealers are present or potential customers or individual collectors as well. Dealers have to add a mark up (discussed in chapter 4 on 'Pricing'), to cover their expenses, time, overheads, and to include a profit, whilst, other things being equal, a collector does not have to allow for a profit and can therefore go to a higher price.

▸ The provenance and condition of the lot. A rare signed work from a famous collection in pristine condition in a superb binding will command the highest price which may be many times the estimate, and vice versa.

▸ The simple economic laws of supply and demand and who is there (or on the phone) on the day.

▸ How well large lots are looked at before the auction. However experienced the auction house cataloguers are there is always the possibility of some gem being missed by them and not itemised, and by others in looking through the lot. This is where your knowledge and experience comes in and perhaps allow you to make a killing. It doesn't happen often but when it does you remember it. I once bought a lot of 50 books for £50 (having looked at most but not all of the titles) and put them on one side for a few months. When I ultimately unpacked them there was a rare work in two volumes I hadn't seen, which I later sold for £750.

2.   PRIVATE PURCHASE

This is without doubt one of the most important sources of stock for any dealer. If you have a shop or other premises open to the public then it is very likely that you will be offered stock on a regular basis by visitors to your shop - what is known as passive purchasing.

To be active in purchasing you have to advertise or use other means to obtain specific types of stock. If you are planning to be a general bookdealer then local newspaper adverts on as wide a basis as you can afford could be one effective method. On the other hand if you intend to specialise, as many dealers do, then it is up to you to tap specialist sources, e.g. advertise in the next issue of the specialist journals (e.g. literary), or society newsletters related to your interests, to the effect that you are interested in buying. One alternative is to print a brochure and distribute it as outlined in chapter 7 on 'Publicity'.

Most academics retire at some time and many have a large library to dispose of. If you get a reputation in a specific field and for giving good prices the word soon gets around. A number of customers over the years have told me that they have given my details to their spouse, for use in the event of their passing on before disposing of their library. This means that the one left behind does not have the worry of disposing of material and also has the confidence that their spouse knew and trusted you and that they will get a fair price.

There is always the possibility that you will be offered stolen books or plates or non-existent books. Where thefts are discovered soon after the event these are usually reported in the trade press and association newsletters. It is important to read and keep such reports for reference. Many libraries will stamp their books for sale as withdrawn, or cancelled but many do not, so you have to be on your guard. Another ploy used by the unscrupulous is to write to you from a foreign country offering you rare books at very low prices under the pretence that the so-called seller does not know much about books. Payment is asked for in advance, and of course the books never arrive.

3.   BOOK-FAIRS

Most dealers probably exhibit at book-fairs in order to sell books. This is fine and is a perfectly logical thing to do particularly if it is their major source of income. Book-fairs however can also be a marvellous source of purchases. If you are exhibiting at a particular book-fair you have the advantage over the general public that you can look at all the other dealers' stands before the public are allowed in and snap up any bargains. Some dealers actually exhibit at book-fairs mainly in order to get this buying opportunity and if they do some selling they regard this as a bonus.

At the end of May and during the first half of June each year there is an enormous concentration of book and other related fairs in London - a tradition that goes back many years. These present a great buying opportunity. Details of these and of all exhibitors are published beforehand in a special bookfairs issue of the *Bookdealer*. One only has to look at the queues forming prior to opening to see a large number of trade buyers both from the United Kingdom and overseas with their cheque-books at the ready.

The ABA and PBFA and many other book-fair organisations throughout the country publish annual schedules of their book-fairs which can be obtained free on request. These schedules can be obtained directly from the head offices of the organisations, from book-fairs organised by them and from their members. A current list of Book-Fair Organisers is published annually in January in *Sheppard's Book Dealers in the British Isles* and in their similar publications for other countries.

4   OTHER DEALERS

One aspect of getting stock from other dealers has been covered above under book-fairs. If you specialise and become well known in the trade, help other dealers by putting business their way or by passing private sellers of specialist books on to them then they are likely to reciprocate. I do my best, if a library coming onto the market is outside my interests, to put the seller in touch with other relevant dealers. Conversely many dealers have done the same to me or if they have actually bought a library then those items relevant to my interests have been offered to me en bloc. This is a *you scratch my back and I'll scratch yours* approach which works extremely well and reinforces and emphasises the friendly nature of the whole secondhand booktrade.

Other dealer's catalogues are an important source of stock for you and it is important that you contact other relevant dealers to arrange a mutual exchange of catalogues.

It is a good idea to keep one or more of the major directories of secondhand and antiquarian bookdealers in your car. Whenever you are travelling to any part of the United Kingdom you can look up in advance to see who is there and make a point of calling in to look at stock. If there are private premises to visit then prior contact is essential to fix an appointment. If you are going a long way to a shop it is also good sense to phone first to check opening hours, that the shop is still trading and is open on the day you are planning to visit. Many shops will have a free printed list and a map of other dealers in their area. Collect these as they form a very useful additional resource.

5   TRADE PUBLICATIONS

One of the major trade publication for sources of stock is the weekly *Bookdealer*. Only bookdealers may advertise in this and though predominantly listing books wanted, it has some 10% of its 100 or so pages each week devoted to books for sale. Similarly the monthly *Book and Magazine Collector* offers thousands of books and magazines for sale and wanted. When bookdealers retire or die, their stock may be offered for sale and similarly if a dealer has a stock sale then such sales are usually advertised in such trade publications. Further details are given in chapter 8.

6.   REMAINDER WHOLESALERS

If you are wanting to deal only in secondhand and antiquarian books and not the occasional new book or remaindered item then please ignore this section. If you are undecided, it is worth getting on to the mailing lists of the twelve remainder merchants in England for a trial period to see what they have to offer. Remainder selling forms a large proportion of many dealers' turnover and is well worth considering.

There are normally one or more annual wholesale remainder fairs in England where future titles for the coming season are displayed. At least one day of the fair is on a Sunday for your convenience so as not to interrupt weekday business. Addresses and other details of remainder merchants are given in *Sheppard's Book Dealers in the British Isles*.

7.   PUBLISHERS' SALES

There are many hundreds of publishers in the United Kingdom, the major ones being listed annually together with their distributors in *Whitakers Directory of Publishers*.

If you are wanting the occasional new title for stock or a customer, then it is up to you to write to them and establish a credit account or to offer payment in advance. In the latter case you will be sent a proforma invoice, and on payment the books will be sent to you or if a pre-publication title, then on publication.

If you are not wanting to stock new books on this basis it is still worth writing to publishers to be notified of any special sales they are planning. Some publishers do this on an occasional basis as a stock clearing or cashflow generating exercise as an alternative to remaindering, and some extraordinary bargains can be obtained in this way.

At one such sale in 1998 I was able to buy stock of a book normally retailing at £215 and sell it at £45, a price that included a generous mark up for me. Such sales are normally for a limited period and though many titles will sell out, those that don't may revert to their normal price after the sale.

8.   THE INTERNET

Though bookdealing and its relationship to computers and the internet is covered in the final section of this book, it is worth mentioning here that at the time of writing (mid-1999), the internet has become a very major influence in the market place for secondhand and antiquarian books and is likely to have an ever increasing effect in the future. With *ABE Bibliofind,* etc., there are an estimated 12 to 15 million books available for purchase throughout the world, and many others on individual bookdealers' websites. All you need is a suitable computer, a modem to connect your computer to a telephone line, the appropriate software, an Internet Service Provider, and at the click of a key, (or mouse) you can see what is on offer and purchase as required.

9   LIBRARIES

As sources of stock there are three major types of library other than private ones:

Academic Libraries. These are by definition associated with universities, colleges and other educational establishments. Details of these are given in relevant directories which may be found in the reference section of most major public lending libraries. Some do from time to time get duplicate material or other items to dispose of. This may be offered to staff first, to an auction house or to a dealer known to them. It is up to you to make yourself and your interests known to relevant librarians. This can be done by letter, fax or e-mail, by sending catalogues, a brochure or best of all, by a personal call to introduce yourself.

Institutional Libraries. Throughout the United Kingdom there are many Art, Literary, Philosophical, Scientific, Technical, Professional and other learned societies, as well as various official bodies that may come under the category of governmental or other national organisations. Many of these have their own libraries some of which may go way back into earlier centuries. Some libraries are bound by their rules or constitution and are unable to dispose of material. Others however are not and a large quantity of material can come onto the market from these sources. As before it is up to you to track these down and make sure such librarians are aware of your existence if you wish to have an opportunity to quote. Ensuring that the staff of such institutions are kept aware of you and your specialities can pay handsome dividends. A major institution recently (April, 1999) decided to scrap all their publications as they needed the room for other purposes. Skips were called in and filled with publications. Fortunately one of the staff saw what was happening, called me in and I was able to take away a very full car load of over 1,000 valuable geological publications that would by now just be pulp paper.

Public Libraries. Many public lending libraries have either a continuous or periodic sale of books to make room for the influx of new material. It is up to you to visit your local libraries on a regular basis to pick up those occasional bargains, possibly at £1 or less, if you wish to stock this kind of material.

10   REVIEW EDITORS

One of the ways in which publishers of new books publicise their latest offerings is to send free review copies to the reviews editors of relevant publications. This is normally on the understanding that the person writing the review is entitled to keep the book, and that the relevant publication publishes a review, a copy of which is then sent to the book publisher. Reviews editors are not always able to find a reviewer and may accumulate unreviewed books. In addition the reviewer may not subsequently wish to keep the book for themselves. Here therefore are two additional sources - it is up to you and your initiative to track them down if you are interested. Some publishers stamp the words: Review Copy on the front free end paper of such items but many do not.

11   EXISTING CUSTOMERS

By providing a good service over the years you will build up a loyal customer base. The time will come when for one reason or another a customer may wish to dispose of some or all of their library. Reasons can vary from falling on hard times, or moving house, to change of interests, and complaints from their partner about the house full of books. If you have treated them well over the years then hopefully you will be their (or their relatives), first port of call. If they go away happy at how much you have been able to give them for their books then this must be good business for both parties and for your future.

12   MISCELLANEOUS SOURCES

Antique Fairs. These are held frequently throughout many countries. Stallholders may have a few books for sale or others may have entirely books.

Charity Shops e.g. Oxfam. These frequently have a section on books or in large towns or cities may have a complete shop devoted to books. They are well worth a regular look as bargains are to be found.

Jumble Sales, Village Fetes, Weekly Markets, and Boot Fairs. These are not to be ignored as there are finds to be made e.g. a first edition of Darwin's *Origin of Species* bought for a few pounds which subsequently sold for many thousands.

PAYMENT

As a general guide when buying books, especially from someone you don't know, it is recommended that you pay by cheque and also obtain the seller's name and address if you don't already have it. This is a precaution to protect yourself, in case there is any future query on the ownership of the books. If you do pay by cash then always ask for a signed, dated and addressed receipt, for the same reason and also to have a record to enter in your cash purchases book. It is all to easy if you do make many cash purchases in a short period, to forget details unless they are written down. You will need this information for pricing purposes anyway.

STOCK VALUATION

Having obtained some stock, you should be aware that for taxation and insurance purposes you are going to need a figure giving the value of your total stock at least on an annual basis. There are several ways of determining this figure. If you follow the guidance given in the next chapter, you will have a price or price code marked in each book indicating what you paid for it. At the end of your financial year you then need to go round your complete stock, making a list and total of all these figures.

An alternative way is to keep a record, either manually or on your computer, of the stock value as a running total figure, which is updated whenever there is an addition to stock via a purchase or a removal from stock via a sale. With sales, this means of course that you have to record the cost price of each item sold to be able to deduct it from the total. If when you start, you do it this way, it avoids the year end chore of a physical stock check, though your accountant will probably advise you that a stock check should be done every year or so to ensure accuracy.

If of course you make a very large purchase that brings your stock valuation well above the figure that you have declared to your insurance company, then they should be advised of this so that they can make an adjustment to your premium if necessary. If you don't do this and you make a claim for loss, in the event of a fire say, then you will find that you are not fully covered.

There are a number of other factors to be taken into account in addition to this. If you have any repairs done or rebinding, then you should get an itemised invoice from your repairer or binder, so you can add the costs to the purchase cost of each book. i.e. bookbinding adds to the value of your stock.

On the other hand the time may come when you have had some stock for some time, it is not moving, it has perhaps been damaged in some way, it may be regarded as worthless, and you feel that it should be written off for stock valuation purposes. If so then this will reduce the value of your stock. For taxation reasons, this is something that you should discuss with an accountant or a business adviser, to ensure that it is carried out properly.

You should remember that a proper valuation of stock plays a very large part in the profit or loss that you make in any year.

TAILPIECE

The amount of capital you tie up in stock is a matter for you and your accountant to decide. A frequently asked question following on from this is 'How do I choose a good accountant?' The answer obtained from one such accountant some years ago is given for consideration:

Select three accountants and ask them all the same question:

What do 2 + 2 make?

The first two are likely to answer 4 but if the third says:

'Well what answer did you have in mind?'

then that's the one you want.

CHAPTER 4

PRICING AND PRICING POLICY

INTRODUCTION

The pricing of any book that you are attempting to sell is usually a compromise between a low enough level to give you a quick sale and yet provide you with a satisfactory return, (which enables you to cover your overheads and make a profit), and the highest level that you think the market will bear. In determining the selling price you may have to take into account one or more of the following factors for each particular book, though there is no substitute for 'experience' which can only come with time and learning from one's mistakes!

What you paid for it.

This should be fairly straightforward as you should record what you paid for each book at the time of purchase and then note it in the form of a pencilled code in the actual book. This is usually at the front at the top of the paste-down endpaper but can be anywhere suitable as long as it is not on the title page. A relatively soft e.g. 2B, pencil should always be used (and also for the selling price) and the writing should be done with a light impression so that the page is not indented, and any notes or prices can subsequently be erased without trace.

Far too many books are spoiled by a pencil being used as if it were an embossing tool. A recent correspondent in the *Bookdealer* likened one such dealer to a latter-day Moses wielding his pencil as if he were engraving tablets of stone. I was horrified once to see someone writing prices in ink (sic) in his books. He obviously had no love of books and needless to say he didn't sell any to me.

There are of course other ways of recording the selling price in a book. A simple method, especially if the endpapers are glossy or coloured is to use small 'post it' self-adhesive labels - obtainable from stationers. Write the price on the label first, away from the book, and then stick the label in the book. These labels subsequently come away cleanly and do not mark the paper. An alternative used by many catalogue dealers especially for higher priced books, is to print out a copy of the individual catalogue or database description (or cut up an existing catalogue) and insert this loosely into the front of the book, either as it is, or mounted on card.

Where you buy a collection of books e.g. at auction, you will not have an individual purchase price for each book unless you have worked these out in advance and the hammer price coincided with your expectations. You should then allocate a purchase price for each book and mark each appropriately. Marking the purchase price in a book serves two purposes: it later acts as a reminder of the price you paid, and it is also an essential element in calculating a subsequent physical valuation of your stock which will be required annually both for accounting purposes and insurance cover.

Unless you keep a purchases register in which you record all individual items bought, it is also strongly recommended when you are entering the price in the book to enter a date also. This is most useful later as it enables you to determine how long any particular book has been in stock. If a book has been on the shelves for a long time you then have the information needed to make an appropriate management or policy decision e.g. on changing its price to move it quickly if required, or to improve your stock rotation or control system.

How common or rare or old is it.

The simple economic laws of supply and demand apply just as much to books as to other commodities. The basic rules are that if a book is common and/or there is little demand for it then the price will be low. Conversely if the book is rare and/or much sought after, the price will tend to be much higher. NB An old book is often thought by members of the public to be valuable just because it is old. This is a common misconception which regrettably often has to be corrected. This applies particularly to nineteenth century works.

Book auction records for the item.

If you look up the book auction records for a particular item and they consistently show the same price over the years, this is a good guide to stability. If however there is a trend either upwards or downwards or considerable vacillation you will have to take this into account. If you only find one price for a book, this should be treated with great caution as there may have been unusual circumstances affecting the price on the day of the sale. The mark up you apply to such prices should allow for the addition of the auction house premium plus your own mark up as discussed below. Details of book auction records are given in chapter 8 on 'Trade Publications'.

Trade bibliographies.

The monthly *Book and Magazine Collector,* has several author or subject bibliographies (UK), in each issue, together with a guide to values of first editions for conditions ranging from good to very good and with or without dust jackets, e.g. the June 1999 issue covers Beatrix Potter; the crime novels of Lindsey Davis; Ann Bronte novels; Cricket Novels and Stories; Elizabeth Bowen novels; and Gunfighter books. Many back issues are available covering a very wide subject range, which enables you to select those relating to your specialities.

How long you expect it to remain in stock.

If you have a long waiting list for a particular book then you can expect to sell it fairly quickly. This means that you could pay more for it than otherwise would be the case. You have several choices here. You can put a modest mark up on the book and sell it quickly thereby generating valuable cashflow. Alternatively you can say that because of the high demand for this book the price should go up in accordance with the laws of supply and demand. This will give you a greater return but may take longer to sell.

Whatever decision you make has to be a management one depending on your own financial circumstances. As a general guide, going for the quick sale-improved cashflow option is strongly recommended at the beginning.

If you expect the book to remain in stock for six months or longer then you are tying up capital in stock. This may be financed by an overdraft or capital loan which attract interest and have to be repaid, or financed by your own capital which needs a return on your investment.

You also have to consider the *opportunity cost* - a term used by economists relating to the investment of your capital elsewhere and of the return that you could possibly expect from this source. This means that in general the mark up that you apply to such a book should be higher than one that you expect to sell quickly. This in turn means that you should pay proportionately less for such books.

Your previous sales and stock record for it.

As you accumulate experience as a bookdealer it is recommended that you record purchase and selling prices for all significant works that pass through your hands. This can be in the form of catalogues, record cards, computer listings or best of all as a computer database. You can then look at your own records to see how many of a particular title you sold, the frequency, the last such sale, how long it stayed on the shelf and the prices. This is essential management information enabling you to make the correct decisions to ensure future profitability and survival.

Other dealers' prices for the same book.

Other dealers who issue catalogues will normally send copies to you on request. Many catalogue prices are issued in *The Clique's* (qv) *Annual Register of Book Values.* These were issued between 1987 and 1999 in six different series: *The Arts and Architecture; Children's Books; Modern First Editions; Science and Medicine; Voyages, Travel and Exploration;* and *Literature.*They concentrated exclusively on books in the English Language, published between the 16th century and the 1980s and in the lower to middle range of the price scale e.g. between £10 and £250. Details of catalogue booksellers who have contributed to any particular annual volume are listed at the back of the volume. Some dealers took the view that they didn't want their prices known and so didn't send any catalogues, whilst others regarded it as valuable publicity and sent all catalogues. These form an important reference source for retail prices. In most cases at the time of going to press, back numbers are available from 1996 onwards and it is recommended that these are obtained. I find that I use my own set of *Science and Medicine* many times a week. The publishers are currently considering whether to issue the data on the series on CD-ROM.

These two sources combined provide a valuable printed guide to what others are charging for particular works. There is often a wide range of prices but only you can decide whereabouts in that range you wish to be. If you issue catalogues and want your prices to be considered for inclusion in future, then you should contact *The Clique* before sending anything.

There are far more books published for the collector than for the bookdealer. An example of one such that is of use to the bookdealer as well, is *Browsing and Collecting Secondhand Archaeology Books* by Michael de Bootman, currently priced at £7.95. This was first published in 1997 and part three comprises a catalogue arranged alphabetically by author of some 2,500 entries of secondhand and remaindered archaeology books with a range of prices for each. Though he does not give his specific sources nor the time period during which the data was collected, de Bootman provides a useful service here, especially if promised future editions and updates are forthcoming. There may well be similar books in other subject areas.

An interesting point is also made by de Bootman in that he suggests that specialist books bought from a non-specialist dealer should on average be cheaper than the price charged by a specialist. This may or may not be valid for Archaeology. In general, for many specialities, based on many years experience I would suggest that the converse is also true in many cases. i.e. other things being equal, the non-specialist may charge more than the specialist. This is not necessarily by intent but may be due to the lack of relevant specialist knowledge and hence to pricing by guesstimate.

Another source of retail prices of exceptional significance is the internet. This is covered in detail later but to whet your appetite, try accessing the website: http://www.bookfinder.com - enter the details of the book you are looking for and see what happens. This is a meta search engine which searches other book databases for you e.g. *Advanced Book Exchange, Amazon.com, Bibliocity, Bibliofind*, etc. Many millions of titles from over 10,000 bookdealers around the world are accessed when you key in an author name and/or title. In a few seconds from 25 to 200 matches per database are listed, giving the retail price and if you wish to order, the dealer details. The lists can of course be printed out as required. The direct costs of this are your time plus your online time at local telephone call rates. Search engines and book databases are explained in part III.

The edition and issue.

When a book is first published there will be a certain number of copies printed initially. This is known as a first edition, first impression. The same edition may be reprinted once or many times; in such cases this is still a first edition but a second impression or third impression etc. The same typesetting, plates or artwork will be used except that second and subsequent impressions may carry additional wording such as 2nd thousand, or second impression, and/or a revised date on the title page. In many cases there is only one impression in which case it is usual to refer to it as a first edition without any qualifying impression number. Where a work has only ever been produced in one edition this is by definition a first edition. Such works are sometimes catalogued as a *first edition*, which description could be regarded as superfluous or as implying that there are subsequent editions. To avoid this problem, if you wish to describe such a book, the preferred wording is *first and only edition*.

I don't wish to get into the minutiae of bibliography here but you should be aware that there are other variations such as *issue* and *state*. If you are interested in further detail, *Book Collecting as a Hobby* by P.H.Muir, 1945, or any of the standard introductions to bibliography such as those by McKerrow or Gaskell, are recommended.

If the text is subsequently revised or reset and republished this will be a second edition, third edition, etc. There is one aspect of publishing that you should be aware of - in the Victorian era and before, if publishers found that sales were slow of a particular first edition, then in order to stimulate sales they would replace the title page with one saying second edition and then bind copies of the first edition and issue it as a 'new' work. You then basically have a first edition but with a title page saying second edition. This is a ploy that publishers today would not be allowed to get away with.

The affect on price of an edition can vary widely. In general, particularly in the field of literature and especially with fiction - a rare first edition may run into thousands of pounds with a second edition only fetching tens or hundreds. Similarly with early scientific or technical works. e.g. A first edition, first impression of Charles Darwin's *Origin of Species* in the original binding would currently sell at well over £15,000 and a second edition at well under £1,000.

Conversely, with many twentieth century works, especially text-books, it is mostly the latest edition that is the most valuable with a first edition the least desirable and hence the cheapest. There are of course all shades of gradation between these two extremes. It is up to you to determine what applies to the range of books you are planning to stock.

Where no date or edition is printed in a book, then this information can usually be found in a particularly useful reference work: *The British Museum General Catalogue of Printed Books.* (qv chapter 8). Such dates are conventionally put in square brackets e.g. [1834] or as n.d. [but 1834], meaning: *no date is present but from other sources it is known to have been published in 1834.* You should be aware however that some dates may refer to the date the work was acquired by the British Museum.

The condition, completeness and binding.

In most cases the *condition* of a book has a great influence on its price. Books in mint to very fine condition are always at a premium over copies which are foxed or stained, faded or heavily used, soiled, brittle, torn or buckled, etc. There are fortunately those who are interested in a working or reading copy only and are not worried about condition and are therefore happy to pay a low price for such items. With some works e.g. first editions of certain twentieth century fiction and the *New Naturalists* series the presence or absence of a dust jacket, and if present, its condition, can have an extraordinary influence on the price. A good dust jacket can add hundreds or thousands of pounds to the price in exceptional cases. e.g. In the summer of 1999 at Sotheby's, London, one of only two known copies of a first edition of one of Conan Doyle's works with a dust jacket, fetched some £87,000, compared with the few thousands expected for a normal first edition.

The *Book and Magazine Collector* publish a useful graded ready reckoner to prices and conditions each month for prices ranging from £200 to £2 and from Mint condition down to Poor. They also give their definitions of the terms used to describe condition. It should be appreciated however that this is only a guide, as others may use alternative definitions and different interpretations of values or prices.

Many books from institutional or public libraries have evidence as such, e.g. library plates on the covers or end papers, library stamps on the title page, throughout the book, or on plates, shelf or classification marks on the spine, tape marks on the spine particularly at the head or tail or even colour coding in paint. Such ex-library delights obviously detract from the price and other things being equal, add to the time any particular item is likely to remain on the shelf. If a book is rare or much sought after and the library marking is minimal then it is quite possible that the price may not be affected at all. Some collectors will not buy any ex-library items because of their appearance, whilst others are happy to have them for their contents and may change them over later if a better non-library copy becomes available.

With regard to *completeness*, a work that is lacking a plate or two or the odd page is obviously worth far less than a complete one, similarly a multi-volume work lacking one or more volumes is worth far less than the pro rata value. e.g. a two volume work lacking one of the volumes will not be worth half the value but more likely something in the region of a quarter to one fifth of the value of the complete set. This is of course subject to the old adage that *any item is worth what you get for it*. The *Bookdealer* offers a useful service here as once a year it takes advertisements for odd volumes both for sale and purchase. This gives great satisfaction if you are able to make that set up after waiting for years.

The *binding* and its condition can greatly influence price. Works in the original cloth binding with the original end papers and in good condition are usually preferred to those which have been rebound, rebacked, recased, or otherwise repaired e.g. head or tail repairs, split hinges attended to, fading restained, new spine labels, sections reglued or plates tipped in. Leather and similar bindings whether in a full, half or quarter state, half calf being one of the most common, usually but not always, fetch higher prices than cloth versions. For further details please see chapter 6.

With older works, an original or contemporary leather binding, provided it is in good condition, normally fetches a higher price than a recent rebind. In many but not all cases the best prices are obtained for gilt prize bindings and highly ornamental bindings. A book may be sold as a fine binding rather than for its reading matter as there are collectors and interior decorators who value the container more than the contents. There is absolutely nothing wrong in this as it illustrates that books can be objects of beauty as well as storehouses of knowledge or providers of recreation.

With the advent of the internet you should be aware that what one dealer from another country describes as **good** or **fine** on one of the databases could be highly euphemistic compared with the accepted usage of such terms in the UK. There are as yet no internationally accepted standards for such descriptions - **let the buyer beware.** For further details please see chapter 6 - on 'Running a Book-Catalogue Business.'

The provenance and any associations.

If a book has evidence to indicate that it comes from a famous library or from the library of a famous person, or from an author's library or from the library of a respected lecturer or professor, then other things being equal, this will add to its value.

Such evidence can be in the form of a bookplate, a signature, a presentation inscription, a name stamp, a written dedication, or an inserted letter. In some cases there may be a succession of ownership signatures over 50 years or more on the front end papers, particularly in the academic world where a particular work has been handed down from one professor to another. As one indicated to me once *'Old professors never die, they simply loose their faculties.'*

The percentage mark up you apply.

There are no hard and fast rules determining the mark up you apply to the price you have paid for a book. From your business plan you will have a good idea of your fixed costs, your variable costs, your expected sales revenue and your break-even point. If you are a one-person organisation working from home, then your overheads will be far smaller than a multi-employee organisation with a shop in a prime position and paying huge business rates with a large salary and insurance bill. The mark up you apply will be determined by your needs and your aspirations.

Earlier indications in this chapter can give an idea of the maximum price you can ask for a particular book and how long you expect it to stay in stock. From this you can work backwards by applying your mark-up in reverse. e.g. your mark-up could vary from as little as 15% to 20% for a highly-priced item you expect to sell very quickly to perhaps several hundred percent for something you expect to stay on the shelf for a very long time. An average mark up could perhaps be in the range of 50% to 100%. As one experienced dealer put it to me many years ago: *Anyone can sell good books, it's selling the 'rubbish' where you take the risk and make your money.* i.e. As an entrepreneur you are by definition a risk taker and the greater the risk the greater the return you should expect. In comparison, for new books most publishers give a trade discount varying between 10% and 40% with most in the range 20% to 35%. e.g. a 33 1/3% discount gives a mark up of 50% if you are sticking to the recommended retail price.

The market you are pricing for.

In general it is likely that most dealers will price their books at a level where they expect them to sell to members of the public. Such a price structure would normally allow for a built in 10% discount given to other bona fide bookdealers who buy from them. This discount incidentally, though it is a convention, is a courtesy and not a right in itself. If you have a shop then your prices will have to reflect the environment in which you operate. e.g. in an economically depressed area prices are likely to be lower than in highly affluent ones. If the question of whom is or is not a bona fide dealer who qualifies for a discount arises, I give for consideration the answer given to me once by a long-established dealer: 'If you are working whole-time at bookdealing, or are a member of the ABA or PBFA or are listed in *Sheppard*, or *Cole,* etc, then you qualify, otherwise no.'

There are some dealers however who price their books at a lower level to appeal to the trade. e.g. at a large bookfair such dealers will do most of their business with fellow dealers, both exhibiting and visiting, rather than with the general public. Such dealers obviously have to have appropriate sources of supply or to live in a part of the country where prices are less than in London and the south east or to be operating on lower margins than others.

What your current cashflow situation is.

An adequate cashflow is the life blood of your business. If cashflow is good then you may have no worries. To stay in business it is vital to have the ready cash to pay your day to day trading expenses and the interest and repayments on any loans. Your business plan and particularly your cashflow forecast will indicate what you expect to achieve in any time period. You have to monitor the progress of this very closely and if there are any variations from your business plan you can then make a management decision to try to correct an adverse situation or to take advantage of a beneficial one.

In an adverse situation you will need to improve your cashflow. To do this you have to consider various options such as reducing prices, publicising yourself with advertisements, etc, increasing the frequency of catalogues, or having a sale. The trade press frequently has notices of such sales.

Whatever you do in an adverse situation do not just do nothing. Money tied up in stock may represent future profit, whereas stock sold at a low profit margin or even at cost, represents cashflow which can keep you going till things improve. *Remember that most businesses that go out of business do so not for lack of potential profit but for lack of cashflow now.*

Inflation

National inflation levels should be monitored and also book price trends from the sources above. Adjust your retail prices periodically in accordance with these. Whether or not you increase the purchase or cost value of your stock because of inflation is a matter between you, your accountant and the Inland Revenue, bearing in mind that your stock valuation at the end of your financial year is one of the major factors in determining your profit or loss for the year and your profitability.

Summary

In practice, as your knowledge increases, you will find that you tend to work backwards from the selling price more and more. You will be able to determine a selling price fairly quickly and from that work out a fair or reasonable purchase price that is equitable both to you and the seller.

TAILPIECE - The Gambler and the Tax Inspector

It is no use making lots of money and then paying unnecessary taxes. It is legal to *avoid* paying tax by certain means but illegal to *evade* paying taxes. Your accountant should advise you here.

A gentleman who's life style had improved dramatically, put gambling (which is non-taxable), on his tax return as his source of income. In due course his tax inspector made an appointment to see him to check this out. 'I'd like to see some evidence of how you make your money' said the inspector. 'OK' said the gambler, 'I'll bet you £5 that I can bite my left eye.' The inspector accepted and the gambler took out his glass eye and bit it. 'I'm not convinced' said the inspector. 'I'll bet you £10 that I can bite my right eye' said the gambler. Thinking he was on to a good thing the inspector accepted. The gambler took out his false teeth and bit his right eye. 'I'm still not convinced' said the inspector. Alright said the gambler 'I'll bet you £50 that you have a three inch scar on your left thigh.' The inspector knew he hadn't a scar so he accepted. 'I'll need to see some proof' said the gambler, so the inspector dropped his trousers to reveal a clean left thigh. Just then a man appeared from behind some curtains and handed the gambler £1,000. 'What's this all about?' said the inspector hastily pulling his trousers up. 'Well, just before you arrived I bet him £1,000 that within five minutes of you being here you'd have your trousers down!'

48

Plate 2

The author in book-fair mode at an international scientific meeting at Southampton in 1992, where he was the only book exhibitor.

CHAPTER 5

BOOK-FAIRS AND SPECIALIST EXHIBITIONS

INTRODUCTION

Book-fairs are extremely popular both from the point of view of the dealer and the collector. There are a number of book-fair associations, (see your country Sheppard's for details and chapter 8 on 'Trade Associations'), who operate nationally or locally by booking venues, managing fairs and carrying out a considerable amount of other helpful activities for their members. The largest of these in the world is The Provincial Booksellers Fairs Association (PBFA), based in the United Kingdom.

Of all the options available to you, this is the one recommended for beginners to start with as it involves the least outlay and you can start with only a few hundred books in stock.

THE ADVANTAGES OF EXHIBITING

- You come in contact with a much wider range of potential customers than you could expect if you were static in one location.
- You meet and get to know colleagues in the trade.
- You have great opportunities to buy stock from other dealers before the general public are allowed in and of course to sell to other dealers. This, for many, is one of the major benefits.
- By other dealers getting to know your specialities they are more likely to pass details of special collections to you if they are outside their own interests.
- You have a wonderful opportunity of getting additions to your mailing list and of meeting customers face to face for the first time.
- By cultivating customers and inviting them to come, you can bring stock relevant to their interests or even orders for specific items placed in advance. This is likely to greatly increase your selling chances.
- You do not have the overheads associated with a shop.
- Cashflow is instant.
- With a two-day fair there may be very pleasant evening social occasions after set up or fair closing.
- If you are attending a fair some way from home it gives you an opportunity of visiting other dealers or sources of stock en route and perhaps making some useful purchases.

▸ If the book-fair is near to your home or premises then you have superb selling opportunities by inviting colleagues to visit you after the fair. At one recent (1999) book-fair I doubled my day's takings and cleared some bulk stock by doing this.

THE DISADVANTAGES OF EXHIBITING

▸ Unless you are operating on a 'book-fairs only' basis, in which case your stock may live in boxes, it can be very time consuming getting ready for one beforehand. i.e. selecting and packing stock, and unpacking afterwards.

▸ A certain amount of physical strength is needed in carrying heavy boxes of books into and out of your vehicle and possibly up several flights of steps at the book-fair. If you are handicapped or not particularly strong, the organisers may have porters available to help if required but this cannot always be relied upon.

▸ Additional expense may be involved if you need to hire a van to carry a large volume.

▸ If you are running a shop as well, you either have to have someone there to look after it while you are away or to close. If the latter then you have to take into account your potential lost sales to offset against increased sales through your attendance at the book-fair.

SELECTING STOCK

Don't just pack up some books and go to a fair hoping to sell. Think about what stock you should take. If it is a thematic fair then this should be relatively easy to do; local topography is always likely to be of interest and if you study the list of other dealers who will also be exhibiting you can take material likely to be relevant to them. (A high proportion of sales at any book-fair is to other trade exhibitors). You will have many opportunities to invite specific customers to the fair. By knowing their interests you can bring items specifically for sale to them. Think about any associations of the town you are exhibiting in or near. e.g. If Chatham or Portsmouth then naval history would be appropriate, if at Swindon in Wiltshire then railway history, or if near a famous racetrack then horseracing, etc. As a general guide, books with bright spines and large lettering are easier to see, and hence more likely to attract attention, than those with dull spines and small lettering.

AIMS AND OBJECTIVES

Try to think beforehand of your general aims, your specific

objectives, and how you propose to realise those objectives. A typical and highly laudable aim is to increase your profit and profitability. Your objectives are likely to include one or more of the following:

▸ To let visitors know of your existence and specialities. You might do this by advertising in the fair-catalogue, producing a special catalogue for the fair, or by making sure that your specialities are incorporated into your fair-signboard.

A properly produced signboard is usually mandatory and is a reflection of your professionalism. A sign saying Alan Bloggs, 6, The Avenue, Mychester, does not do much selling or informing. A sign saying Bloggs Books, is better; Bloggs Books, specialist in Literature is better still, whereas incorporating your speciality into your name and then qualifying it does even more selling for you. e.g. Bloggs Literature Books. Specialists in English and American Literature from the 18th Century to the 20th Century.

Bear in mind however that if you have some general stock as well - which is always advised for a book-fair, then this can be counter productive, as visitors may by-pass a stand if they are not interested in the speciality advertised. One way round this problem which is used by many exhibitors, is to have subject shelf-labels.

▸ To sell some stock. To do this you first of all have to sell yourself and your stand as outlined below.

▸ To buy either some stock for your business or some items for your own library.

▸ To get additions to your mailing list.

▸ To distribute recent catalogues.

▸ To distribute brochures promoting your business, your shop and your website.

▸ To encourage future visits to your premises.

▸ To increase your knowledge of books, authors and the trade.

▸ To help others by running or managing the fair or assisting.

▸ To help establish a reputation as a knowledgeable professional.

▸ To let visitors know that you are always interested in buying relevant books ranging from single volumes to complete libraries.

▸ To enjoy yourself financially and socially.

THE MECHANICS OF EXHIBITING

Book-fair organisers will let you know in advance the details of their forthcoming fairs for the year. It is up to you to decide those you would like to attend and to apply for. Space may be allocated on a first come first served basis, on a lucky draw basis or on a points basis depending on past service to your association.

If the book-fair organisers are issuing a catalogue for the fair, or the trade press e.g. the *Bookdealer,* are producing a special book-fairs issue for the June fairs in London, then there are opportunities for you to book advertising space should you so wish. The costs of this should be budgeted for well in advance.

The collapsible three-shelf wooden bookstands seen at book-fairs are standard equipment and are usually a mandatory requirement. They may be obtained through your book-fair association or through advertisements in the trade press. There are usually several arrangement possibilities for these at any one fair. You may be allowed two or three complete bays (at fairs where space is at a premium you may be restricted to a maximum of two bays) - a bay being one bookstand on top of another, giving you a maximum of six shelves.

The standard modular bookstands are usually made of beech and are of a good design. Unfortunately these are sometimes poorly made, resulting in them being more collapsible than intended with possible disastrous results. It is important to take a number of replacement screws of different sizes and an assortment of screwdrivers with you so you can make last minute adjustments (particularly to the hinges and shelf supports), which are usually necessary during stand assembly.

As an alternative to bookstands you are usually allowed to use a cloth covered table replacing the lower tier of one or more bays. If you require additional security or presentation possibilities, many organisers will provide glass showcases with glass shelves for you to rent. These are often on a table replacing the upper tier or may be large ones taking up a complete bay. Tables and showcases are usually allocated on a first-come first-served basis also, so early application is advised if you would like one of these.

Setting up times are specified and are either in the morning of, or the evening prior to the fair opening, or a combination of both. By setting up early this gives you a chance to have a good look around before opening time or to visit local shops or other book-fairs nearby, e.g. at the May/June book-fairs in London. Where there are both options, travelling and setting up in the morning rather than the previous evening enables you to reduce your overnight accommodation expense, though it also reduces your pre-opening viewing time.

Transport of you and your stock and stand to and from a venue has to be thought about in advance. If you are only ever going to do two-bay fairs and carry a relatively small stock then an ordinary hatchback would probably suffice. If however you are regularly going to do three-bay fairs then a large estate vehicle is needed with a good carrying capacity. If I mention that a typical book-fair in the UK looks as if it were a Volvo Estate convention this perhaps will give a broad hint as to what many choose. Some models have the big advantage that they have self-levelling suspension which means that even when fully loaded they stay practically horizontal. If you are going to have an assistant with you and do a three-bay fair, then one of the many types of vans able to carry at least a tonne is recommended. Whether you buy a van or just rent one for the fair is up to you.

Hint. Rain in the UK when you are unloading or loading at a fair is not unknown. It is a practical insurance policy to have some rectangles of polythene sheet cut to size to place over your books if using open boxes, or to place inside the lid if you are using closed cardboard boxes, as these are rarely water-tight.

Many book-fair venues are not particularly well lit and it can be a great advantage for you to have individual lighting for your stand. This should always be checked out in advance to see if it is permitted and to see if there are power points within reach of your stand. Any lighting you provide must comply with the current Electrical Engineering, and Health and Safety Regulations of the country in which you are exhibiting. e.g. In the UK your lead should be fitted with an earth-leakage-trip-plug.

Access to book-fair locations is rarely all on one level. You therefore have to be prepared to transport boxes of books, sometimes up several flights of stairs. A portable folding trolley or sack barrow is an essential piece of equipment. Books are heavy and it is much better to pack them in small to medium-sized boxes which you can carry easily, rather than in fewer, larger boxes which involve the possible risk of injury to your lower back. When lifting or putting down any box of books, keep your back vertical, i.e. do not bend over; and use your leg muscles for lifting and lowering rather than your back muscles.

Book-fair venues are not renowned for the flatness or levelness of their floors. Two essential pieces of 'high tech.' equipment can help you to overcome the potential problem of top-heavy bays falling over. **a.** Buy four metal G-clamps of appropriate size to enable you to clamp adjoining bays to each other, both at the top and at the mid-point where the corners of four stands meet. This greatly strengthens and stabilises a three-bay arrangement. With two bays you would only need two G-clamps. **b.** Make or get made for you, a selection of very thin wooden wedges about an inch or 3cm wide and up to 2 inches or 5 cm long and take them to every book-fair. Where necessary these can be strategically placed under the legs of each bay to help ensure verticality and stability. If you are fortunate enough to have a wall position it is recommended that you tilt each bay a few degrees back towards the wall. These vital pieces of equipment should be fitted in alphabetical order.

Where you are in a central position you will usually back onto another set of stands. In such cases clamping each set at the top to the other or just tying with polypropylene string will give improved stability. Whenever possible these two simple operations should be carried out before loading books onto the shelves as it becomes difficult or impossible when they are fully loaded. **Hint:** Check with your association and your insurance company or broker the potential public liability you may have at such a venue away from your normal premises.

With regard to organising the layout of stock on your shelves there are two main schools of thought. One puts all books on the same subject together on the same shelf with perhaps shelf subject labels; the other spreads them as widely as possible to encourage visitors to look at all the books on the stand. The choice is yours. A compromise some dealers use is to move their stock around periodically so that on their second trip round the book-fair visitors may see something they missed on their first.

When the fair opens, stand attendance is usually mandatory at all times. If you are on your own and you need a break, a nearby dealer will usually look after your stand and vice versa. Most associations will ask you to record sales to the public, to exhibiting trade and to visiting trade, so you should be prepared to record your sales accordingly. You will need to record totals for accounts purposes anyway. If you have a brochure on your business or a recent catalogue, you may be allowed to display copies of these near the entrance where visitors can pick one up if interested.

CONDUCTING YOURSELF AT A BOOK-FAIR

Having run the exhibitions section of IBM UK for five of my last seven years with them, I was heavily involved in planning for, setting up and running major exhibitions at venues such as the National Exhibition Centre and in training staff to man the stands. (One of the particularly enjoyable annual events, where there was a great demand from colleagues to help out, was Cowes Week on the Isle of Wight where IBM provided a yacht race results service. In an Admiral's Cup year we would put terminals on board the Royal Yacht *Britannia* for the use of the Royal Family).

Resulting from this experience, the following positive actions are recommended to help you to achieve your objectives as outlined above.

Encourage visitors to come to your stand and look at your stock by:

▸ Being smartly dressed.

▸ Having your stand and stock well lit. (It is probably not a good idea to be well 'lit up' yourself). At the planning stage you should check with the organisers the position of your stand and the likely illumination level. If this is low then you should check to see if stand lighting is allowed and the position of the nearest power points.

▸ Avoiding tatty or shabby stock as this gives a bad impression.

▸ Keeping your stand clean and tidy at all times. e.g. coffee cups cleared away as soon as emptied, Thermos flasks, drink cans and lunch boxes tucked away out of sight, and scraps of paper on the floor removed immediately.

▸ Taking an interest in visitors and not ignoring them. I have often heard visitors at a fair comment that they wouldn't go to that stand because ' *he didn't even look up from his paper*' or '*he looked so bored and tired I didn't want to disturb him.*'

▸ Looking bright, alert, happy and welcoming. Conversely don't be over eager, hover or pounce.

Once visitors are at your stand then:

▸ Greet them face to face with a bright and breezy 'good morning' or 'good afternoon' as appropriate. This gives them an opportunity to respond and possibly to ask you a specific question. If you can get into conversation with them you can usually home in on their interests. From then on you can show them what you have of possible interest. If there is no conversational response then let them look at the stock for a while.

▸ DO NOT say 'can I help you?' This is one of the greatest of all put-offs and positively invites a 'No' or 'Just browsing thanks,' which makes further questioning more difficult.

▸ After an appropriate pause try to initiate a conversation by asking an open question - one that cannot be answered by a simple yes or no. Starting with an adverb or pronoun can set you on the right track. My memory of the childhood rhyme goes something on the lines of:

...I have six serving men,
who and **what** and **why**
and **how** and **where** and **when**.

e.g.' **How** may I help you? **What** does your range of interests cover?' If the visitor is already carrying bags of books then:' **How** is the fair going for you?' If it's someone you recognise then: **'How** are you?' etc. It is up to you to think of a range of questions that you are comfortable with and that are appropriate. A determined non-talker will always get round this type of question, but for many who are reticent or shy it does give them an opportunity to break the ice. An alternative technique is to watch what books are being removed from the shelves for inspection. This enables you to point out others of similar interest or to mention that catalogue you have just produced on that topic.

> If you can't help the visitor directly, try to get details of their interests, you can invite them to go on your mailing list, or to visit your premises or website, or you can point them in the direction of other dealers at the fair who might be able to help them. It could be that you have the book they are looking for back home or at your shop. In that case you can take their details and quote them after the fair. Without getting into conversation with them this would otherwise be a missed opportunity.

> During the fair make notes of all the actions you have to take afterwards e.g. sending catalogues and quotes, sending that parcel off to a colleague or posting that item a customer was unable to take away. Carrying these out as soon as you return is good business and creates a good impression of efficiency.

N.B. An excellent training video written by Dennis Norden, called *How Not to Exhibit Yourself* is available from Video Arts. I used it in IBM for training my staff. It is recommended that all book-fair associations obtain a copy of this video to show to their members. For details of this and the accompanying booklet, please see the appendix.

SPECIALIST EXHIBITIONS

If you are going to specialise in a particular subject or range of subjects then exhibiting at 'private' book-fairs, conferences or exhibitions (as opposed to those open to the public) can be very profitable. If you have an interest in your subject then you are likely to be a member of a number of related societies e.g. scientific, literary, sporting, collecting, etc. Such societies hold regular meetings at which members are welcome. If you can make a name for yourself by speaking or lecturing at such meetings or by contributing to their written proceedings then you will find many opportunities for displaying your stock for sale at appropriate meetings for the mutual benefit of other members and yourself. (Sixteen of the societies I belong to are listed on my website under <u>Background</u>).

On average I attend about one book-fair per month of which about half are private. These latter involve meetings of geologists, palaeontologists, natural historians and historians of science and in many cases I am the only dealer there, e.g. see the illustration on page 48. I take stock relevant to the meeting, have a captive audience and my takings are usually far higher than with public book-fairs. The societies like it as it provides a service to their members, exhibiting fees are often not charged or are minimal, and it provides an excellent opportunity to get additions to my mailing list. Once you have become a known regular, members will often bring spare material from their own libraries to sell to you. One other big advantage is that you may have a very large space available including tables and benches, which means that you can take a full van load of material. There are also large national annual events such as the Chelsea Flower Show, though with these, booking space for a stand can be highly expensive and you need a very large specialist stock to cover your overheads.

International conferences are frequently based in the UK and north America and may have over 1,000 delegates all interested in one special subject. If you can exhibit at one of these then you have superb selling opportunities, can meet overseas customers and prospects, and will obtain many additions to your mailing list. If you think about it early enough you could produce a catalogue or advertising literature for the organisers to insert into the delegates packs, even if you were unable to attend the conference yourself. Over the years I have found that such conferences are the most enjoyable, financially, intellectually, and socially.

The ball is in your court - it is up to you to contact the meetings organisers of the societies you belong to. Your interest in the society and its activities should be a primary consideration and you should not join purely for potential commercial considerations. Remember that for such private meetings you still need public liability insurance cover.

THE INTERNET

By cataloguing your books and listing them on an international internet database such as ABE, you get sales potential equivalent to displaying your stock at 10 or more different British book-fairs concurrently, for 24 hours a day, for every day of the year, with over 25,000 visitors every day; and all this for just a very modest monthly charge -much less than you would pay for the average single book-fair. Please see part III for further details.

TAILPIECE

Having a stand at a book-fair is a little like a NASA space launch at Cape Canaveral. NASA's objectives are likely to be to increase the prestige of the USA and say, to study the violent volcanicity of Jupiter's proximal moon *Io*. You have the book-fair as a launch pad to project yourself, your personality, your knowledge and your stock towards new business opportunities and customers, so that hopefully you too will soon be over the moon.

CHAPTER 6

RUNNING A BOOK CATALOGUE BUSINESS

INTRODUCTION

Whether you are considering producing book catalogues either as your entire operation or just as one activity of several, there are many separate issues to consider. Based upon some 30 years of catalogue bookselling experience, this chapter outlines some comments, suggestions and recommendations on how to run an efficient and profitable business. Even if you are not planning to issue catalogues, there is much in this chapter be of interest to anyone starting secondhand bookdealing.

THE ADVANTAGES OF CATALOGUES - A Check-list.

- Can be quick and easy to produce.
- Extremely beneficial to cashflow.
- Moves stock quickly.
- Enables you to build up records of wants lists. e.g. If you get more orders for any item than you have stock for, you can keep records of those who want them on a waiting list for when further copies come in.
- Can go on selling for years afterwards.
- Can be circulated to non-customers enabling you to build up your customer base.
- Data entry can be carried out at any time and by relatively inexperienced staff.
- Can easily be combined with some or all other methods of operating.
- Can be timed to suit your marketing and cashflow situation.
- Can help to establish your reputation as a serious dealer in a specialist field, e.g. customers may keep your catalogues and use them for reference for years to come.
- Mini-lists as a subset of catalogues are very easy, quick to produce, and are highly cost-effective.
- You can give your customers first choice before putting material on the internet if you so wish.
- Much cheaper than running a shop, provided you can get suitable stock.
- Can easily be carried out operating from home.

- ▸ Can act as a very useful form of advertisement both for selling and buying, and can be an excellent form of publicity for you.
- ▸ Can be used to draw attention to your website.

THE DISADVANTAGES OF CATALOGUES

- ▸ Producing major catalogues e.g. with over 1000 items, can be expensive, time consuming, and possibly wasteful.
- ▸ Label production, envelopes, envelope stuffing, and mailing costs have to be covered.
- ▸ Mailing lists have to be created and maintained.
- ▸ No social intercourse with customers other than on the phone.

BUILDING AND UPDATING A MAILING LIST

Unless you are buying an existing mail-order catalogue business, it is likely that you will have to start from scratch in building up a list of names and addresses of potential customers that you subsequently hope to convert into a customer list. There are many ways or sources of list building, and some of the major ones are outlined below.

Other Dealers.

The standard directories and registers e.g. *Sheppard*, *Cole*, etc., can give you a head start here. It is up to you to select those related to your specialities and interests. *Cole* for example, has a very useful separate section for catalogue dealers with whom you might wish to enter into a reciprocal agreement for exchanging catalogues.

Trade Directories.

These are covered in chapter 8 on 'Trade Publications'. Many of these are purchased annually by collectors, libraries, and the book-buying public. It is therefore essential to ensure that your details are included in these as early as possible in your business life.

You will of course only be included in the ABA and PBFA directories and relevant ones for other countries, if you join these associations. The very powerful advertisement value of this is only one of the many benefits you obtain from such membership.

Direct Mail.

Writing a direct mail shot and to whom it should be sent is covered later in chapter 7. In this instance your specific objectives will include getting additions to your mailing list. It is strongly recommended that you design an appropriate form as specified under 'Customer Profile' below and send copies out with your mail shot to make it easy for recipients to reply.

Mailing lists or labels are available for purchase at so many £s (or $s) per hundred from specialist mailing houses. In addition there are many specialists belonging to the hundreds of thousands of individual societies and associations throughout the World. Directories of these e.g. *Directory of British Natural History and Related Societies in Britain and Ireland,* can be found in most reference sections of major public libraries or can be bought from the publishers. There are even Directories of Directories to help you. With many societies you can contact them to find the cost of including a mail shot or brochure in their next mailing to their members. (I have recently carried out just such an exercise with mailings of over 40,000 coloured brochures to the members of 10 different scientific societies. The results have been highly satisfactory. Further details of this are given in chapter 7 on 'Publicity'.

Some direct mail experts suggest that a 2% to 3% response from a mailing to the general public is the expected norm. By selecting your target audience to include only those interested in your speciality, the rate of response can be greatly increased thereby making it much more cost effective.

In order to monitor your success rate with each different method you use it is important to ascertain where people heard about you from. i.e. Ask them or if using a prepaid envelope or reply service include a code in the address to give you this information. You then have the information to know your success rates for each, which helps with future management planning.

Use of a Customer Profile.

This is basically a form you design yourself to include at least the following data: Your name, address, phone, fax, e-mail, website address; spaces for the potential customer to give their data as above including their title e.g. Mr, Dr, etc., and a date; a summary of your business and details of your subject categories and any subdivisions so that those of interest can be marked appropriately. You can of course use it to advertise past and forthcoming catalogues as well and any sales or major recent purchases or other news items.

If you are proposing to hold customer or potential customer records on a computer, or in any written form, then in the UK, under the provisions of the 1998 Data Protection Act you require explicit permission from the customer to do so. It is essential to include wording such as: *The provision of your name and address on this form will be taken as implicit permission for your details being held on our files.* Customers also like to be assured that their details will be used for your mailing purposes only and will not be passed to third parties - we have all suffered from junk mail. In addition to this, from the Autumn of 1999 anyone keeping such a mailing list has to be registered with the Data Protection Registry, currently at a cost of £75 for three years. For details of their address, and other contact information please see the appendix.

While on the subject of junk mail you should be aware that if you receive large numbers of unsolicited and unwanted faxes, British Tele-communications (BT) will change your number free of charge. Towards the end of 1998 I found I was getting up to six of these every day. This wastes a lot of paper and time. I complained to BT, they gave me a list of 20 or so new numbers to choose from and within a few hours I had a much better fax number than I had previously. The problem was solved for just the cost of changing some stationery which I was about to reprint anyway. Similarly if you wish to stop junk mail or junk faxes (the problem of junk e-mails has yet to be resolved) then contact the Direct Marketing Helpline on 0345 034599 or write to MPS, Freepost 22, London, W1E 7EZ

An alternative remedy is to contact the Office of Telecom-munications (Oftel), an independent body and obtain their advice. You should refer to Oftel's Consumer Representation Section who's phone number can be obtained from your telephone directory. In May 1999 new legislation was introduced in the United Kingdom, providing heavy financial penalties for those sending unsolicited faxes after being asked not to do so.

If you are only ever going to issue catalogues or lists to everyone on your mailing list, then the form can be relatively simple such as a postcard with your name and address on one side. If however your stock covers a wide subject range it is likely that from time to time you may issue monotopic catalogues or shorter lists on individual subjects. You will then need a more detailed customer profile. In this case it is highly advantageous to keep your mailing list on your computer in the form of a database with separate categories for each subject. You then have the facility to print out selective names and addresses for only those interested in the subject matter of the catalogue or list.

A wide range of self-adhesive label stationery suitable for computer printers is available from stationers or computer suppliers. It is a relatively simple matter to organise your customer name and address computer files into two or three columns, have a set number of lines per address and adjust the point size so that each name and address fits conveniently onto the label stationery you have chosen.

If you don't want to bother with labels to start with, you can always print on plain paper, cut out the names and addresses, and Sellotape or glue them to the envelopes.

An example of a customer profile can be seen on my website by clicking on <u>Mailing List</u>, though a more detailed one (A4 sized) is available for sending through the post. Since I have had a website and publicised it, an ever increasing proportion of the weekly additions to my mailing list come via the internet.

Book-fairs.

Though mentioned earlier, it is relevant to emphasise here that if you are proposing to sell at book-fairs as well as through catalogues, then one of your prime objectives at any book-fair should be to obtain additions to your mailing list. Visitors will readily give you a visiting card on request; you can have a blank sheet of paper on which you can write their details, or a notebook, or you can have a supply or pre-printed customer profile forms for visitors to complete on the spot or to take away and return later. It is of course very helpful to have a supply of your last one or two catalogues to hand to give away which can help to convince visitors of the benefits of being on your mailing list. If they are just giving you a visiting card or you are writing their details down and you are proposing to put their details on your computer, or in other form such as a card index file, then you must obtain their verbal permission to do this, in accordance with the legal requirements outlined above.

Lists of Collectors and Special Libraries.

There are a range of special publications specifically devoted to providing the names and addresses of individual collectors throughout the world and their interests, or details of libraries which are interested in acquiring certain material. It is up to you track these down via your local library or adverts in the trade press. e.g. *International Directory of Book Collectors 1998-99,* 6th edition, compiled by Roger Sheppard and published by Trigon Press in 1998 at £32. This contains details of around 1,500 collectors with an index of authors and subject collecting interests. The publishers or their distributors should be contacted directly for details of the latest edition. A survey of the subject-area requirements in old, rare and collected books of certain libraries and other institutions in the United Kingdom was published by The Clique in 1989 under the title *U.K. Libraries Interested in Old Books.* It is now out of print but can be obtained through the public library lending system.

Buying an Existing Business.

If you are ever thinking of buying another business there are a four major considerations to bear in mind of which obtaining the mailing list is only one:

Why is the business up for sale?

If the proprietor is elderly and wishing to retire this is likely to be well worth considering. The business may have declined in the later years possibly in parallel with the proprietor(s), but with the vigour you will be injecting into the business this reverse can soon be halted. If the business is declining for any other reason then a very careful look should be taken. This should be backed up by insisting on receiving copies of at least the last three years accounts e.g. trading and profit and loss, and balance sheets, preferably produced by an accountant. This will give the trends of the business. Note that it is easy to adjust figures for one year to give superb results but much more difficult for three years in a row. Get an accountant to check them out for you if you don't feel qualified. If taking over a shop or shop lease then a solicitor should be used to check out possible future changes such as new parking restrictions or the impact of nearby buildings or road widening.

The Mailing List.

This can be the most important part of your purchase. If a dealer has been in business for many years and is well known, then in buying it you are also buying the goodwill of the business which comprises the reputation of the seller and the customer relationship that has been built up, together with the mailing list. Some years ago I bought out another dealer who was retiring. His stock and reference library were minimal but it was his mailing list and goodwill I was after. If such a mailing list is more comprehensive than you need, then those names and addresses you don't want can be passed to an appropriate specialist dealer, for cash, or an exchange, or for brownie points.

The Reference Library.

Every dealer needs reference works to be able to operate efficiently. These may vary from a few volumes to a library of hundreds. Such a library may comprise as much value as the stock and can give a considerable impetus to a fledgling business. If in buying such a business you find that you don't need all the reference works there is normally little trouble in disposing of them to other dealers or to collectors.

The Stock.

There can be an enormous variability in the amount, quality and value of stock. It is up to you to decide what it is worth to you and to see if this is what the seller is looking for. If it is a good buy then you may need to seek additional sources of finance such as a long term capital loan from a bank, a second mortgage on your house, a short term increase in your overdraft facility, or a loan from another source as recommended by your accountant. Even if you don't advertise your purchase (and it is strongly recommended that you do), the word soon gets around and you will find a rapid rise in your cashflow.

Press Release.

Though this is covered in chapter 7 on 'Publicity' it is worth reminding you here that one of your objectives in issuing a press release is to obtain additions to your mailing list. The press release should accordingly carry appropriate wording.

The Internet.

If you decide to put some of your stock on one of the internet book databases such as ABE or Bibliocity then hopefully you will receive orders from many parts of the world. Each of these can represent an addition to your mailing list and can be particularly useful if you obtain details of their interests by the use of a customer profile as outlined above.

Updating and Organizing a Mailing List.

Additions and changes to and deletions from your mailing list are usually very straightforward to implement particularly if you have them on a database. It is getting the information enabling you to do this that is a little more difficult. Additions are fairly well covered in this chapter. For changes, particularly to addresses, it is important to remind customers periodically to notify you of any change of address. This can be done textually in the body of your catalogues or by including an appropriate form in with your catalogues when you mail them. There is no greater waste of time, money, and effort than to get many catalogues returned marked *Address Unknown* or *Gone Away*.

The implications of this are, that you should always include your name and address on the mailing envelope so that the Royal Mail know to whom the envelope should be returned, or you should use transparent plastic envelopes and print your name and address on the outside of your catalogues so that they show through; and that on receipt of such returns you delete the details from your mailing records.

As part of your customer records you should monitor and record the individual response to each catalogue mailing and then, via a management decision, you may if you wish, carry out a pruning exercise if you have not received any response from say the last three catalogues. This can be done by writing directly to the individuals or institutions concerned, asking if they wish to be retained on your mailing list. React according to their response and if none then delete them.

If you have a small mailing list then much file organisation may not be needed. With a large and complex one, especially if you have many customers abroad it is important to divide it into UK and Overseas and with the latter into European countries and at least into the Post Office airmail zones 1 and 2 for the rest of the world. Full details can be obtained from the Royal Mail. This makes it much easier to work out the postage costs for each division and how many of each denomination of stamp you will need to buy if you are using stamps rather than a franking machine. You should be aware that for Europe at certain weights in the lower range (currently at up to 60g), it is actually cheaper to send items at airmail letter rate rather than airmail printed paper rate. If you are going to do selective mailings to only part of your mailing list e.g. all institutional libraries say, then your database file organisation must allow you to do this and the appropriate features be incorporated at the design stage.

If you have a large overseas mailing list for catalogues and are likely to be spending £100 or over (at the time of going to press), on overseas airmail postage, then it is worth enquiring about the savings to be made by using International Unsorted mailings. You should contact your nearest Royal Mail International business centre whose address and phone number is given in the leaflet *The easy way to mail abroad for businesses,* obtainable at most post or sorting offices. If speed of sending catalogues abroad is not essential then sending them via surface mail is far and away the cheapest alternative. There is a flat Royal Mail rate for any item up to 100g (currently 54p) from the UK to any country in the world.

Other deletions are usually notified in instances such as 'retirement' or 'no longer wanting to collect.' If you are on the ball here you will of course immediately contact the customer to wish them a long and happy retirement and just mention in passing that if at any time they are thinking of disposing of all or part of their library you know just the person to help them.

With notices of deaths it is always sad to hear of the passing of customers, many of whom over the years have become well known to you or even become personal friends. It is not a time to intrude when a family member has just lost a loved one but there may be a large library there whom those left behind may not know what to do with. To avoid this situation, it is recommended that you get to know your customers well so that whilst they are still alive they will make sure that their family is aware of your existence so that in due course they know where to contact you.

CATALOGUE ORIGINATION AND CONTENT
Catalogue Origination.
The advent of the in-house Personal Computer (PC) with word-processing and database facilities has such enormous advantages over handwriting and the typewriter or sending copy out to be typeset, that other methods will not even be considered here. One of the big advantages of word processors is that spelling *missteaks* (regardless of whether or not they are due to you or a keying error), are automatically highlighted, facilitating proof reading and corrections.

Catalogue Content.
It is usual to have a title page giving your trading name and address and your phone, fax, e-mail and website details together with a catalogue title and number. There may be an illustration if you wish. On the title page or verso (= reverse) or on the rear cover, it is normal to include your terms of trade, (e.g. payment on receipt of goods), ordering information, how payment may be made, postage and packaging costs, details of abbreviations used, contents with page numbers and/or item numbers and any advertisements you may wish to add.

It is important to include in your catalogue and on your invoices, a printed statement to the effect *that all items remain our property until payment has been made in full.* This is a legal requirement to protect your title to the goods in the event of a dispute over ownership, especially when payment has not been made e.g. in bankruptcy and insolvency cases. This applies when goods are supplied on approval or on an invoice for payment later. It does not apply if payment is made in advance.

If you wish to illustrate your catalogue, it is usual to do this with illustrations taken from one or more of the works you have catalogued. Here modern technology comes to your aid in the form of a digital camera. It could be well worth your while investing in one of these if you are going to be using many illustrations in the future, as it can greatly reduce your overall costs and produce high quality results.

You should be aware of the copyright situation. For books aged 70 years or older no permission is needed, but for those younger than this you do need the permission of the publisher and possibly other copyright holders.

If as a policy decision you are going to offer trade discount to other dealers after say two weeks then here is a good place to put it. If you are expecting to be VAT registered and to have customers in the EEC, then you should ask that those who are registered for VAT in the EEC should supply their VAT number when ordering. It is worth stating that books are currently zero rated in the UK and that there is therefore no tax to be added to the price. It is strongly recommended that you ask customers **not** to send a remittance with their order. If customers do send payment with their order this presupposes that all items ordered are still available, which is often not the case, and can involve you in writing back and sending a full or partial refund and unnecessary accounting paperwork and expense.

The rest of the catalogue, forming the bulk, will be the detailed catalogue entries. If you examine a range of dealers' catalogues you will soon get the idea. One useful tip is to ask customers to specify alternative items in case the one(s) they want have already been sold. It is also worth while entering general information here particularly if you are not using a database. e.g. *All items are complete, bound in cloth or hardback printed boards, are in fine condition, octavo and published in London except where otherwise described.* This saves repeating these data in every entry.

CATALOGUE DESCRIPTIONS.

The basis of a catalogue description is to give a unique reference by which each entry can be identified, in combination with a more or less detailed description of the item including its physical condition and any relevant comments. The recommendations given here are not all mandatory but they are based upon common usage over many years and they are commended to your attention.

Examples of other dealers' catalogue entries can be seen in their catalogues, and in Cole's *Annual Registers* which were issued up until 1999. Abbreviated ones can be found in trade publications such as the *Bookdealer*. An important reference work here is John Carter's *ABC for Book Collectors*, 7th edition, 1994.

If you are dealing in antiquarian books then the article in the Antiquarian Booksellers Association *Handbook 1999-2000* by Roger Gaskell - *The Terms of the Trade,* is essential reading. Your entries should be considered under the following headings and sequence which includes the twenty three most common descriptive categories used. Categories **i, ii, iii, xvi,** and **xxii** are mandatory for all entries. Your choice from the remainder will depend on the details of the book and its price and how much space you can afford to allocate.

i. Item Number.

This will usually be a straightforward sequential number from 1 or 001 onwards. Though it is the first item in any catalogue entry it is strongly recommended that it is the last to be keyed in if you are doing this manually. When compiling a catalogue, new material may come in which you wish to catalogue or a particular item may sell before the catalogue is finished. Any of these situations can play havoc with your numbering system unless you leave numbering to the last minute. There are also situations where you may wish to include letters as well, to give an alphanumeric identifier. If you manually put the numbers in on your computer do check every page before moving to the next. There can be mistakes of duplication or omission and if these occur unnoticed near the beginning you have to slog through the whole catalogue again altering numbers.

Most modern word processing software packages, e.g. *Corel WordPerfect 8* and *Microsoft Word 97* and subsequent updates, provide the facility to do automatic item and page numbering for you which makes life much easier once the essentials of this have been mastered. Automatic numbering has the advantage over manual numbering that additions and deletions are taken care of and far fewer key strokes are needed.

ii Author or editor name(s).

The surname should be given first followed by initials e.g. Odell, N.E. Where the author is famous or well-known you may like to give the forename in full e.g. Ray, John. To emphasise a catalogue entry you can put the surname in upper case and/or bold e.g. **BOYD, L.A.** or by underlining. Where there is more than one author you have to decide how many you standardise upon. e.g. if there are two then both may be entered e.g. **WAGER, L.R. & DEER, W.A.**, or if three or more you may just put the first plus *et al.* e.g. **HOEL, A. et al.** If the author is not known then **Anon.** is a suitable entry or in some cases details of the publisher. (Between them, *et al* and *Anon.*, are amongst the most prolific authors of all time). The catalogue entries should follow in alphabetical sequence of the first author's or editor's surname. If an author or combination of authors has more than one entry then these should be strictly in date of publication order.

With editors the same principles apply as above except that it has to be made clear that the name(s) given are editors and not authors by putting an appropriate abbreviation after the name(s) e.g. **(ed.)** or **(eds.)**. If an author is also the editor of another publication in your catalogue, you should consider putting this after the authored works rather than in date sequence within them.

iii. Title.

With a short title this should be entered in full e.g. ***Systematics of the Green Algae.*** How you emphasise this or not with bold, italics or underlining is up you. If there is a subtitle as well it is entirely a matter of choice whether or not this is included. You are trying to communicate to the readers sufficient data to enable them to identify the book or to be attracted to it and yet at the same time not take up unnecessary space.

With many older works there are extremely long descriptions. If the book is valuable then you can afford space and time to enter details in full. A compromise is often entered into especially where a work is well-known, by entering the first part of the title followed by an ellipsis: ... to indicate that there is more but it has been left out.

Where the main language used in the text is foreign e.g. French, this is normally apparent from the language of the title and the place of publication. If there is any doubt the language should be specified or where applicable a general statement can be given e.g. *all books are in printed in English or in the language used in the title*.

iv. Number of Volumes or Parts. (Vols., pts.)

Where a work has been issued in more than one volume this is a convenient point at which to say how many, e.g. if a work had been issued in four volumes then put **4 vols.** Some volumes may be issued in two or more parts each of which can confusingly also be called a volume. In such cases state the number of issued volumes and the number of bound volumes. e.g. SARTON, G. *Introduction to the History of Science.* **3 vols. in 5**. Some works have a number of plates which may be bound in with the text or bound separately as an atlas. Such distinctions should clearly be stated in your descriptions. e.g. **text and atlas volumes.** With multi-volume works the stated collation of pagination and plates can be omitted.

Some works were issued in parts, to be bound later on completion. This is common with many Victorian works such as those of Charles Dickens and scientific works such as the monographs of the Palaeontographical Society. If complete the number of parts can usefully be given. If such a work is incomplete then the number of parts must be given. e.g. **Parts 1-6 (of 8).**

v. Edition, Impression, Variations. (Ed., imp., variant.)

Appropriate detail should be included as outlined in chapter 4 on 'Pricing and Pricing Policy'. If a volume is a book club edition, then this must be stated in your description including the name of the book club, as in general such books are much less desirable than standard editions, other things being equal.

vi. Frontispiece. (Frontis.)

Where one is present it should be mentioned e.g. **Frontis.**, unless you have made a policy decision with books under a certain retail price, say £10, not to include this amount of detail. If you do use the term it may be qualified in various ways. e.g. Portrait frontis. = **Port. frontis.**, or Coloured frontis. = **Cold. frontis.** In cases where a work contains plates, the frontispiece is sometimes numbered as a plate, e.g. pl. I, or it may be unnumbered but still included in the plate count. It is a good idea to indicate this e.g. (= **pl.I**) so that later when the number of plates is given the reader is aware that the frontispiece has been included as one of these.

vii. Title Page. (T/p.)

Title pages came into general use in the early 16th century and for most modern works, unless it is lacking or has faults to be described, this needs no description or mention. In 19th century and earlier works the title page may be particularly ornamental or have a small decorative illustration or woodcut. Where this is not within set borders or squared off at the edges, this is called a Vignette. e.g. **T/p vignette.**

Prior to the 1830s if a printer made a mistake on a title page a replacement page was usually issued with instructions to the binder that the original should be discarded. This was often not done, or both put in, or the wrong page discarded, resulting in the book being found in three separate states. e.g. In John Ray's first work: *Catalogus Plantarum circa Cantabrigiam nascentium*, 1st edition, 1660, [Keynes 1] as indicated in Geoffrey Keynes's Bibliography of Ray, 1951 where both title pages are illustrated. This bibliography incidentally is an essential reference work for those interested in Ray.

viii. Pagination. (pp.)

In early books the pages were often erratically numbered or not at all, and if you look at bibliographies of early works or any of the standard works on bibliography you will find that collations are given by the signatures, which are letters and/or numbers at the foot or tail of each gathering or section.

Most books, at least within the last two centuries, follow a standard practice of having some or all of the preliminary pages numbered in Roman numerals (usually lower case e.g. **viii**) with the main text in Arabic numerals. There are many variations within this, e.g. some publishers use no numbers at all for the preliminaries and the main text suddenly starts at page 15 or some similar number. There may also be Roman numerals at the end and in many 19th century works there may be publisher's advertisements at the back to be described. As many of these are important for bibliographic work it is important to include the pagination of such advertisements in your descriptions. Where preliminaries are unnumbered these can be counted and the number given in square brackets, e.g. **[viii]**.

The use of square brackets [ ] anywhere in a catalogue description is, by convention, normally reserved for data which is not explicit in the book, e.g. where the name of the author or date or place of publication is not given on the title page, but can be determined from other sources. e.g. *Vestiges of the Natural History of Creation* was first published anonymously in 1844 and it was not until the 12th edition forty years later that Robert Chambers put his name on the title page. References to the authorship of any of the first eleven editions should therefore be: **[Chambers, R.]**.

How much detail you include is entirely up to you but it is recommended that at least the main pagination is included. e.g. **pp145** or **145pp** or just **145**. For books of say retail price £15 and over you could use the preliminaries as well. e.g. **pp xii, 256.**

ix. Illustrations. (Ills.)

Text-figures are printed within the text, and whole-page illustrations are mainly but not always referred to as plates and sometimes as figures. Up until about 1600 most text-figures were in the form of wood-cuts. Copper engravings followed but wood-cuts continued until late into the 19th century. A serendipitous discovery in Munich in 1796 by Aloysius Senefelder, led to the development of lithography though this term did not come into use until 1804. Lithography literally means printing from stone. The term has been retained though coated aluminium plates are now used instead of stone. Limestone from Solnhofen in Bavaria, which had a very fine-grained texture, was the only entirely satisfactory lithographic stone available and enabled great detail to be obtained in the printing process.

Quarrying this limestone had a very significant subsequent impact in the world of palaeontology. The fine-grained limestone and the unusual circumstances of its deposition in an anoxic lacustrine environment, produced exceptional circumstances for fossil preservation within it, e.g. remains of the late Jurassic bird *Archaeopteryx* were first found at Solnhofen in 1860 and tens of thousands of other superb fossils subsequently. Many institutions have displays of fossils preserved in exquisite detail in this limestone, e.g. the Sedgwick Museum in Cambridge and the University Museum of Natural History in Oxford.

Coloured plates first appeared at the end of the 17th century but were not common until the mid-18th century. For the next hundred years plates were mainly coloured by hand with water-colours; then from the mid-19th century, chromolithography and subsequently other forms of colour-printing gradually took over. The coming centuries will undoubtedly see technical advances as yet undreamed of.

Some publishers have a habit of giving details of all illustrations. e.g. Text-figures 108, Plates 45, (of which 3 are coloured), Maps 5, Tables 15. This is extremely helpful to the cataloguer and votive offerings should be made to all such publishers. Others are less helpful and it may be up to you to do some counting.

With works containing coloured or other plates it is vital to check that all are there, as a missing plate can make a vast difference to the price. If you have incorrectly described a work as complete when it is not, then a customer is perfectly entitled to return it at your expense or to negotiate a much lower price. Many dealers abbreviate the term text-figures to just figs. and the entry above could appear as: **figs. 108, pls. 45 (3 cold.), maps 5, tabs. 15.** With a cheap book or where the illustrations are not numbered then just **some ills.** or **many ills.** may suffice.

x. Ex-Library. (Ex-lib., or E)

This term is used for books mainly from public or institutional libraries which show evidence of their provenance. Books from public lending libraries almost invariably have library book-plates or labels on the end papers, stamp(s) on the title page and possibly on plates and other pages as well. A cancellation stamp may also be present. On the spine of the book or dust jacket, there is invariably a shelf mark or plastic tape in one form or another, and the condition can often leave much to be desired. These characteristics inevitably lessen the appeal and value of a book but have to be described. Despite this there is a market for such books provided the price is right. Items from reference sections of public libraries are usually in far better condition and much less marked and hence are considered more desirable.

Those from institutional libraries tend to be in better condition than those from public libraries though many may still have library plates, stamps and shelf marks. If you are lucky some may be completely unmarked. In general they tend to be of a more serious nature and if scarce can command a good price.

Works from private libraries may at most have an ownership bookplate on the paste-down front end paper and do not need to be described as ex-library. An interesting book-plate can add value however and could be worth a mention. e.g. **Armorial Bookplate of Lord Avebury (John Lubbock).** See also under **Provenance** below.

xi. Dust-Jacket or (Dust-Wrapper). (d.j., or just J.)

Carter (1994) suggests that dust-*jacket* should be preferred to dust-*wrapper* as this avoids any possible confusion with the term *wrappers*. Where appropriate, the chosen abbreviation should be used, and any defects present described, e.g. small tear Sellotaped, or **slightly chipped** which means a number of small pieces are missing.

xii. Size and Format. (Imp., Roy., Cr., Folio; & 4to, 8vo, 12mo, etc.)

Books are printed on sheets of paper of various sizes, which are then folded and sewn, or stapled, or glued. An unfolded sheet is called a broadsheet or broadside. These were originally printed on one side only and used for royal proclamations, official notices and even for speeches by criminals about to be executed at the scaffold. Broadsheets can come in many sizes the most common of which are: imperial (30" x 22"), royal (25" x 20"), medium (23" x 18") and crown (20" x 15").

The naming of book sizes and formats originates in the way in which the sheets of paper comprising the book are folded, i.e. folded once to give four pages or sides = folio (Fo., fol. or 2^0); folded twice to give eight pages = quarto (4to or 4°); folded three times to give sixteen pages = octavo, (8vo or 8°) and by right-angle folds as well to give 24 pages = twelvemo or duodecimo (12mo or 12°), etc. It should be emphasised that terms such as 8vo refer to the number of folds and not to the finished book or page size, though the trade does use these terms loosely to indicate size. A leaf comprises two pages, one on each side of the leaf. For any leaf the right hand page is called the recto and the left-hand page the verso. Normally, but not always, the recto is an odd numbered page and the verso an even number.

The vast majority of books published today come into one of the several octavo categories and they are usually described collectively as 8vo. Obviously, depending upon the size of sheet you start with and the number of folds, you can finish up with many different combinations of page size and format. Through long common usage, these terms are used for book sizes though technically they apply to the page.

75

Some of the more common ones are listed below:

Some Standard Average Bound Book Sizes and Formats

Name	Size (Inches)	Size (mm)
imp(erial) folio	22 x 15	556 x 380
folio	18 x 12	453 x 305
sm(all) folio	15 x 9	380 x 228
roy(al) 4to	13 x 10	330 x 254
4to	12 x 9	305 x 228
cr(own) 4to	10 x 7.5	254 x 190
roy(al) 8vo	9.25 x 6.25	234 x 156
8vo	9 x 5.75	228 x 147
cr(own) 8vo	7.5 x .5	190 x 127
sm(all) 8vo	6.5 x 4.5	165 x 115
12mo	7.5 x 4.5	190 x 115

There are some minor differences in size between American and British usage of these terms and the above sizes should not be taken as absolute. If a book falls in between two of the above categories, choose the nearest and you are unlikely to fall foul of the *Trades Description Act*. This book is a royal octavo with a page size of 234mm x 156mm.

When describing the size and/or format of a book it is particularly useful to have to hand a large imperial folio sheet (22" x 15") of white faced cardboard or foamboard marked with all the above sizes. This enables you and any of your staff who are entering catalogue data to check the size of any book by simply placing it on the sheet.

Where the normal dimensions of a book are reversed, i.e. the width is greater than the height, then this is referred to as oblong, e.g. **oblong 8vo** or **obl. 8vo** (= 9" width x 5.75" height.) Where the dimensions are equal the format is described as **square**, e.g. **sq. 4to** (= 10" x 10".)

xiii. Binding.

The earliest bindings comprised thin wooden boards held together with strips of leather and were used for protecting medieval manuscripts. These were laid flat, and hence any ornamentation was applied to the front cover only. Calf skin and parchment or **vellum,** (usually obtained then from the skin of sheep or goats) became popular during the 15th century. Around 1500, cardboard began to replace wooden boards particularly in Italy, and were often covered in **morocco** (imported goatskin). By the end of the 15th century books had become more affordable and hence more common and were being shelved on their tails as we now do. As a consequence this led to the initiation of spine decoration.

Full brown calf bindings were the most common up until the middle of the 18th century when half leather bindings became popular. With half bindings the back (or spine) and the corners are covered in leather and the rest of the sides with paper (often **marbled** q.v.below) or cloth. A quarter binding has a narrower backstrip and no corners and can be either in leather or cloth.

For the last two hundred years calf has been the most popular choice for leather bindings. It has the advantage of being easily dyed but if left in a dry atmosphere, or exposed to sunlight, with time it becomes brittle and cracks, particularly at the outer hinges, unless periodically treated with a suitable leather cream. [I spend several days each year applying cream to the leather books in my own library].

When a calf book comes into stock it is always a good idea to give it one or more applications of leather cream. This quite often has a dramatic effect on both its appearance and feel and can greatly enhance its value. Please see the appendix for a source of supply. Such creams are also useful for treating other leather items such as shoes, gloves and handbags.

The earlier books were generally published in paper covers called 'wrappers' or in 'boards' (paper-covered cardboard), so that they could subsequently be bound in leather according to the requirements and purse of the purchaser. In England from about 1830, **publisher's cloth bindings,** (q.v.) below, became common, though many works continued to be issued in paper-covered parts till the 20th century, and some still continue today. From about 1840 gilt embossing of cloth covers by machine (blocking) became firmly established and the Victorian era was truly a golden one as far as book cloth decoration is concerned.

Most modern books are issued bound in one of two main cover types:

a. With paper covers called **paperbacks** or softbacks.

The dawn of the modern paperback era dates from the first Penguins produced in England in 1936. Even paperbacks were issued with dust jackets in those days. [As a young schoolboy in the mid-1930s I earned my first pocket money by folding dust jackets and placing them on paperbacks produced by The Anchor Press near to where I lived at Tiptree in Essex. The princely sum of one penny (1d = 0.417p in today's money) was paid per 100 copies. No money for Tiptree jam here! The book - *Mein Kampf* by one Adolf Hitler. I'd dearly love to see a copy of this again one day].

b. With hard covers called **hardbacks** which may comprise:
- publisher's cloth glued to boards (cases), or
- boards covered with printed paper, or
- boards covered with a synthetic material, or
- boards with a full or half calf cover.

You should be aware that some modern publishers state in their descriptions that a particular book is bound in 'cloth' when in fact it is not bound in a fabric at all but in some synthetic material which may be embossed to resemble cloth.

Some of the more common terms used in catalogue descriptions relating to bindings and pages are given below.

- **All Edges Gilt** (aeg): The head, fore-edge and tail have been gilded.
- **Backstrip:** A synonym for the back of the book or spine.
- **Binder's Cloth:** This differs from publishers' cloth q.v. below, in being less ornamented and is lettered from standard type or dies. It is unique to a particular book and is normally of a higher quality. If a book from an earlier period is subsequently rebound in cloth then the term **new cloth** is an alternative description.
- **Buckram:** A superior quality strong book cloth with a characteristic appearance. It is favoured by libraries for its durability - hence the term *library buckram*. It may be made of linen, cotton or jute.
- **Calf:** Leather made from calf skin. It has a smooth finish and has been used for books since about 1450.
- **Cased:** A term applicable to most modern hardbacks where the binding material is glued to two boards with a hollow between forming the spine. The case is subsequently attached to the book by means of a coarse muslin called mull or a strip of calico, and paste-down endpapers. The first such book issued by a publisher in England with a cloth case and lettering on the spine was by John Murray in 1832.
- **Contemporary:** The binding, usually calf, is from the same period as the date of publication.

- **Disbound:** Once bound but now removed from the covers. This may apply to a whole book or to a part removed from an annual volume.
- **Hinges:** The interior junctions of the spine of a volume with the boards or sides. The term external hinge is in common use however as an alternative to joint.
- **Joints:** The exterior junctions of the spine of a volume with the boards or sides. These are normally only referred to if defective. e.g. rubbed, cracked, split.
- **Marbled:** The effect produced when sheets of paper or edges of books are decorated by transferring floating colours from the surface of a bath of gum or size.
- **Publisher's Cloth:** A uniform cloth case used by a publisher for binding an edition for issue to the trade. It started in the early 1820s and rapidly superseded paper covered boards. Cases could readily be blocked in a production run and hence are normally much more ornamental then binder's cloth. q.v. above.
- **Rebacked:** Replacement of the original spine with a new one, usually when the backstrip has become detached or the joints severely split or cracked.
- **Recased:** The original case has become partly or wholly separated from the book and is refixed using fresh mull or calico and new endpapers. It is also used as a means of repairing minor joint splits by additionally lining the spine with a cloth matching the original, to minimise the unsightliness of the splits.
- **Relaid:** With cloth, where a detached backstrip is complete or nearly so, it is glued to the new spine after rebacking. This gives a better colour match, saves the need for new spine lettering and is usually preferred by collectors. With leather rebacks, if the original spine label can be removed intact it can be replaced or relaid on the new spine.
- **Rexine:** A cloth with an imitation leather surface.
- **Top Edge Gilt:** (teg) As for aeg but the head only is gilded. This improves the appearance and prevents staining from accumulated dust.
- **Tipped in:** An item is fixed into a book by paste or glue along the inner margin. This can apply to separate illustrations, maps, etc, as part of the book, or to an author's letter, or errata slip. Pages sometimes come loose from a book and these can usually be tipped back in. Chapter 9 explains the tipping-in procedure.

▸ **Unbound:** The book has never been bound or cased. c.f. *wrappers* above.

▸ **Uncut:** The edges of the paper have not been cut by a guillotine or plough and are left rough or ragged. It is often confused with *unopened*.

▸ **Unopened:** The section folds on the head and sometimes the fore-edges as well, have by intent or by accidentally missing the guillotine, been left uncut. To open them they need to be slit by hand using a paper-knife. A specially sharpened one is strongly recommended. It is often confused with *uncut*.

Sheppard's Directories of Book Dealers, give a useful checklist of other generally well-known descriptive terms and their abbreviations.

xiv. Publication Series.

Where a book or monograph forms part of a series it is relevant to give details with the abbreviated publication name in italics and the number in the series in bold. e.g. Symposium of the Zoological Society of London number 31 would appear as: *Symp. Zool. Soc. Lond.* **31**. You can do your own abbreviations or follow the guidelines sometimes given in the publication or the standard abbreviations given in works such as the *World List of Scientific Periodicals published in the years 1900-1960.* 3 volumes, 4th ed., edited by P.Brown & S.B.Stratton, 1963, and subsequent supplements.

xv. Place of Publication.

This is where you have to make a policy decision. Some dealers omit this altogether, while others include it for books over a certain retail price only. If in your general statement you have said that all are published in London unless otherwise indicated, then this can save much repetition. Where a book is published in several towns in different countries at the same time, the preliminaries usually indicate the major country and hence which town to use.

xvi. Date of Publication.

This is normally given on the title page or its reverse. If it can not be found there, then sometimes a date will be given at the end of an introduction. Care has to be taken here as the date may be the date the introduction was written and not the date the book was published. The *British Museum General Catalogue of Printed Books to 1955* and subsequent supplements is an invaluable reference source for dates. (The compact edition produced by Readex Microprint Corporation, is the most convenient to use.) Where a date is not given but can be inferred then square brackets are used as before e.g. **[1868]**. If a work is reprinted or reissued then the original date should be given in round brackets. e.g. **(1945)** reprinted, **1998.**

The date and place of publication are often placed after the title and before the contents in a catalogue entry. The choice of position is yours.

xvii. Reference Works.

One of the major working tools of a catalogue bookdealer is a comprehensive reference library. Many of these will be bibliographies of particular authors or subjects or catalogues of books from a particular time period. Where relevant, quoting a particular authority and reference number, will both add authority to your catalogue entry and at the same time leave the reader in no doubt as to which edition, impression or issue is being offered. e.g In the section on title pages above, **Keynes 1** is an example. For works by Charles Darwin you should refer to - Freeman, R. *The Works of Charles Darwin...* and for early printed books the *Short-title catalogue...* by A.W.Pollard and G.R.Redgrave and its continuation by D.Wing are very frequently quoted. Bookdealers love to find issues not in these works and then delight in wording such as: not in *Wing.*

Where such references are used it is a nice touch to include a list of the books quoted in the catalogue or alternatively on your website as exemplified by the natural history bookdealers Wheldon & Wesley Ltd. on http://www.users.dircon.co.uk/~wheldwes. All of these references will of course form an important buying guide for you in building up your own reference library.

xviii. Condition.

The general condition should be described ranging from mint which means indistinguishable from new, down to poor. Several different terms are in common use and the usage of these terms apart from mint which is unequivocal, differs from dealer to dealer and from country to country. e.g. In descending order: **Mint, very fine, fine, very good, good, fair, reading copy, (= working copy or binding copy), poor.** There is a need for standardization here though Carter, 1994, includes much useful guidance. It may be necessary to describe both the exterior of the book e.g. **a fine bright copy,** meaning the covers are in excellent condition and the lettering and or embossing are outstanding; and the interior e.g. **a clean, sound copy,** meaning the pages are unmarked and the binding is firm and not loose.

xix. Description of any Specific Faults.

Apart from the general condition, a description of any faults should be given unless with a cheap book, minor faults such as library stamps or minor soiling are stated not to be described. Some of the more common terms used are:

Browning: Due to the acid or chlorine content of the paper used for books produced in earlier years, pages may go brown - a process that usually starts at the outer edges and progresses inwards. It is the result of a chemical reaction involving atmospheric oxygen which is greatly accelerated by sunlight. (Try leaving a newspaper in sunlight for a few days or weeks and you will readily see the browning effect). In some cases this may only be unsightly but all too often it results in brittleness, the older the book the greater this effect is likely to be.

Damp buckling or staining: Water is one of a book's worst enemies and can cause covers and pages to become buckled and stained, colour to be lost or high gloss art pages stuck together. There is no cure though stuck pages can sometimes be freed from each other.

Faded or Sunned: Through exposure to sunlight, the colour on the spines may become faded compared with the rest of the cover. This is particularly marked with red covers. It is sometimes possible for a restorer to restain the spine to give an appearance approaching the original. This should be described as **spine restained.**

Foxed or **foxing:** brown marks on pages or plates or the head and fore-edge caused by storage in damp conditions enabling certain moulds to grow. The products of mould metabolites react chemically with the paper to produce localized brown patches. This may range from **light spotting** to **heavily foxed.** Commercial products are frequently advertised in the trade press for the removal of such marks.

Loose: One or more gatherings may become unsewn or unglued, or the case may become partly detached from the book. This occurs most frequently at the inner hinges where the end papers may become split as well. The cure is resewing or regluing, combined with recasing and new end papers.

Rubbed: Means the cover is a little worn or abraded, usually at the head, tail, spine, hinges, fore-edges or corners.

Shaken: Similar to **loose** but to a lesser degree.

Shaken but not Stirred: As above but is applied only to the James Bond novels of Ian Fleming.

xx. Provenance

This is an indication in the book of previous ownership, such as a signature, a bookplate, a library stamp, or details of auction houses or salerooms with dates where the book was previously sold. A characteristic collector's binding may also indicate provenance and similarly dealer's catalogues.

xxi. Association Copy

An association copy is one that belonged to either: the author or editor and may be signed or annotated by them; or to someone associated with the author or editor; or someone in some way connected with the subject matter or contents of the book.

This term should not be confused with **Presentation Copy** which means that there is written evidence that the copy was presented by the author, and **Inscribed Copy** which means that the author has signed the book but has not necessarily presented it.

xxii. Price(s)

Most catalogue entries will have just one price, i.e. the retail or asking price, e.g. **£50,** which forms the last item of the main entry. Where a work is fairly recent and is either still in print or is a review copy or has been remaindered, then it is sometimes appropriate and a sales aid as well, to quote the published price additionally. e.g. In print or published at £40 or just [£40] followed by the catalogue price - usually flushed right as in this example:
£28

If the book is out of print (O.p. or oop) and is in demand, then the asking price may be higher than the original price in accordance with the laws of supply and demand. In such cases it is probably better not to put the original price.

xxiii. Commentary Notes.

These normally follow after the main entry which finished with the retail price and usually only apply to books of particular interest or above a certain price. They may range from simple one - liners such as: **Copy number 254 from a limited edition of 750 copies** or **page x introduces the word** *Carboniferous* **into the English Language,** to biographical details of the author or a long description of the place of the book in history and its subsequent intellectual impact. Notes are usually in a smaller point size than the descriptive text.

DATA ENTRY

This is something you can do yourself - a quick course in keyboard skills can be most beneficial and cost effective in the long run and avoids the tedium of two-finger typing. As an alternative you should consider the use of part-time staff for data entry. Such staff should have keyboard or typing skills and should preferably also be trained in the use of PCs, with wordprocessing and in particular with *Windows 98* or later and databases.

As a training guide for such staff it is useful to provide them with a printed checklist of the 22 descriptive categories given above. (Numbers **ii-xxiii.**)

Some dealers design a form to be completed for each entry which can be done by relatively inexperienced staff for straightforward books. This form is then used by the keyboard operator for data entry.

TERMS OF TRADE

This is a simple statement, which can be repeated on your invoices, of when customers should pay and details of any discounts. In the interests of cashflow make your terms as tight as possible. With new customers you should insist on payment in advance by issuing a **Proforma Invoice** and with all overseas internet customers too; i.e. you get your money before you send the books.

Payment due on receipt of goods please, is the next step. This is appropriate for private customers but for educational establishments and other institutions this is impractical and you will almost certainly have to allow them 30 days (They often take 60 days or more). Unless you are allowing discounts then the phraseology should be **30 days net.** Whatever you do, avoid the use of the term **net monthly.** This means that payment is not due until the end of the month following the month of issue of the invoice; i.e. if you issue an invoice on say the 1st of June, then this is not due for payment until the end of July, and with people going on holiday you may not get paid for three months or more.

ORDERING INFORMATION

You should include a simple statement of how orders may be sent: e.g. by phone, fax, e-mail, and by post. It is recommended that you state that all orders will be dealt with in strict sequence of receipt. If there is likely to be a long time between receipt of order and despatch it is courteous to acknowledge receipt of orders.

To facilitate ordering, each catalogue should have a unique identifier such as a number, and many dealers give a code for use when ordering. e.g.

'Gems' 25, means please sent item number 25 from catalogue number 48. This is important if you have more than one catalogue current at any one time.

PUBLICITY

Announce in all catalogues, separate lists of all current catalogues available, and include details of forthcoming ones. The trade press e.g. *Bookdealer, Antiquarian Book Monthly, Book and Magazine Collector*, etc, have a special section for new catalogues and copies should be sent to these as appropriate. There may be a charge for this with some publishers. Catalogues may also be sent to relevant societies of which you are a member. Catalogues should be taken to book-fairs and details should be posted on your website where you have one. The space available on your website should have room for several large catalogues and if you are using a database cataloguing system it is a relatively short step to having an on-line search and ordering system incorporated into your website.

FINAL COPY AND PRINTING

Editing on screen is quick and easy but is not infallible. It is essential to print out a hard copy of your catalogue for final editing. Errors of typing, spacing, spelling, omission, etc., are much easier to see on paper than on a monitor, even if you have a 17" high resolution screen. This incidentally is a reiterative process and may have to be repeated several times.

Most catalogue dealers choose to have a coloured cover in a heavier weight paper than the main catalogue. Because of the way in which printers operate, it is more economical for the main body of the catalogue to have a number of pages which is at least exactly divisible by four, and preferably by eight or sixteen.

One of the problems encountered in preparing the final copy is that you either have too few or too many entries to fit the number of pages you have chosen. Apart from adding or deleting entries or adjusting the line spacing, one easy solution is to change the point size of your text so that it will exactly fit your pages. Word processors allow you to adjust to fractions of a point. A point is the unit of measurement used for type; one point is 0.0138" giving about seventy two points per inch. Bearing in mind that not all customers will have your acuity of vision, it is recommended that you do not go below about 6 to 7 point in your final printed version. The choice of type face is up to you; a good standard such as Times New Roman being commonly chosen, as used in this book at 11 point.

One recommendation that can save up to 10% to 15% of catalogue space is to use two columns. This is a standard feature on word processors. For data entry and editing it is easier and quicker not to use the columns feature, but once you get to the formatting stage just initiate *columns on* and you will see an instant reduction in the number of pages and a pleasing layout.

There are a number of printers who specialise in catalogue work and these regularly advertise in the trade press. Having selected a printer it is recommended that you contact them as the catalogue is nearing completion to let them know that you have one in preparation and the expected completion date. They will in return give you their present schedule and turnround time and expected delivery date to you. When sending copy you must follow the printer's instructions regarding the margin sizes they require - these should be obtained beforehand and your page margins set accordingly.

Having finalised your text, at present you have the option of sending or delivering it to your printer either as A4 camera-ready hard copy or on a floppy or zip disk. Do not send your only copy. Make a back-up copy to retain in the unlikely event that the original gets lost in the post.

Printers have a wide range of cover colours and weights and paper weights available and it is up to you to get their recommendations and samples at the planning stage to enable you to plan the optimum catalogue size and final weight. Try to avoid a strong red as a cover colour as this can make any text on it extremely hard to read.

CATALOGUE SIZE AND DISTRIBUTION FREQUENCY

It is most economical to choose either an A4 or A5 format as these are commonly used standard sizes. If choosing A5 then it is quite acceptable to send hard camera-ready copy in A4 size for the printer to reduce. This reduction is approximately two thirds, so if you want a final type size of say 8 point then your A4 copy should be around 12 point.

The number of entries in a catalogue will obviously depend on your stock, but other things being equal you should plan to get the greatest cost effectiveness from the postal system and from the printer. Having chosen a weight of cover and weight of paper and an appropriate envelope it is then a relatively simple calculation to work out the maximum number of pages that will bring the total weight to just under the Royal Mail postage breaks e.g. 60g, 100g, etc. (Don't forget to allow for the weight of the wire stitches). After a little experience you will soon find the average number of catalogue entries that will meet these criteria. It is much better to do this at the planning stage than to find that your printed catalogue works out at 62g which means you have to pay the 100g rate. At the 100g rate you may have been able to add another 1,000 entries for no extra mailing cost, though with some extra printing and cataloguing cost.

Another important factor in determining your size of catalogue is your cashflow. If this is good then you can afford to wait and go for a larger catalogue. If it is poor then it would be politic to do smaller catalogues and get them out more frequently. It is a trade off between your need for cashflow and the additional proportional costs involved in mailing out catalogues.

An A5 catalogue can easily contain some 2,000 entries and still be under the 100g postage break. There is a limit however to the number of pages than can conveniently be stitched. This will vary from printer to printer and with the weight of paper chosen, but a maximum will be of the order of 80-90 pages. Above this a catalogue will need to be perfect bound - a process where the back folds are sliced off and a polyvinyl acetate or thermoplastic glue applied to the spine. This is a more expensive process than the wire stitching used for smaller catalogues, but does give a superior product. Remember that if your catalogues are good then collectors are more likely to keep them for future reference, which acts as a long-term advertisement for you.

ENVELOPES AND MAILING

If you are going to be using large numbers of envelopes then there are economies of scale in buying in bulk. Additionally it is strongly recommended that you print on the envelope 'If undelivered please return to: followed by *your name & address.*' Unit printing costs are greatly reduced if this too is done in bulk. Gummed envelopes are cheaper than self-adhesive and do not have the disadvantage that the latter sometimes loose their adhesion if stored for some time.

Putting catalogues into envelopes and fixing labels is straight-forward, all you have to bear in mind is that if you have overseas mailings then these should be sorted as discussed above so that the appropriate postage and air mail stickers can be applied.

The Royal Mail and Parcel Force offer various services e.g. they will stick stamps on for you at no charge other than the cost of the stamps, or collect parcels daily, or twice a week, from you if you have sufficient. Call your local Royal Mail Business Centre on 0345 950950 and ask for details.

DEALING WITH ORDERS

When a catalogue has been sent out there can be a flood of orders during the first week or two. Your order pulling, invoicing and packing will be at their peak and you need to be properly organized to cope with this. If you don't have one already, a part-time secretary can help with the invoicing and customer labels unless this is something you are planning to do yourself.

For ease of getting orders up it is vital that you have separate shelving where all the catalogue items are stored in strict catalogue order. It is useful to have a master copy of the catalogue in an A4 ring binder in which you can note where you have more than one copy of any one item and where you can mark off copies as they have been sold. It is vital to keep up-to-date with this as there is nothing more annoying for a customer to be told that a catalogue items is theirs only to learn later that it had already been sold.

Where you get more than one order for any one item this gives you an opportunity to create a 'wants file' in which you record the item details and the details of the customer(s) wanting it, for use when further copies come in.

If you have a database catalogue system then you should ensure that it includes a field for the number of copies of each item that you have in stock. This number can be reduced manually for each sale or automatically if you have an integrated stock control and invoicing system.

It is useful to have a separate packing area with a flat bench about waist high and storage space for packaging materials and some accurate scales that will weigh up to 20kg. Packaging can be obtained from local packaging distributors who will normally be found in Yellow Pages or your local Thomson Directory. Supermarkets can be a very cheap source of cardboard boxes for outside packaging.

Hint. If you have a college or university or industrial premises near you with a large chemistry department, it is worth checking with them what they do with all the plastic material that is delivered packed around glass bottles. (Sausages, leaves, chips, etc.). One near me used to throw it out till I asked them to save it for me. I now collect a car full per month on average, it is ideal for packing between books and an outer carton, and I save some £40 per month on packaging materials.

INTEGRATED SYSTEMS

A number of different integrated software packages are available offering you a complete service for cataloguing, invoicing, stock control, customer records, etc. It is up to you to assess your needs and to look at the cost effectiveness of what is available. Trade organisations such as the ABA and PBFA will be able to give recommendations but before you take the plunge, talk to at least three other dealers who have been using the package for some time, to get their reactions to it.

INVOICING AND AN INVOICE REGISTER

If you don't use an integrated system then you should at least have a preprinted invoice for typing, or design a suitable layout for use on your word processor. It is customary and good business to thank customers for their orders, and it is strongly recommended that the wording: **Thank you for your order**, is preprinted on your invoice.

With regard to keeping records, an accountant or your local Business Link can advise you on book-keeping, but at its simplest you should have an invoice register in which all invoices are entered sequentially. You should record as a minimum the invoice number, the date, the goods value, the post and packaging, the invoice total, the running monthly total, the date paid, and any exports with a separate column where goods have been supplied to VAT registered customers in the EEC.

The date and invoice number can conveniently be combined if required e.g. 001004.2 = invoice number 2 on the 4th October 2000. Such registers with an appropriate number of ruled columns can readily be obtained from most stationers.

CUSTOMER RECORDS

The legal aspects of keeping customer records have been covered earlier. It is good sense to record how much a customer spends with you and when and how prompt they are in paying, as well as details of their interests and what catalogues they have been sent. Such records form an important pool of data on which you can base future management decisions.

PACKAGING AND DESPATCH

If you are going to be sending out parcels on a regular basis it could be well worth while negotiating a contract with ParcelForce or one of the many other delivery services such as Omega. This can give you substantial savings over the normal parcel rates you would pay at a post office.

The PBFA have for example negotiated a special low rate with ParcelForce for their members and I save my annual PBFA membership costs each month through using this service. In some cases parcels may be collected on a daily basis which saves trips to the Post Office, and charges are by direct debit, which saves paperwork and bank charges. Such contract parcels are sent on a 72 hour recorded-delivery basis, though faster services are available at extra cost.

Postage for any parcel can easily be determined by weighing it and/ or looking at your contract. Packaging costs and packaging labour are a little harder to calculate. A padded bag may cost beteween 40p & 80p at today's prices depending on the size used, plastic bubble pack and other materials costs can be determined from your packaging supplier's invoices or price lists. Labour both for invoicing and packing should be charged at an appropriate hourly rate.

With your insurance policy you should have a clause to cover in-transit goods both whilst in the post or in your vehicle. The additional costs of this have to be spread over your invoices for the year. All of these costs may add up to several pounds per item. It is up to you to decide how much of this you pass on to the customer directly and how much you build into the price structure of your stock as part of your general overheads.

EXPORTING

If you are exporting for the first time then the Royal Mail have many publications to help you. A large Guide to International Direct Marketing, of over 330 pages called *Marketing Without Frontiers* is available from Marketing Without Frontiers 4, Royal Mail, 12-25 Fenton Way, BASILDON, Essex, SS15 6SL, or by calling 0345 950950. Similarly *Starting in Export* is available from Royal Mail, Royal London House, 22 Finsbury Square, LONDON, EC2A 1NL. Your local Customs and Excise Office will also provide you with all you need to know about VAT registration or dealing with VAT-registered customers in the EEC.

PAYING SUPPLIERS

You will of course as a normal part of your business, receive invoices from suppliers. These will give their terms of trade and you should wherever possible pay by the stated date. If you are beginning in business it is always worth asking for a little extra time in which to pay as this can help with your cashflow. If however, as sometimes happens, when you have been trading for a while, your cashflow situation may not be as good as your forecast, your overdraft or loan facility may be near its upper limit and you have bills to pay. In this situation the one thing you must not do is nothing. If suppliers don't hear from you, you are likely to get ever increasing demands for payment with ultimately, solicitor's letters.

What you should do is to notify your suppliers that you have a temporary setback in cashflow and ask for a little more time to pay. Most people are reasonable and are likely to agree to this. What will not be tolerated is silence. Alternatively, via your business plan, take steps to improve your cashflow as soon as possible by bringing forward that next catalogue or booking into that book-fair with some spare spaces, etc., or request a temporary increase in your overdraft or other loan, with your revised business plan to show how you will repay it and when.

CHASING OVERDUE ACCOUNTS

Quite often of course the ball is in the other court and it is your customers who are late in paying you. A gentle reminder two weeks after your deadline will nudge those who have genuinely forgotten. Check your outstanding invoices at least once a week and produce an aged debt list, i.e. whom owes you what and for how long, with the longest at the top. You can then write with increasing urgency requesting payment. If customers persist in late payments then you can make appropriate policy decisions. e.g. consider sending them proforma invoices in future with possible increased postage & packing charges to compensate you for the additional interest charges you have incurred on your overdraft or the costs of writing chasing letters. For further details on chasing please see page 154.

THE INTERNET AGAIN

With the advent of the internet you will have to make certain policy decisions with regard to issuing printed catalogues or putting your books on to an internet book database or onto your own website. This is discussed more fully in the final section of this book but two points for consideration are given below.

A lot will depend on the value of the books you are cataloguing. There appear to be relatively few books on the internet at the lower end of the market e.g. priced at under a few pounds. If most of your books fall into this category then you may as well issue a printed catalogue as outlined above.

If a proportion of your books are above this value then you could consider issuing a printed catalogue to your customers to give them first choice and only after a certain time period, put what is left of the more expensive ones on to the Internet.

SUMMARY

Considerable detail has been provided on the running of a catalogue bookselling business as seen by one bookdealer at the end of the second millennium. It is felt and hoped that such operations will continue well into the third millennium and that the advent of the internet will not have such disastrous consequences for catalogue bookdealers as has been forecast by some merchants of doom.

TAILPIECE

There are times when suppliers do make mistakes and chase for an invoice that has already been paid. I commend to your attention the answer of one bookdealer who was in just such a situation. He had written and posted a cheque, he checked his monthly bank statement and his cheque had been presented. Ergo he had paid his bill, yet he was still chased for payment with an ultimatum that unless payment was forthcoming this matter would be placed in the hands of their solicitors. He replied:

'It is a matter of complete indifference to me whether this is placed in the hands of your solicitor, or in any other part of his anatomy which your ingenuity can devise and his complacency permit.'

CATALOGUE ENTRY
An example of a typical bookdealer's catalogue entry for this book:
Baldwin, S.A. A Beginner's Guide to Secondhand Bookdealing. Cold. frontis., pp x, 214, pls. 5, figs. 2, d.j., roy. 8vo, hardback, Witham, 1999. A mint copy.   **£24**

92

Plate 3

Botanist David Bellamy cutting the tape at the opening ceremony of the new fossil
museum attached to the author and his wife's bookshop and factory at Fossil Hall, in
September 1988. The author is on the left with his wife Pam holding the tape. An
audience of invited customers is in the background.

CHAPTER 7

PUBLICITY

> *'He who whispers down a well*
> *about the goods he has to sell*
> *will not make as many dollars*
> *as he who climbs a tree and hollers.'*
> Mark Twain

INTRODUCTION

You have started or are just about to start in business, how then are you going to communicate this fantastic piece of good news to the world at large and to the book buying public in particular. You need to get the maximum publicity for yourself and your business so that potential customers know of your existence, what your offerings are that could be of benefit to them, and where to contact you.

You should not think of publicity as an end in itself but as a part of your marketing plan, which in turn is part of your overall business plan. As such you should have set yourself very specific quantified objectives for your publicity campaign to achieve. These should be foremost in your mind in deciding how you are to realise them. This chapter is concerned with how, when, and where to holler, to whom, and what about. It concentrates on a number of topics.

OBTAINING FREE PUBLICITY

This is obviously the most cost-effective method available to you. Let me illustrate with an example: In June 1979 when I was seconded by IBM to the London Enterprise Agency, I had been running a small spare-time manufacturing business for ten years which was internationally known in a specialist field. IBM wanted to use my experience to help others expand existing small businesses and in advising would-be entrepreneurs in start-up situations.

My initial brief was to design, organise and run courses for those wishing to start and run their own businesses. One-day courses were organised to give a taster of what was involved and longer courses spread over 4 weekends. Extensive advertising was done and I interviewed many potential candidates for the longer courses. As the deadline for the first of these approached, the course was still not full. Inspiration struck and I phoned BBC Radio Two in London and asked to speak to the researchers for the John Dunn Show which then went out nationally on weekday evenings between 5pm and 7pm. I explained the situation and was immediately invited to the studios, was interviewed by John Dunn and recorded a broadcast which went out that evening. The result was instantaneous and the switchboard at the London Chamber of Commerce, where The London Enterprise Agency was based, was subsequently jammed for several days with enquiries. Several course members spoke later of their excitement on hearing the broadcast on their car radios and how they pulled over to write down the details.

There was a double touch of serendipity here as not only were quite a number of courses filled but on the first of these a very genial gentleman by the name of Reg Peplow appeared. He was wanting to change direction from having been a publicity consultant and offered to give a talk on dealing with the media, writing press releases and getting free publicity. This offer was immediately accepted and turned out to be one of the most useful and fascinating talks I have ever attended.

Following Reg's advice I have subsequently obtained over 100 mentions in the press, both local and national, have appeared on local TV several times, on national TV once, and am frequently invited on local radio stations. My most recent appearance was on BBC Essex Radio just before Christmas 1998, at their invitation, to talk on secondhand books as Christmas presents. What more could a bookdealer wish for! (Reg Peplow incidentally is currently well-known in the secondhand book world as the Business Correspondent of the *Bookdealer*). Through chance and luck with the John Dunn Show I had tapped a golden seam but Reg showed us how to do it professionally and a superb example he gave us forms the tailpiece to this chapter. If you would like to know more then I would strongly recommend Reg's book *The Good Publicity Guide*, 1987. Another excellent book is *Successful Media Relations* by Judith Ridgway, 1984. These have both been long out of print but are well worth getting through the public library lending system.

The basic idea behind getting free publicity is to write and issue a press or news release. Many whole books have been written on this subject, and the following is just a summary of some of the basics.

PRESS AND NEWS RELEASES
The media are always interested in a news story, particularly if it has a human interest angle. The fact that you are starting in business is news, (news = **new** with an s on the end!), the more unusual you or your business

are the more newsworthy the event. First then **whom** should you tell? There are probably hundreds of possibilities, but the following are suggested to start with:

▶ **Local Newspapers**: within a twenty mile radius of your premises. These are always short of good stories and a local person starting a business is news, - you will never have a better opportunity. Look in your local newsagents, get the details of the local papers and who the reporters, writers and editors are by name and send your press release to a named individual. They may have a range of reporters or feature writers such as a business correspondent or a sports reporter. If you were specialising in sports books then contact the latter. **Hint**. Check *Benn's Press Directory* or *Willing's Press Guide* and related publications in the reference section of your local public library to see if you have missed anything.

As an alternative you could sketch out details and visit the editorial office in person with your story. This can sometimes produce excellent results with perhaps a staff photographer being sent to your premises for some photographs. When this book was published I used all my contacts in the local press and radio to help spread the word.

You should always try to think of the readers when writing. Editors are there to sell newspapers. They therefore want stories that will interest their readers and persuade them to buy the paper.

▶ **The Trade Press.** Details of these are given in the next chapter. You should consider joining at least one of the major trade associations e.g. the PBFA, as even if you are not necessarily going to exhibit at book-fairs your name appearing in their newsletters and annual directory of members is excellent publicity for you. The regular publications such as *Bookdealer* and *Antiquarian Book Monthly* in the UK have a wide readership so you reach a target audience for just the cost of a letter or press release.

▶ **Specialist Societies.** If you are a member of or know of any societies whose interests coincide with your specialist stock subjects, then let them know. Newsletters from such societies usually contain details of book dealers of relevance to their members.

▶ **Specialist Journals and Periodicals.** If you have some specialities then the chances are that there a number of appropriate publications who might see your existence as a useful source of information or interest to their readers. In the same way that your business is selling benefits to customers you should try to look at your press release from the point of view of the journal readers.

▶ **All Relevant Libraries.** Local ones should definitely be covered and any specialist ones nationally. From your market research you will already have identified these. e.g. In *Libraries in the United Kingdom and the Republic of Ireland,* published annually.

▸   **Tourist Information Centres.** Many visitors on entering an area will make a beeline for the nearest TIC to obtain a list of local secondhand bookshops and businesses in the area. Make sure that you are included on their lists.

▸   **All your local radio stations.** You can find out details of these in *Willing's Press Guide* and similar publications such as *British Rate and Data* (BRAD). If you are successful there are three likely possibilities.

i. You may be asked to record an interview over the phone, either as a live broadcast, or for later transmission. If you are not used to this then you can prepare beforehand by thinking of some likely questions, running through the answers and practising speaking them out loud to your partner or a friend. A little rehearsal can take some of the nerves out of that first broadcast and also some of the *ums* and *ers* that are so irritating to listen to. If you have a tape recorder then record a pretend interview and play it back to yourself afterwards and reiterate as required..

ii. A reporter may visit you with a tape recorder and record the interview. This is easier as if you do make a mistake or become tongue-tied it is very easy to do another take.

iii. You may be asked to a studio to do a live broadcast face to face with a well-known local radio DJ. You will be given plenty of time, music is usually played between chat or news items, coffee, etc, is laid on and you will be put at your ease. You will be sat at a 'table', will wear earphones and will have a microphone in front of you. The DJ will do a test run with you off line, usually while a track is playing live. It's great fun!

Most such interviews will be of the order of five minutes or so with possibly up to ten minutes. It depends on what other news stories have broken that day. If you are on a local BBC Radio then do not attempt to push yourself too commercially. The interviewers are skilled in asking the right questions to draw you out. Once you have finished, the interviewer will round off the story by saying who you were and where you can be contacted. You won't get paid for your time incidentally but you are reaching a large number of people just for a few minutes of your time. If the radio station like what you said and particularly the way in which you said it, then this will be registered and if in future they want a speaker on your subject you may be invited back many times.

Results may not be instantaneous but for up to a year after such a broadcast you may find visitors commenting 'I heard you on the radio and

I've been meaning to come for ages.'

Secondly **how** do you tell the story, i.e. write a news or press release, and what should be in it? A release has a definite structure and sequence which it is strongly recommended that you adhere to:

▸ **Heading** to the first sheet. This should have PRESS RELEASE on it, the date and possibly the name of your business if it is a meaningful one. You do not need to put your address, name, phone or fax number at the top as there is not a human interest story in these. (You are selling books not addresses).

▸ **Headline** to the story. This should be concise yet long enough to convey the main idea of what your story is about. The idea is to grab the attention of the readers so they will want to read on. e.g.

Top executive leaves rat-race to start local secondhand book business.

Don't try to be too clever with your heading; editors have seen it all before and if your story is used the heading would possibly be rewritten anyway. If you can't condense it all then a subheading can be added with extra data. The emphasis in your headline can be changed to suit your target audience.

▸ **The story.** In your first paragraph you should provide as briefly as possible a summary by answering the five basics - Who, what, when, where and why. e.g.

Who	Andrew Browser
What	is opening a new shop specialising in secondhand Art and Literature Books
When	today
Where	at 256 Pages Street, Bibliotown
Why	to meet the needs of local and national book collectors.

The remaining paragraphs will expand on these with perhaps some relevant information on you the proprietor. How you emphasise each of these five categories and what angle you use depends on whom your release is aimed at, e. g. if for a local newspaper or radio then the emphasis should be on the local angle, if to a radio station then it should be very short, topical and to the point and perhaps sent a few days in advance so that it becomes an up-to-date news item. (In these cases you would head your sheet News Release.) If you are sending it to a national monthly specialist magazine then you can play down the local aspect and the topicality and concentrate on the specialist aspects. In your use of prose try to think of the readers, and write accordingly. You could be far more technical in a release to an arts magazine than say to a local free newspaper. If you can, get it all on one side of one page.

Your press release should end with a standard sentence such as:

▸ **For further information please contact:**
Your name, phone, fax, e-mail, etc. For phone you should give both your daytime and evening numbers if they are different. When you have issued a release then it is essential that you are available for the next few days for people to be able to contact you.

▸ **The Conventions and Practicalities of Layout.** Use A4 sized paper, leave wide margins and use double spacing - giving room for editors to mark up. Type (or computer print) on one side of the sheet only - your text may be cut out for pasting up. If producing your release on a word processor then use a standard font, preferably at 12 point - all editors don't necessarily have your visual acuity. Don't underline, as to a printer this is an instruction to use italics. If you want to add emphasis use *italics* or **bold**. If using more than one page then number all, and at the bottom right of all but the last put - **More follows.** For numbers one to nine spell them out, for 10 and above digitise. Don't split sentences or paragraphs over two pages. Put **End** at the bottom right under the text on the last page. This should be apparent by the - For further information - line but it doesn't hurt to make sure. Your address, business information and website details where available, can be included at the bottom of the last sheet.

Have a last look at your release - have you answered all the questions an editor or his or her publication's readers are likely to ask?

▸ **Photographs.** By all means include a photograph. This will normally be a black and white glossy print which should be sharp and preferably avoids stark contrasts of dark and light. A picture as we are told, is better than a thousand words. It should be apposite and must have a caption giving as many of the five basics as possible. The photo should not be written on the back either in ink or pencil or anything else. The caption should be typed or printed on a separate piece of paper which is then fixed to the back of the photo along the top edge of the caption only. Masking tape is recommended for this rather than Sellotape.

▸ **Back-up Material.** The essence of your story goes into the main press release. You can however have additional background material if required which can be slanted towards the various media you are aiming at. (Media is a commonly used term which simply means people.) This should answer all the additional questions that may be asked and which haven't been covered in the release. Your cv is relevant with the emphasis on your book background and interests. The objectives of your publicity campaign could be included and a statement of the gap in the market you have identified and how you are hoping to fill it. Editors may use this material to answer reader's queries or file it for a possible follow-up story later.

▸ **Timing.** Your mailings will have to be timed and dated according to the respective lead times of the media. This will range from the daily radio broadcasts, through your local weekly newspapers, to the monthly glossy magazines or the quarterly newsletters of specific societies. Though a magazine may appear monthly or bi-monthly the lead time for stories may be many months. This should be taken into account in planning your campaign. As part of your plan you should decide when the first mailings should go out and the last. Between these dates see what national or local events are taking place that you can either cash in on or avoid. e.g. National Book Week or World Book Day would be good events to take advantage of, or the Football Association cup final a good day to avoid as many people's attention will be elsewhere then.

End.

As an alternative to End in the USA, use # # # centred on the page.

Hint. In writing, any copy, whether it is for a press release or for an advertisement, make a list of the main points you want to make, then write a first draft and put it on one side for 24 hours before looking at it again. Almost invariably you will find a better way of phrasing something, or see an improvement that can be made. I have found that this works every time - I don't know why, but assume it must be something to do with the way the human brain works.

An example of one of the press releases used to promote this book is included in the appendix, though double spacing has been removed and the point size reduced to fit the pages.

GETTING INTO TRADE PUBLICATIONS

Though this has been mentioned before it is worth repeating because of its importance. There are a number of annual directories of book dealers published in the UK and in many other countries and also in regions such as Europe. These are covered in chapter 8 on 'Trade Organisations and Publications.' You should ensure that your details are included in these directories as soon as possible, as many collectors and dealers buy these on a regular basis and they form a vital method of communicating your details to customers.

DIRECT MAIL

Direct mail is one of the most widely used methods of promoting business, and in the UK is the third largest publicity medium after the Press and TV. There is a vast literature on the subject and many courses are available for those wishing to learn more about organising and running a direct mail campaign and what it can do for you. It is not proposed to give you much detail in this section but just to point you in the right direction if you wish to know more and to outline the structure of a direct mail letter which has much in common with a press release. Successful direct mail has three major ingredients:

▸ An accurate and up-to-date mailing list.

▸ You have something that people want or will want to do when they have read your letter.

▸ Your letter gets the reader's <u>attention</u>, attracts their <u>interest</u>, creates a <u>desire</u> to buy from you or to contact you and makes it easy for the reader to take <u>action</u> e.g. by including a reply paid envelope or freepost address.

Before starting such a campaign you should of course work out your objectives and quantify them so you can plan accordingly. Is it to get visitors to your shop, to come to that book-fair, to be added to your mailing list or to buy that book that you have just purchased in bulk?, etc. Are you going to do a test mailing first (absolutely essential), and are you going to make any special offers e.g. additional discount if replies are received by a certain date?

To find out what to do, go to your local lending library and scan the business section (Dewey decimal classification 658 & 659). There you will find large numbers of books on all aspects of starting and running a small business. General books may have a useful chapter or more specific books may cover marketing, advertising or direct mail only, e.g. *How to Advertise* by K. Roman and J Maas, 1983 or the *Post Office Direct Mail Handbook* edited by L. Andrews, 1984. These are excellent, the latter covering where and how to build a mailing list and the detail of creating, producing and testing a letter.

In the UK the Royal Mail provide a wealth of literature and various courses to help the beginner. To find out about these and the special discounts they offer to first-time users, contact your local Head Post Office and ask to speak to a Postal Sales Representative. Look in your phone book under Royal Mail - Customer Service Centre.

Psychologists have studied the way in which people read a direct mail letter. It seems as a general guide that the heading or first paragraph is looked at first. If there is something there to make them want to read on then they will turn to the bottom of the letter to read there next. This then is why those special offers such as *reply by a certain date to get an extra xx% off* or to obtain that *free gift*, are placed as a PS at the end. If their attention is still held the reader will then return to the top of the letter and read on. Ideally your letter should cover just one page and should finish with a specific request for the reader to take some action such as sending a cheque, responding immediately, requesting a catalogue, sending you a wants list, or to note your next book-fair or opening hours.

The direct mail letter, as with the press release, has a tried and tested structure. Using headed paper is fine and also a heading as before. The pundits say that there are four key works that can be used to obtain the attraction and interest of a reader: YOU, NEW, NOW and FREE. Try to incorporate one or two of these into your heading or your first paragraph. The main body of the letter follows. What then should this consist of? You will remember from chapter 2 on 'What Business Are You In?', that you are selling benefits. These benefits appropriately angled towards your target audience and objectives should form the bulk of your letter and can continue till you have no more. You then wrap up the letter with a request for action and add a PS as indicated above. If you are opening a bookshop then a direct mail letter to a specific audience could invite them to the opening and you could offer a special discount for all purchases that day or week.

After your test shot, analyse the results, modify if required and you are then ready for the big mailing. Remember that a well-directed mail-shot is like an arrow at a specific target and is quick and extremely flexible. Direct mail is of course just one facet of advertising.

ADVERTISING

So far in this chapter various more-or-less cost-effective ways of advertising have been looked at. These are the ones that you should try first, and you should only resort to paid advertising if you feel that you need more exposure. You should therefore be very careful beforehand to decide what your specific objectives are and to quantify them and then decide how you are going to achieve them. With the methods used above you may not be involved in much expenditure but with advertising it can be very easy to waste resources. If you are involved in a major book-fair such as those in London in the May-June period, then it is more sense to book advertising space in the *Bookdealer* for their June Fairs Issue than at other times because there is a much larger print run than normal, these are available free at all the book-fairs and they obviously reach your target audience as most visitors to book-fairs are book buyers. If as in the press release above you are selling art and literature books then you would look first at the cost of space in related journals or literary or art supplements rather than trying blanket coverage in a national newspaper. The basic principles are as before, i.e. your copy must capture their attention by showing the readers what is in it for them by doing business with you.

Hint. If you are planning to advertise in a newspaper or periodical then consider budgeting for a series of at least 3 insertions. Experience has shown that the cost-effectiveness of this is far greater than that of a single insertion.

THE HUMBLE BOOKMARK

I was just going to give this a passing mention as a useful and simple way to advertise or publicise yourself by giving them to customers or placing in books when you post them. However on re-reading Reg Peplow's *Good Publicity Guide*, apart from giving much more additional valuable information on publicising yourself, I was reminded of the marvellous story he tells, of the lady running a gardening business who had some inexpensive bookmarks printed with details of her services and where she could be contacted. She then visited her local libraries and placed a bookmark in all the books on gardening, flowers, plants, etc. Whether she obtained permission from the librarians is not sure but they were her first customers and business boomed rapidly.

With a little thought this simple technique is easily applicable to your specialities. I leave you to think of the extreme cost-effectiveness of this and related methods and how you can apply them to your business.

Hint. If you are going to produce a bookmark, apart from the essential basic data, try to make it a selling document by putting in some of the benefits to customers as outlined earlier, and if you can, get all this on one side only. This then leaves the other side for you to print a location map of your premises, making it easier for customers to find you.

THE INTERNET

Setting up a website and publicising this as widely as possible, especially on the internet, is rapidly becoming a major element in many successful bookdealers' marketing campaigns. There is much that you can do for yourself, which is covered in chapter 16. Bear in mind in reading the following case study, that much of it is applicable to website design and publicity.

PRODUCING A BROCHURE - A Case Study.

I make no apologies here for using myself as a case study as most of the thinking behind my brochure and its results are applicable to any secondhand book business.

In revising and updating my business plan during 1998 I decided to plan ahead for the next seven years. (I'll be 75 by then and may want to wind down a little). My shop is in a small village in the middle of rural Essex with relatively little passing trade and I decided that it was time for a some publicity to boost business. A two-pronged attack was decided upon - a brochure and a website. My overall aim, as usual, was to improve my profit and profitability whilst retaining liquidity. For the brochure I set myself some very specific objectives:

▸ To attract 300% more visitors to my shop and 500% more to my website.
▸ To obtain 30% additions to my catalogue mailing list in one year.
▸ To sell 500% more stock from the shop at the lower end of the market. i.e. Stock that would otherwise not be catalogued or put on the web.
▸ To sell from my website by putting recent catalogues on.
▸ To notify people of my interests so that I would be offered material on my special subjects.
▸ To make it easy for visitors to find me by providing a map.
▸ To show what else is of interest to visitors to the area.
▸ To make the brochure of interest to other local tourist attractions, museums, and libraries by including their details to encourage them to stock my brochure on a reciprocal basis.
▸ To design the brochure in parallel with my website as the objectives have much in common.
▸ To tell prospective customers about the type of books I stock.
▸ To promote other local secondhand bookshops.
▸ To make it colourful, different, and attractive.
▸ If possible, to amuse.

With these objectives in mind, I collected some 50 different tourist leaflets from as wide a range of attractions as possible. I studied these to see what others were doing. They gave me a few basic ideas, but no one had exactly what I wanted. I thought through how to achieve my objectives, drafted some copy, revised it over the next few days, took a few photographs and presented it all to a local design and print company. They laid it out, suggested a colour scheme and after a few reiterations the design was complete. (An A4 sheet was used folded into three to fit standard business envelopes, and the leaflet dispensers found in tourist attractions, hotels, etc.).

The next step was deciding where to send them and hence how many to print. I approached 10 of the scientific societies I either belonged to or was associated with, and obtained quotations from them for sending them to their members with their next newsletter or circular. The local tourist centres and attractions, museums, libraries, hotels, and other bookshops were analysed and also various national organisations, and relevant university departments. The total came to 45,000 so a print run of 50,000 was ordered to give a few spares.

Distribution took place during the first five months of 1999 including all PBFA members. The results were and continue to be phenomenal. By the middle of 1999 all the objectives had been attained, including the longer-term one, and the not inconsiderable costs of printing and distribution had been more than covered by increased sales. There was a great acceleration in the rate of hits on my website, additions to the mailing list continue to pour in at a very steady stream, much material has been offered to me and my exports in particular have had a considerable boost.

I was delighted to have my thinking confirmed when a senior member of staff of The Royal Society, one of the major scientific institutions in the world, commented that it was the finest brochure he had seen in over 40 years. Your situation and many of your objectives are likely to be different from mine, but I commend a brochure to your attention as a very cost-effective way of publicising your business. If you'd like a copy of the brochure for reference, I'd be delighted to send one on receipt of a SAE (1/3 A4 size.) or international reply coupon.

TILBROOK TOM TAILPIECE

Some years ago Reg Peplow had a farmer friend who wanted to advertise the services of his bull - Tilbrook Tom, by entering him into the grand parade of animals that opens the East of England Show each year. The bull was not of a well-known local breed and the organisers wouldn't let him into the parade as there was no class for him. Reg was called in to help and with the aid of a photographer went with the farmer to see Tilbrook Tom. It was a fine sunny day and the photographer clicked away. Reg then spotted an attractive young lady in a summer dress and straw hat working in a nearby field. She was asked if she would mind being photographed standing by the bull and after some extensive persuasion and on being assured of his docility, she agreed. The photographer clicked away again and then quite spontaneously the young lady put her straw hat on the bull's head.

Plate 4   **Beauty and the Beast**

Accompanied by a story written by Reg on the lines of *Beauty and the Beast*, that was the photograph that hit the local paper that week.

This attracted so much attention that not only was Tilbrook Tom allowed into the parade, he led it, and the demand to see him during the show was so great that he was given a special pen in the centre of the showground with a collecting box, which raised several thousand pounds for charity.

NB I hasten to add that not everything I write is a load of bull.

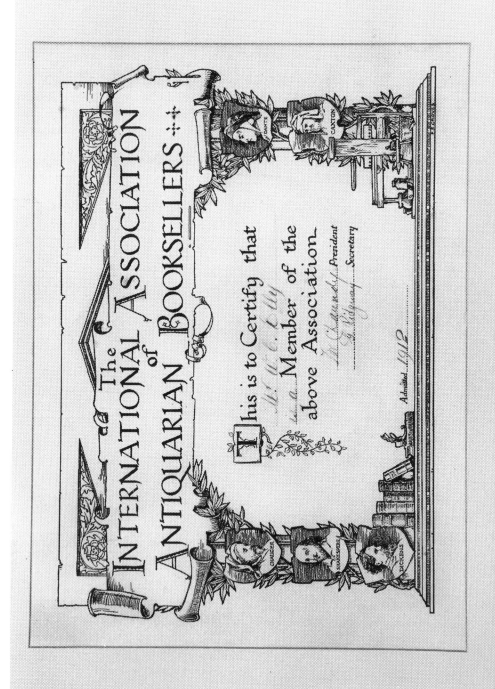

Plate 5   International Association of Antiquarian Booksellers Certificate.

This is the only known copy of the IAAB certificate of membership, 1912. Before this date the ABA was called the Association of Second-Hand Booksellers, and no certificates were issued in that name. In 1912 the name was changed to the Antiquarian Booksellers Association International, coinciding with a large committee shuffle, and a new membership certificate was issued, of which there are plenty of examples.

CHAPTER 8

TRADE ASSOCIATIONS, PUBLICATIONS, PERIODICALS AND REFERENCE WORKS

INTRODUCTION

Some of the more important names, addresses and publications likely to be of interest to a bookdealer, have been selected and in some cases annotated, to give an idea of the type and range available, though this chapter is not intended to be an exhaustive or definitive list. For more complete details in many areas please refer to the various Sheppard country and regional directories listed below.

TRADE ASSOCIATIONS

Australian and New Zealand Association of Antiquarian Booksellers. (ANZAAB) P.O. Box 279, Cammeray, NSW 2062, Australia. **Tel:** 02 9331 1441 **Fax:** 02 9361 3371

Antiquarian Booksellers Association of America. (ABAA) 20 West 44th Street, Fourth Floor, New York, N.Y. 10036-6604 U.S.A. **Tel:** 212 944 8291 **Fax:** 212 944 8293 **E-mail:** abaa@panix.com

Antiquarian Booksellers' Association (International). (ABA) Sackville House, 40 Piccadilly, London, W1V 9PA.
Tel: 0207 439 3118 **Fax:** 0207 439 3119
E-mail: info@aba.org.uk **Website:** http://www.aba.org.uk

The ABA, founded in 1906, is the senior trade body for dealers in rare and fine books, manuscripts, and allied materials in the British Isles and elsewhere. It is also the oldest trade association in the world, and is affiliated to 20 associations throughout Europe, the Americas, and the Far East which form the International League of Antiquarian Booksellers (ILAB).

It is a non-profit making organisation, and provides many services for its members including running a major reference library, and organising annual international book-fairs at Olympia in June and Chelsea in the autumn. Biennial branch fairs are held in Bath and Edinburgh. A monthly newsletter is sent to all members of whom there are over 200 in the UK.

Membership is currently restricted to booksellers who have a minimum of five years trading experience. Applicants for membership must be proposed by two full members and seconded by two other full members. The current entrance fee is £75 plus VAT and an annual subscription of £325 including VAT.

A handbook containing a directory of members and details of the ABA code of good practice, is produced annually and is available on request. The most recent handbook, 1999-2000, contains a ten-page section *The Terms of the Trade* by Roger Gaskell. This is an erudite and comprehensive description of the ten most important elements used in the catalogue descriptions of antiquarian books.

Antiquarian Booksellers' Association of Canada. C/o Alphabet Bookshop, 145 Main Street West, Port Colborne, Ontario, Canada, L3K 3V3

The Provincial Booksellers Fairs Association (PBFA) The Old Coach House, 16 Melbourn Street, Royston, Hertfordshire, SG8 7BZ **Tel:** 01763 248400; **Fax:** 01763 248921; **E-mail:** pbfa@dial.pipex.com **Website:** http://dspace.dial.pipex.com/pbfa

The PBFA is the largest association of antiquarian and secondhand booksellers in Great Britain. With over 700 members it is also the largest in the world. From origins in 1972 it had an inaugural meeting in 1974 and celebrated its 25th anniversary in 1999. It is a non-profit making organisation catering for a wide range of book-collecting interests, and aims to promote a broader interest in antiquarian and secondhand books. To members it represents an association that is co-operatively managed by the members for the members through national and regional committees.

The PBFA began in 1974 from a need for a regular London shop window for dealers with shops in the provinces. Monthly fairs were established in London, and fairs in various towns and cities around the country soon followed. The PBFA today not only mounts the only monthly two-day fair in London, but also provides a national programme of events for its members. Apart from those who wish to exhibit at book-fairs, the association offers a wide range of services to members, negotiating advantageous rates for insurance, parcel postage rates, equipment, and credit card processing. e.g. one dealer's Barclaycard merchant's rate went down from over 3% to 2.5% thanks to the PBFA.

Booksellers are welcomed at all levels though they must have been trading for at least two years prior to membership. Candidates must be proposed by two full members, and on election they become Associate Members. After two years they may apply for full membership. The annual cost of membership is currently £90 including VAT, and once you are a member you may exhibit at any of the PBFA fairs. There are over 200 members who never exhibit at book-fairs and who belong for the other benefits including a high public profile and a respected position in the trade.

A *Newsletter* is issued ten times a year and forms a very valuable source of information to members on a wide range of topics ranging from details of books stolen, reports on fairs, new and improved services to members and importantly, enabling members to keep in touch with each other. An inexpensive *Directory of Members* is issued annually. The 14th edition covering 1999-2000, was issued in May 1999 at £3. Apart from an alphabetic list of members with their details, geographical and speciality listings, sections are included on Supplies and Services and on Literary and Book related Societies. A free *Calendar of Book Fairs* for the whole of the UK is available on request.

The PBFA is organised into 8 geographical regions:
1. *Scotland & Northern Ireland.*
2. *The North:* Cumbria, Durham, Cleveland, Greater Manchester, Lancs., N. Yorks, W. Yorks, S. Yorks, Cheshire, Tyne & Wear and Merseyside.
3. *The Midlands:* Notts., Derbyshire, Leics., Staffs., Salop, Northants., Warks., W Midlands, Hereford & Worcs., Glos. and Wales.
4 *Eastern*: Cambridgeshire, Norfolk, Suffolk, Essex and Lincolnshire.
5. *Home Counties North:* Berks., Beds., Bucks., Herts., and Oxon.
6. *South East:* Kent, E Sussex, W Sussex, Surrey, Hampshire and Isle of Wight.
7. *South West:* Avon, Devon, Dorset, Cornwall, Somerset and Wiltshire.
8. *London:* London and Greater London (within North/South Circular)

Welsh Booksellers Association, c/o Hay Castle, Hay-on-Wye, Herefordshire, HR3 5AA **Tel:** 01497 820503   **Fax:** 01497 821314

Established in 1987, current membership is of the order of 50. A current list of members is available on request.

OTHER ASSOCIATIONS AND BOOK-FAIR ORGANISERS

The Exhibition Team Ltd., Events House, Wycombe Air Park, Booker, Marlow, Bucks., SL7 3DP   (Organisers of HD Book Fairs.) **Tel:** 01494 450504 **Fax:** 01494 450245

HD Book Fairs. 38 Fleetside, West Molesey, Surrey, KT8 2NF **Tel:** 0208 224 3609 **Fax:** 0208 224 3576

HD organise book-fairs in London (monthly), and at other venues in England at various times throughout the year. e.g. during 1999 at Bath, Cheltenham, Farnham, Hatfield, Hertford, Harrogate, Kempton, and Rickmansworth

Fine Press Book Association. Carol Grossman, Four Rivers Books, 7228 Four Rivers Road, Boulder, CO 80301, USA, or Nigel Roberts, The Celtic Cross Press, Ovins Well House, Low Street, Lastingham, York, YO6 6TJ **Tel:** 01751 417298

PUBLICATIONS AND PERIODICALS

AB Bookman's Weekly, PO Box AB, Clifton, NJ 07015, USA.
Tel: 973 772-0020 **Fax:** 973 772-9281
E-mail: abbookman@aol.com **Website:** http://www.abbookman.com

It has frequent special topic issues, lists bookdealers catalogues, book reviews, auction and book-fair calendars, plus books wanted and for sale with a useful library-wants section. Current annual UK subscription is $80 for surface mail.

Antiquarian Book Monthly, Countrywide Editions Limited, P O Box 97, High Wycombe, Buckinghamshire, HP10 8QT
Tel: 01494 817600; **Fax:** 01494 817666
E-mail: editor@abmr.demon.co.uk

This is the leading monthly publication for both dealers and collectors covering all aspects of antiquarian and rare books. The magazine encourages interest in the pleasures of finding, collecting and preserving books. Coverage of related topics such as book-binding and printing presses also feature, together with articles and profiles of the many and varied book-world personalities, both old and new.

Also to be found is comprehensive coverage of auctions, exhibitions and fairs, together with catalogue and book reviews. There is plenty of news and views, as well.

Facilities for dealers include use of the 'Diary' section for dealer announcements and news, catalogue review section, auction/fairs/exhibition listings and reports, and a full advertising service including 'Classifieds'.

The Book Collector. (Quarterly). The Collector Ltd., 20 Maple Grove, London, NW9 8QY **Tel/Fax:** 0208 200 5004

Established in 1954, it is aimed at collectors at the top end of the market, bibliographers, antiquarian booksellers and rare book custodians, with an emphasis on bibliophily and the book world. Current annual UK subscription is of the order of £40.

Book and Magazine Collector. (Monthly). 43-45 St. Mary's Road, Ealing, London, W5 5RQ. (Published by Parker Mead Ltd. for Diamond Publishing Group Ltd). **Tel:** 0208 579 1082 **Fax:** 0208 566 2024

This has books and magazines for sale and wanted and also articles and bibliographies on subjects and authors e.g. The August 1999 issue includes features on Ernest Hemingway, Alfred Hitchcock, Star Wars, and Sue Grafton. The current annual UK subscription is £33. It also contains book value information, of which further details are given in chapter 4.

Bookdealer. (Weekly). Suite 34, 26 Charing Cross Road, London WC2H ODH. **Tel:** 0207 240 5890 **Fax:** 0207 379 5770

This is the leading trade weekly magazine for the British secondhand and antiquarian book trade. In addition to a dozen pages of editorial that include business articles, notes on catalogues and auctions, interviews, book reviews, letters and general trade notes, *Bookdealer* contains approximately 10,000 Titles Wanted and For Sale, classified, display advertisements and an Author and County Index of Books Wanted. It is an indispensable trade paper for both the newcomer and experienced antiquarian booksellers. It is available on subscription only at a cost of about £1 a week. A specimen copy is available on request.

For dealers holding some or all of their stock on a database *Bookdealer* additionally offers each week's Books Wanted on disk or by e-mail. Under the trade name *BookMatch*, users are supplied with free software, a manual, and two weeks free trial. Thereafter *BookMatch* is available at less than £2 a week. Matches created between a dealer's stock database and that week's Books Wanted from *Bookdealer,* are printed out in a form compatible with the publisher's weekly Wednesday free mailing of report slips. For further information please contact the *Bookdealer* office.

The Bookseller. (Weekly). Published by J. Whitaker and Sons Ltd. 12 Dyott Street, London, WC1A 1DF. **Tel:** 0207 420 6000 **Fax:** (Editorial) 0207 420 6103 **E-mail:** letters.to.editor@bookseller.co.uk **Website:** http://**www**.theBookseller.com

This is the main UK weekly for news, features and updates on new books with a very useful classified section: publications of the week. The current UK annual subscription is £142.

Book Source Monthly, 2007 Syossett Drive, Cazenovia, NY 13035-9753, USA. **Tel:** / **Fax:** 315 655 8499

This contains auction and book-fair calendars, mainly for the USA and UK, articles, catalogues received (free entry to subscribers), specialist bookdealer directories, and virtual bookshops, but does not contain books for sale or wanted. The current annual UK subscription is £15 (surface), £25 (airmail).

The Clique, 7 Pulleyn Drive, York, England, YO2 2DY **Tel:** 01904 631752; **Fax:** 01904 651325 **E-mail:** cole@clique.co.uk **Website:** http://www.clique.co.uk. Publishers of *Cole's Registers*: *Cole's Register of British Antiquarian & Secondhand Bookdealers*. An annual directory of some 3,000 book-trade members and bookshops in Britain and Eire.

Annual Register of Book Values. An exceptionally useful resource for book values and pricing, abstracted from dealers' catalogues. Six titles were published annually between 1987 and 1999 and are unlikely to be published in future. At the time of going to press, the 1999 editions and back numbers from 1996 onwards are still available from the publishers, who are also considering whether to issue the data from the series on CD-ROM. It is strongly recommended that these are obtained whilst still available.

The Arts & Architecture. Including art reference, illustrated, Private Press books, applied arts, the book arts.

Children's Books. From the 18th century until the present day; classics, rarities, old favourites - a wide range of collectable children's books.

Modern First Editions. Modern collected authors. Cut-off date 1900. Includes some detective, fantasy and science fiction.

Science & Medicine. Including natural history, agriculture, technology.

Voyages, Travel & Exploration. Including topography and local history.

Literature. Including titles from the 17th century to mid-20th century, with emphasis on the 19th and early 20th centuries. Has a minimum overlap with *Modern First Editions.*

The Clique's sister organisation: The British Internet Bookdealers Centre, also provides a wide range of computer and internet services for bookdealers which are described in part III of this book.

Skoob Directory of Secondhand Bookshops in the British Isles. Skoob Books Limited, 15 Sicilian Avenue, Southampton Row, Holborn, London, WC1A 2QH **Tel:** 0207 404 3063, **Fax:** 0207 404 4398
E-mail: books@skoob.demon.co.uk   Current price is £7.99 (trade £5) This is published every few years. The current edition is 6th, 1996. It has a mainly geographical layout, with an index of shops, subjects and towns, and contains an ABC of Book Auction Terms plus a Glossary of Bookselling Terms.

Scottish Book Collector (Quarterly), c/o 36 Lauriston Place, Edinburgh, EH3 9EZ **Tel:** 0131-228 4837; **Fax:** 0131-228 3904

It has reviews of catalogues, short stories, auction reports, articles on collectors, secondhand dealers, authors, and Scottish books. Current UK annual subscription is £11.

Sheppard's Directories. Published by Richard Joseph Publishers Limited, Unit 2, Monks Walk, Farnham, Surrey, GU9 8HT
Tel: 01252 734347 **Fax:** 01252 734307 **E-mail:** rjoe01@aol.com
Website: http://members.aol.com/rjoe01/sheppards.htm

Sheppard's Book Dealers in the British Isles. A Directory of Antiquarian and Secondhand Book Dealers in the United Kingdom, the Channel Islands, the Isle of Man, and the Republic of Ireland. It is published annually. Currently £27. All active dealers are eligible for a free entry. Companion volumes include: *Sheppard's Book Dealers in: Europe; Japan;*

Australia and New Zealand; North America; India and the Orient which are published less frequently.

Other Directories: *Sheppard's International Directory of Print and Map Sellers*, currently covering 40 countries; *Sheppard's International Directory of Ephemera Dealers,* currently covering 20 countries.

Sheppard's Collectors Guides. A series of international subject guides providing listings of dealers who stock antiquarian and secondhand books on specific subjects: I - Art; II - History; III- Science; IV - Literature; V - Special Editions; VI - Topography and Geography; VII - Transport; VIII - Military; IX - Children's; X - Travel. e.g. Volume III - Science, covers Archaeology, Biology, Botany, Chemistry, Geology, Medicine, Mineralogy, Natural History, Natural Sciences, Pharmacy, Science. This series is very useful for collectors and it is important for dealers to ensure that their details are entered.

Book Data's Archive BookFind-CD: A unique reference source for those searching for out-of-print books, distributed by Richard Joseph. Dealers get a free entry. It contains half a million records - including descriptions, contents lists and detailed subject classifications where available. Information culled from the eight main Sheppard's Book Dealer Directories, gives details of the dealer's name, address, telephone, fax and e-mail numbers. Contact details for book dealers and their specialities are available alongside out-of-print title information, on a single CD-ROM. (CD-ROM = Compact Disk with Read-Only Memory). This is currently one of the major forms in which computer software is supplied for use on PCs.

It is marketed to all booksellers and libraries around the world and is available to dealers listed in Sheppard's at £145 currently, compared with the usual retail price of £225. This allows booksellers, i.e. of NEW books, to offer listings of specialist book dealers to the book buyer in the subject of the book they seek to buy but which has gone out of print. The CD contains most of the books which have gone out of print in the last 14 years, complete with all the usual details used by the new book trade. Also included are all distributors of new books, and all publisher's names and addresses. The search criteria include 'words in title', 'publisher', and 'author'.

International Directory of Book Collectors 1998-1999. 6th edition, compiled by Roger Sheppard. £32. Trigon Press, 117 Kent House Road, Beckenham, Kent, BR3 1JJ. **Tel:** 0208 778 0534 **Fax:** 0208 776 7525

A directory of book collectors in the United Kingdom, Ireland, America, Canada and the rest of the world. For details of the latest edition please contact the publishers. It is of use to obtain additions to dealer's mailing lists or to track down fellow collectors.

Trigon Press also have in preparation for 2000, a directory of some 3,000 dealers in Science Fiction/Fantasy. If you wish to be included in this or future editions please contact Trigon Press directly.

REFERENCE WORKS (For bookdealers and collectors).

Introduction. A number of the works cited here are from my own library collected over many years. Some will therefore be out of print while others may have more recent editions available than those cited. Apart from reference purposes this section serves to illustrate the point made in the introduction, that there are many more books for the collector on collecting than there are for the bookdealer on bookdealing. Many works, though they are aimed at collectors, contain extremely useful information of interest to bookdealers. Where possible, books have been selected for inclusion here because they represent a particular class or type, e.g. bibliographies of authors or subjects or a certain time period. A number of titles are present that are not strictly reference works but are included because they are reminiscences of bookdealers and are therefore relevant and of interest.

American Book Prices Current. (ABPC) P.O. Box 1236, Washington, CT 06793, USA
Tel: 860 868 7408 **Fax:** 860 868 0080 **E-mail:** abpc@snet.net

This is published in annual volumes e.g. Volume 103 covering the Auction Season September 1996 - August 1997, was published in 1998. It is not just a transcribed record of titles and prices but claims to be the only work in English in which every listing of printed material has been checked for title, format, date of publication, and edition. Bindings are described, with condition where relevant, and whenever possible maps and plates in books are verified. Sales of autographs and manuscripts are also reported.

It is an accurate, and essential tool for the secondhand bookseller and collector for buying, selling and evaluating books, serials, autographs, manuscripts, broadsides, and maps, based on actual figures realized at auction. ABPC is composed of two parts. Part I, Autographs and Manuscripts, includes original illustrations for printed books, documents, letters, typescripts, corrected proofs, signed photographs, and signatures as well as manuscripts. Part II, Books, includes broadsides, single-sheet printings, maps and charts, and uncorrected proof copies of books.

Entries are listed alphabetically by author whenever possible, by title when the author's name is unknown, or by private press, printer, or publisher headings. There is a lower value limit of hammer prices below which entries are not included. e.g. volume 103 only includes books and manuscripts which sold for at least $50 or its equivalent in other currencies.

ABPC is only available direct from the American publishers, the most recent volume costs $139.10 plus shipping.

It is also available on CD-ROM at $2001.95 with a dealer/library discounted price of $1680.76. The CD-ROM covers the years 1975-1998 and is updated annually. The update, which is cumulative, is available to subscribers for roughly the price of the annual volume.

Andrews, Les (ed.). *The Post Office Direct Mail Handbook.* Exley Publications Ltd., 1984. (This unfortunately is the only edition as it was never reprinted. It is well worth getting through your local library).

Barker, Nicolas. *The Oxford University Press and the Spread of Learning, 1478-1978.* Oxford, 1978, reprinted 1979. A work typifying a wide range of books on printing presses, their history and influence.

Bernard, P. & L & O'Neill, A. (Compilers and eds.). *Antiquarian Books; A Companion for book-sellers, librarians and collectors.* Scolar Press, 1994. Reprinted with minor corrections 1995. List price £59.50. Orders should be sent to Bookpoint Ltd., 39 Milton Park, Abingdon, Oxon., OX14 4TD **Tel:** 01235 400 400 **Fax:** 01235 832068.

An important work which should be in the reference library of any secondhand bookdealer. It contains a glossary of the major bookselling and bibliographic terms, biographies of individuals from the early days of printing to the 1990s and a series of longer articles on a wide range of subjects including Science, Literature, Natural History, Bookplates, Computers for booksellers and Book auctions.

Bland, David. *A History of Book Illustration.* The Illuminated Manuscript and the Printed Book. Faber and Faber Ltd., London, 1958.

Block, Andrew. *The Book Collector's Vade Mecum.* Denis Archer, London, 1932.

Bloomfield, Barry (ed.). *A Directory of Rare Book and Special Collections in the United Kingdom and the Republic of Ireland.* 2nd ed., Library Association Publishing, hardback, 1997. List price £98. Orders should be sent to Bookpoint Ltd., at the address two items above.

This is the only comprehensive guide to libraries and collections of rare or special books throughout the UK and Ireland, and contains details of over 1,200 libraries. It includes the many collections in major national and university libraries, public libraries, schools, cathedrals, private societies, institutions and accessible libraries of private individuals, and covers books from pre-1850 plus some modern material. It is an essential tool for researchers, academics, collectors, and antiquarian booksdealers.

Bondy, Louis W. *Miniature Books.* Their History from the beginnings to the present day. Richard Joseph Publishers Ltd., 1981. £24.

Book Auction Records. (BAR) A Priced and Annotated Annual Record of International Book Auctions. Published by Dawson Publishing, Cannon House, Park Farm Road, Folkestone, Kent, CT19 5EE. **Tel:** 01303 850101 **Fax:** 01303 850440

BAR covers all book and map sales of the major British and American Auction Houses, plus most British provincial sales and significant sales in Europe. It is issued in large annual volumes with a general index volume every five years covering the most recent five-year period. The annual volumes are in two parts: I, Printed Books and Atlases; II Printed Maps, Charts and Plans. BAR is compiled from the season's auction catalogues from around the world. Book entries are arranged alphabetically by author or by title, private press or other associations. For each entry a bibliographic description is followed by the auction sale record which provides details of the auction house, sale date, lot number, buyer's name (where given by the auction house), and the hammer price which excludes any buyer's premium. Where known, the amount of Buyer's premium charged by each Auction House is given as a percentage in the listing of Auction Houses and their addresses.

Cross-references are made for items such as pseudonyms, joint authorship, compound names and also for the more important illustrators, editors, translators and private presses. Each volume has a lower lot value under which records are not included. e.g. Volume 90 issued in 1993, records only those lots which realised £70.00 and over (U.K.), $140.00 and over (U.S.A. Canada and Australia), or the European equivalent of £150.00 and over. BAR is not only an invaluable source of international auction prices going back many years, but is also important for general bibliographic reference.

The current retail price is £99 (£84.15 to the trade). Volume 95 covering the year 1997 was issued in July 1999 and will be the last issued by the present publishers. Its future, at the time of writing, is unknown. Back numbers are available from the Folkestone address at the following trade prices: Vols. 61-71 £10 each; vols. 72-81 £20 each; vols. 82-86 £30 each; vol. 87 £40; vol. 88 £45; vol. 89 £50; vol. 90 £60; vol. 91 £70; vols. 92-94 £84.15. The general index volumes are available from (1968-72) at a trade price of £85, to (1990-94) at £347.50. BAR is not available on CD-ROM. Current volumes should be ordered from Dawson UK Ltd., Book Division, Crane Close, Denington Road, Wellingborough, Northants, NN8 2QG. **Tel:** 01933 274444 **Fax:** 01933 225993

Note. In using ABPC, BAR and other auction records for pricing purposes it should be remembered that a buyer's premium has to be added, and in certain countries there may be taxes as well. In addition, whether or not the item was bought by a dealer for resale or by a collector for himself is significant in determining a retail selling price. It is recommended that any auction prices are used in connection with the guidance given in chapter 4.

The British Library's Automated Information Service - BLAISE
National Bibliographic Service, The British Library, Boston Spa, Wetherby, West Yorkshire, LS23 7BQ **Tel:** 01937 546585 **Fax:** 01937 546586
E-mail: blaise-helpdesk@bl.uk
Website: http://portico.bl.uk/services/bsds/nbs/blaise

This is an online information retrieval service that provides access to 21 databases containing over 19 million bibliographic records via the web. Items range from the earliest printed books to the most recent scientific reports. If you visit their website you will find instructions on how to access the data and if you would like further details, please ask for their leaflet 'Connecting to Blaise'. An incredibly useful service.

British Museum General Catalogue of Printed Books to 1995. This is available on CD-ROM from Chadwyck-Healey Ltd, The Quorum, Barnwell Road, Cambridge, CB5 8SW, **Tel:** 01223 215512, **Fax:** 01223 215514. You should contact the distributors for the computer specification required for this (it runs under *Microsoft Windows*) though at £11,000 for new purchasers it is hardly likely to interest the average bookdealer. It is worthwhile checking at your local main library, however.

What is more useful is the READEX compact edition in book form, unfortunately now out of print. This was produced in 27 volumes to 1955 with nine volumes of supplements to the end of 1975. It occasionally comes up at auction (A set sold for under £1,000 in London during 1998), and is strongly recommended as one of the most useful sources of information for any secondhand bookdealer, particularly on dates and editions. I use my set many times a week.

Bury, Richard de. *Philobiblon.* 1344. Reprinted with translations and introductions, Basil Blackwell, Oxford, 1960.

Carter, John. *Taste and Technique in Book Collecting.* Private Libraries Association, Pinner, 1970.

Carter, John. *ABC for Book Collectors*, 7th edition, revised by Nicolas Barker, 1994. A very useful work with over 450 entries defining and analysing the technical terms of book collecting and bibliography. Currently priced at £12.95 it is available from the publishers - Werner Shaw Ltd, or from the PBFA office. The addresses of both of these are given above.

Carter, John and Muir, Percy H. (eds.). *Printing and the Mind of Man.* A Descriptive Catalogue Illustrating the Impact of Print on the

Evolution of Western Civilization during Five Centuries. 2nd edition, 1983 Karl Pressler Publisher, Roemerstr. 7, 80801, Munich, Germany. Currently in print at a list price of £80. This is the standard reference for first editions of great books and is of interest to book-collectors, booksellers, librarians and scholars.

Dunkin, Paul S. *How to Catalog A Rare Book.* American Library Association, Chicago, 1951, ninth printing, 1970.

Feather, John. *A Dictionary of Book History.* Croom Helm Ltd., Beckenham, 1986.

Gaskell, Philip. *A New Introduction to Bibliography.* Oxford University Press, 1972. This is basically a successor to McKerrow, (q.v.). It gives an account of the printing practices and textual problems of the last 200 years and also serves as an advanced manual of bibliography for students of librarianship.

Gilbert, Colleen B. *A Bibliography of the Works of Dorothy L. Sayers.* Macmillan Press Ltd., London, 1979. This work is included as exemplifying the many hundreds of author bibliographies available. (Dorothy L Sayers lived in Witham, some 3 miles from my premises, where there is a statue of her, and a special centre devoted to her books and life).

Glaister, Geoffrey A. *Glossary of the Book.* George Allen and Unwin Ltd., London, 1960. A substantial book of nearly 500 pages which I found invaluable in writing parts of this book.

Hickin, Norman. *Bookworms, The Insect Pest of Books.* Richard Joseph Publishers Ltd. £24.

Honeyman, Robert. *The Honeyman Collection of Scientific Books and Manuscripts. Parts I to VII.* Sotheby's sale catalogues, London, 1978-1981. One of the greatest collections of scientific books ever sold.

Horblit, Harrison D. *One Hundred Books Famous in Science.* Based on an Exhibition Held at the Grolier Club. The Grolier Club. New York, 1964. This is often cited but the title is misleading as there are 130 books illustrated. There are collations but no commentaries.

Howard-Hill, T.H. *A Bibliography of British Literary Bibliographies.* Oxford, 1969.

Hunter, Dard. *Papermaking. The History and Technique of an Ancient Craft.* Alfred A. Knopf, New York, 1947, reprinted Dover Publications Inc., New York, 1978.

Jackson, Holbrook. *The Anatomy of Bibliomania.* Faber and Faber Ltd., London, 1950.

Johnson, Arthur W. *The Practical Guide to Book Repair and Conservation.* Thames and Hudson, Ltd., London, 1988

Joy, Thomas. *Bookselling.* 1952. *The Truth about Bookselling.* 1964. *The Bookselling Business.* 1974. Joy was Managing Director of Hatchards Ltd, Piccadilly, London and these three books are predominantly on dealing in new books.

Lewis, Roy Harley. *Antiquarian Books.* An Insider's Account. David and Charles, 1978.

Linklater, Clive. *Reflections from a Bookshop Window.* Hole in the Wall Publishing, St. Leonards-on-Sea, 1994.

McKerrow, Ronald B. *An Introduction to Bibliography for Literary Students.* 1927, second impression with corrections, Oxford, 1928 with many subsequent reprints. For many years this was the standard work on bibliography and is a classic of scholarship. It is still an excellent guide up to about 1800 but has now been superseded by Gaskell, (q.v.).

McLean, Ruari. *Victorian Publishers' Book-Bindings.* Gordon Fraser, London, 1974.

McMurtrie, Douglas C. *The Book.* The Story of Printing and Bookmaking. 3rd revised ed., 1943. Oxford University Press, New York, reprinted 1976.

Meenan, Audrey. (Compiler & ed.). *A Directory of Natural History and Related Societies in Britain and Ireland.* British Museum (Natural History), London, 1983. An example of one of the many directories of scientific societies. This is the only edition to date.

Merryweather, F. *Somner. Bibliomania in the Middle Ages.* London, 1933. Reissued by Benjamin Blom, Inc. New York, 1972.

Miller, Stephen. *Book Collecting.* A Guide to Antiquarian and Secondhand Books. PBFA, Royston, 1994.

Minet, Paul. *Late Booking.* My First Twenty-five Years in the Secondhand Book Trade. Reminiscences from one of the most senior dealers in the UK. Frantic Press, Frant, 1989. £12.

Muir, Percy H. *Book-Collecting as a Hobby in a series of Letters to Everyman.* Gramol Publications Ltd., 2nd edition, 1945. Percy Muir was one of the greatest of secondhand dealers and writers on books of the 20th century. Anything written, co-authored or edited by him can be highly recommended.

Muir, Percy H. *Book-Collecting. More Letters to Everyman.* Cassell and Co. Ltd., 1949.

Muir, Percy. *English Children's Books 1600 to 1900.* B.T.Batsford Ltd., London, 1954, 4th imp.,1985. An example of a subject bibliography.

Muir, Percy. *Victorian Illustrated Books.* 1971. B.T.Batsford Ltd., London, new edition, 1989.

Muir, Percy H. (ed.). *Talks on Book-Collecting.* Delivered under the Authority of the Antiquarian Booksellers' Association. Cassell and Co. Ltd., 1952.

Munby, A.N.L. (General editor). *Sale Catalogues of Libraries of Eminent Persons.* e.g. Volume 11: *Scientists,* edited by H.A.Feisenberger. Mansell Publishing Ltd., / Sotheby Publications Ltd., London, 1975.

Peplow, Reginald. *The Good Publicity Guide.* Sheldon Press, London, 1987.

Peters, Jean (ed.). *Book Collecting. A Modern Guide.* R R Bowker Co, New York and London, 1977.

Pitcher, M.A. *Management accounting for the lending banker.* The Institute of Bankers, London, 1979. This is one of the major guides used in training bank managers in dealing with small businesses. It is highly relevant if you are in the position of needing to present a case for finance.

Plomer, Henry R. *A Dictionary of the Printers and Booksellers who were at Work in England, Scotland and Ireland from 1668 to 1725.* Bibliographic Society, Oxford, 1922.

Pollard, Alfred W. *Fine Books.* Cooper Square Publishers, Inc., New York, 1964.

Pollard, A.W. and Redgrave, G.R. *A Short-title Catalogue of English Books 1475-1640.* London, 1926. A revised three volume edition was published between 1976-1991. This is known as STC. It is also available on CD-ROM.

Porter, Roy. *The Earth Sciences. An Annotated Bibliography.* Garland Publishing, Inc., New York and London, 1983.

Quayle, Eric. *The Collector's Book of Books.* Studio Vista Ltd., London, 1971.

Rees-Mogg, William. *How to Buy Rare Books.* A Practical Guide to the Antiquarian Book Market. Phaidon. Christie's Ltd., London, 1985, 2nd imp., 1988. An excellent book with a particularly useful section on 'Further Reading' giving details of many bibliographies with comments.

Ridgway, Judith. *Successful Media Relations.* A Practitioner's Guide. Gower Publishing Co. Ltd., Aldershot, 1984.

Roman, Kenneth and Maas, Jane. *How to Advertise.* A professional guide for the advertiser. What works. What doesn't. And why. Kogan Page, London, 1979.

Shep, Robert L. *Cleaning, Repairing and Caring for Books.* Revised edition. Richard Joseph Publishers Ltd. £10.95

Uden, Grant. *Understanding Book-Collecting.* Antique Collectors' Club Ltd., Woodbridge, 1982, reprinted 1983 and 1992.

J. Whitaker and Sons Ltd., 12 Dyott Street, London, WC1A 1DF. **Tel:** 0207 420 6000 **Fax:** (Editorial) 0207 420 6103
E-mail: sales@ whitaker.co.uk or custserv@whitaker.co.uk

Whitaker are primarily concerned with new books and data relating to them. As a dealer in secondhand books you may often be asked to provide new books for customers. Whitaker provide a wide range of excellent publications and services to help you. e.g:

Whitaker's Directory of Publishers - is a best-selling reference work for all who are involved in the book-trade. It currently contains a listing of over 34,000 active publishers and distributors in the UK and Ireland with their contact details, ISBN prefixes and index of categories supplied. Also included is a directory of book trade organisations, export booksellers, library suppliers, wholesalers and major international book fairs. It is known in the trade as the Red Book and is published annually in one paperback volume, currently at £25.

Whitaker's Books in Print is the definitive source of bibliographic reference in hardcover and contains details of English language titles published in the UK, Ireland and Europe in alphabetical author, and alphabetical title sequence. It also includes publisher and distributor details, plus a separate alphabetical listing of series. In the 1999 edition there are over 887,000 titles with over 1.2 million changes since the 1998 edition. It is published annually in January in four volumes. (Current price is £449).

Books in Print on Microfiche is an alternative to the above and is available with weekly or monthly updates. Most public libraries have these so it is rarely necessary to buy your own for in-house use.

Whitaker BookBank. A range of CD-ROMs providing reliable, accurate and timely bibliographic information for all English language books. With over 1 million English Language titles in print in the UK and over 2 million in print world-wide, these CD-ROMs let you know what is available, the cost and where to get it from. These are not cheap but if you are planning to stock or supply new books as well as secondhand they are worth investigating. Whitaker will supply an evaluation disc on request.

Wing, D. *A Short-title Catalogue of Books Printed in England, Scotland, Ireland, Wales and British America...1641-1700,* 3 volumes. New York, 1945-51. A second edition was published in the period 1972-1988. This is abbreviated to and just quoted as *Wing.*

The World of Learning. Europa Publications Ltd., 18 Bedford Square, London, WC1B 3JN **Tel:** 0207 580 8236 and 0270 631 3361
Fax: 0207 636 1664   49th edition, 1999, £260.
An essential reference work to the world of academia, giving details of

universities, colleges, learned societies, museums, and libraries throughout the world and of international organisations.

TAILPIECE

In marketing yourself and your books, remember that if you try to do things a little differently from others, people are more likely to take notice of you:

During the early 1930s, an American film studio undergoing lean times, was looking for a child to star in their next film. The producer went on a talent-spotting visit to a local dance school for very young ladies. The children were asked to line up for inspection and all did except for one, who ran and hid under the piano. 'I'll have that one' said the producer, pointing to the piano. The shy little girl, not only went on to become one of the greatest child film stars of all time, but also saved the fortunes of the studio. Her name? - Shirley Temple.

CHAPTER 9

SIMPLE REPAIRS AND REFURBISHMENTS

REPAIRS

With cased books, paperbacks, or books issued in paper wrappers, some of the most common faults are: hinge-splits, the book becoming loose in or partly detached from, its case or wrappers, and loose pages or plates. These faults all detract from the appearance and value of a book. They can however in many cases be easily corrected quickly and cheaply. This makes a book either more saleable or able to fetch a higher price.

There are a number of very simple basic repairs that can be carried out with just an inexpensive container of polyvinylacetate (PVA) emulsion glue and a small, round or flat, nylon artist's paint brush with at least a 10 inch (26cm) long handle. PVA glue is obtainable at most hardware or DIY stores as a white viscous liquid sold as a wood-glue. If it is too thick the glue may be diluted slightly with water as required to give easier spreading. Distilled or de-ionised water as used for topping up car batteries, is the ideal choice, but generally tap water is alright. The glue can be used straight from its container but for ease of access it should be decanted into an empty plastic screw-lid pot - the kind that ladies use for their face cream. If you are planning to repair older books or documents it is advisable to use an acid free PVA with a neutral pH, obtainable from specialist suppliers.

Small splits in the external hinges of cased books. e.g. up to 3cm long.

These should be held open slightly with the point of a penknife or scalpel to allow the brush and glue to be inserted under the cloth on both sides of the split. As little glue as possible should be used, compatible with enough being used to enable the sides of the split to be glued down and held together. Press the sides of the split together and down and if there is any surplus glue exuded, this should be wiped off immediately with a very slightly dampened cloth. Keep pressing on the split with your fingers for about a minute to allow the glue time to penetrate slightly and to harden initially. Put on one side for an hour or two to let the glue dry but do look after 5 to 10 minutes to make sure the split has not reopened. If it has then hold it down again for a further period. The glue, once dry, is transparent and almost invisible. This technique is not advised for head or tail hinge splits unless they are very small. For larger splits, re-casing, lining, or re-backing may be necessary. For these you should look at the appropriate repair manuals (q.v. chapter 8), or consult an expert bookbinder. **Hint.** Though this repair is described first, if there are other repairs to be done as described below, then these should be carried out first.

Book loose in the case or cracked internal hinges.

Where this is due to the paste down end papers becoming partly detached at the inner hinges, but not split, then open the book with the covers roughly in a straight line to open up the hollow back, and stand it on end. With your brush inside the hollow back apply glue at the inner hinges to both the boards and the end papers as far as you can reach, then turn the book upside down and repeat for the other end. Lay the book flat and rub down the inner hinge with a dry cloth to ensure that the formerly loose end paper is in contact with the boards and the mull. Close the book, lay flat, place a weight on, e.g. some other books, to hold it firm and leave for several hours or overnight. This may not work for badly affected items but it often produces a much tighter book.

If the inner end paper hinges are split and possibly some of the mull or muslin holding the case to the book has come away from the book, then access is a little easier. Lift the edges of the split end papers, apply glue underneath, to the mull where it is exposed, and to the spine where any mull had become detached. Care should be taken to avoid getting any glue on the inner surface of the hollow spine of the case. Press down as before but before shutting the book insert a strip of waxed paper slightly longer than the book, at the hinge, to avoid any surplus glue sticking the free end paper to the fixed end paper. Lay flat and place weights on as before.

Loose pages or plates.

Single pages and in particular, plates, are often completely detached. Before attempting to refix these, first place the plate in position to see if it will fit in properly. Quite often the fore-edge may project a millimetre or two. If it does project then remove the amount of the projection, e.g. 2mm, from the hinge side of the plate using a metal or plastic straight edge and a sharp scalpel. Plates can then easily be tipped in or reglued as follows.

Take three pieces of scrap paper larger than the plate, e.g. A4 sized for an 8vo plate. Place one piece (**A**) on a flat surface with the hinge side of the plate (**B**) resting centrally on it. Place the other piece of scrap paper (**C**), which must have a straight edge, over the plate, leaving a clear parallel strip at the plate hinge of about 5mm (3/16"). Apply glue to this strip with the brush (or with a glue stick), as shown in the diagram opposite, and also a little to a 5mm strip at the hinge of the adjacent page in the book, using the third piece of paper as a mask. Place the plate in the book, line up its edges with the rest of the book, and close the book for an hour or two.

If a section or part section of the book is loose but not detached it is sometimes possible by regluing the hinges on both sides of the section to refix it. If it will not sit in its position properly, then removing the case, regluing the spine and refixing the case may be called for if the value of the book justifies the cost. N.B. With any of these simple techniques it is always advisable to try them out first on a cheap or worthless book.

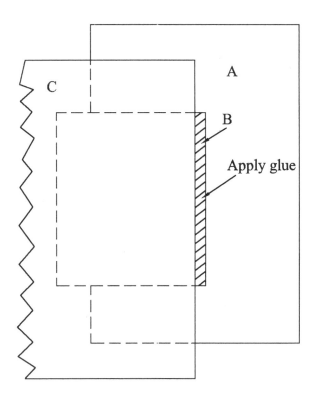

Text-figure 2. Preparation for applying glue to a loose page, plate or cover.

Paper covers or wrappers partly or wholly detached.

Where the covers or wrappers are intact, apply glue both to the spine of the book and the inner spine of the covers. Place the book in the covers, rub the spine with a dry cloth to make both surfaces come together and place the book on its spine with a large book or bookends either side to support it. Leave it for a hour or two, until the glue is dry. If one cover has become detached it can be refixed by gluing as in the illustration above. N.B. With all procedures remember to wash the brush afterwards.

REFURBISHMENTS
Cloth books.

Covers of case-bound cloth books may get soiled or stained with use. There are a number of commercial book-cloth cleaners on the market e.g. *Backus Book-Cloth Cleaner,* (please see the trade press and the appendix for details), which can be used to remove grime and improve the surface finish. These do not work for all types of cloth but in general they can considerably improve the look of a book and brighten the appearance of the spine lettering. The instructions are easy to follow and the contents of one container can be used to clean a large number of books.

Leather books.

Leather-bound books, particularly if they are older than about 50 years or have been stored in poor conditions, may have covers that are dull, dry and brittle. The application of leather creams or dressings can dramatically improve the colour, shine, and the feel of the binding and also prolong the life of the book by delaying or preventing hinge splitting and other forms of leather deterioration. There are many of these on the market but the best I have found, (I use it regularly on my own library), is a neutral Leather Cream made by Liberon Waxes whose address is in the appendix. This comes in 250ml containers currently at a cost of £4.28 plus VAT each. It may be ordered direct from the manufacturers with postage extra, or for the cost of a phone call they will give you details of your nearest local supplier.

Protecting covers and dust jackets.

To give that extra look or protection to your books and to your stock, especially if it is on display in a shop or at a book-fair, the use of polyester clear film is strongly recommended. This comes in rolls of various lengths, widths and thicknesses. One of the suppliers I use has film available with thicknesses ranging from 0.075mm to 0.175mm. A commonly used thickness is 0.100mm which comes in a 15m roll at a width of 610mm. It is simple to use - you just cut the film to size- a little larger than any dust jacket fitted, and wrap it round the book or jacket as if it were a dust jacket. This smartens the appearance of any book, and if you are doing book-fairs this greatly improves the shelf life of any dust jacket. Suppliers frequently advertise in the trade press. Some dealers stock this and if you are both exhibiting at the same book-fair, a prior phone call can save delivery charges.

OTHER REPAIRS AND REFURBISHMENTS

For more advanced work you should consult a professional bookbinder or restorer or some of the reference works mentioned in chapter 8. You should be aware however that many other products are available for lifting labels, removing foxing, removing label and tape (e.g. *Sellotape*) glues, and repairing torn pages or dust jackets. Please see the trade press or appendix for details.

TAILPIECE

RAGS

Make   **Make**

BEGGARS   **PAPER**

Make   **Makes**

LOANS   **MONEY**

Make   **Makes**

BANKS

Anon. Circa 18th Century

PART II

BUSINESS

PLANNING

CHAPTER 10

INTRODUCTION TO BUSINESS PLANNING

This book is structured to have three main parts rather like a sandwich. Bookdealing and the internet are two vital bread and butter elements, but the filling that holds it all together occupying a central position and synthesising it into a unique viable entity, is business planning. There is plenty of meat here, which if digested properly, will hopefully provide jam and cream for you.

During the early 1980s, after two years with the London Enterprise Agency, helping many hundreds start small businesses, I was commissioned by the Anglian Regional Management Centre at Danbury in Essex to produce a guide to business planning for use on their small business training courses at which I was a visiting lecturer. These courses subsequently transferred for the next fifteen years to the Polytechnic of East London, which later became the University of East London.

During this time the business planning guide (with modifications by Ivan Rush who ran the courses), was instrumental in helping nearly a thousand course members start their own businesses, the finished business plans being highly regarded by bank managers to whom they were presented. This second section of the book is based on my lecture notes and the business planning guide, my experiences with the London Enterprise Agency, over forty years of marketing and the practical know-how gained in running two separate small businesses in parallel for thirty years.

Business planning is a common link between success and failure for businesses of all sizes. Trouble shooting for small firms with problems was a part of my brief whilst I was at the London Enterprise Agency. Almost invariably those problems were caused by lack of business planning generally and by lack of cashflow forecasting (or liquidity) in particular. The successful enterprises were those who planned their business. Before getting to the detail of what business planning is and how you do it, let me outline what it did for one young man.

CASE STUDY

Mark, a young college student, came to me some years ago for help with a major project which was an important part of his catering course. The students of his year had been set the task of producing a viable business plan for setting up a small business related to the catering industry. I went over the basic principles with him as outlined in the following pages. He went away, drafted his plan, and then showed it to me again. I was able to make some positive suggestions which he incorporated and his plan was then presented. Mark's plan and those of the other students were reviewed by the college staff and a local bank manager.

Not only did Mark win the top prize for his year for his plan, he was congratulated by the staff and the bank manager for one of the finest business plans they had ever seen from a student over many years. Top students were sometimes rewarded by being allowed to spend two weeks (unpaid), obtaining practical experience in the famous kitchens of the Savoy Hotel in London. When he got to the Savoy, Mark was so highly regarded that he actually spent seven months there and after qualifying at college was offered employment by the Roux Brothers restaurants in London. He turned this offer down to follow up his own plans and he now runs a very successful outside catering business, and a flourishing restaurant. Needless to say, the red carpet is laid out when my wife and I go to eat there and the service is fantastic.

THE BUSINESS PLAN

The preparation of a detailed business plan is an essential element in starting any small business or in running or expanding an existing one. It is not a one-off exercise, i.e. something you do once and then forget. It should be constantly monitored and updated and it forms a very powerful management tool in the running of a business once it has been established. It will help you to clarify your thoughts, identify and plan for potential problems and enable you to assess whether or not your proposed business is suitable for you, your personality and your circumstances, and will provide you with an acceptable return on your investment of time and capital. It will help you to avoid the trial and error process and may possibly save you from making unwise decisions and disastrous mistakes.

A completed business plan should enable you to determine whether or not you have a viable proposition. On the positive side it is always hoped that you will have and it becomes successful. One valid outcome of a properly prepared plan however, is that your business is not potentially viable and that therefore you should forget that particular business. By doing this at the outset you could be saving much heartache and stress to yourself and your family and avoid losing your hard-earned capital.

Producing a business plan is something that you owe to yourself and your family, because it is your future that is at risk, and a plan will help to reduce or minimise this risk. At its simplest a business plan is a statement of your aims and objectives, where, when and how you are going to achieve these and your best estimates of the skills and resources required e.g. premises, people, stock, equipment, and finance. It is also very much concerned with the profit and cashflow you forecast and how and when you will be repaying any money borrowed for the business. A business plan is also a document that can be used as a yardstick to measure your business performance once you have started.

The main way in which you will use your business plan is keeping tabs on and controlling your business by comparing what actually happened with what you forecast or budgeted would happen, and then taking the necessary steps to correct an adverse situation or to take advantage of a favourable one. This could be weekly or should be at least monthly.

Apart from being a management tool in the running of your business, the most common use of a business plan is to support an application for a loan from a bank or other source of finance or for a grant. Even if you are in the happy situation on not needing finance at present, once you have produced your plan it is always a good idea to make an appointment to see your bank's small business manager and do a formal presentation of your plan to him, (or her will be taken as read from now on). The bank manager will hopefully be suitably impressed and if the time does come in the future when you do need a loan, e.g. for that very large library which has just been offered to you, you are far more likely to get what you are after and more quickly. Remember that the best bank manager is the best informed one.

Other important uses of your business plan include informing your accountant, your solicitor, potential business partners and potential investors in your business.

In drawing up a business plan, you should aim to produce a main document of not more than 10 to 12 single sided pages. Where you feel that your case would be helped by providing more detail, then this can be done in the form of appendices, e.g. as a part of your marketing section, you could consider enclosing a draft press release to show how thoroughly you have thought through the publicity aspects of your business.

There is one important element of your plan presentation that cannot be written down. It is you and how you present yourself and your plan. You should show enthusiasm, smile, inspire confidence with your manner of presentation, anticipate questions so you won't be stumped and dress appropriately. A mediocre plan well presented will do better that a good one poorly presented. The bank manager is assessing you as a person, your skills, and your business knowledge, just as much as your plan.

If you are needing a loan to start with then the source, typically a bank, will need to be satisfied on a large number of points. These are covered in the next chapter plus some practical hints on approaching bank managers. Try if possible to avoid the 'curate's egg' situation with your plan, i.e. make it good in all parts.

There is a very considerable amount of help, much of it free, to assist you in business planning. A few examples of some of the multiplicity of publications are given below. Where not specified, the addresses for obtaining these are given in the appendix.

Business planning - a quick guide. Department of Trade and Industry publication no. URN 99/659. Free.

Business Plan. Part of a larger guide: *Setting up and running your business*, available free from branches of Barclays Bank.

Starting a business. From Midland Bank branches. Free.

For those living in the London area: *Getting started in business* including *Business Plan Guidelines.* London Enterprise Agency in conjunction with Barclays Bank. A very fine 40 page outline guide with many pointers to other sources of help. Free.

Your Business Plan. Lloyds Bank branches. Free.

Business Start-up Guide. A Guide to Business in Scotland by Brian McVey and Ronnie Scott. An excellent and very comprehensive guide of 144 pages, available free in Scotland through the Scottish Business Shop Network.

How to Prepare a Business Plan. By Edward Blackwell. 3rd edition, 151 pp, paperback, 1998. Kogan Page Ltd., 120 Pentonville Road, London, N1 9JN, in association with the Royal Bank of Scotland. £9.99

UNDER THE TAILPIECE.

One of the major parts of your business plan will be concerned with marketing, i.e. about finding or creating opportunities, of which the following is a fine example.

Some time ago Chester Zoo were planning a new elephant house, but had two problems: lack of money and three tons of elephant dung to dispose of each week. Someone pointed out that this was an excellent garden fertilizer, (apparently it produced mammoth results), and so project 'Zoopoo' was born. The product was advertised packed in plastic containers, and orders rolled in, (no doubt via many trunk calls). Parcels of pungent pachydermous poo were soon popped in the post, and both problems were solved. The project still continues, (it hasn't bottomed out yet), and for price and quantity details please telephone 01244 380280 or just turn up with an empty dustbin or two.

CHAPTER 11

THE BANKS AND PRESENTING A CASE FOR FINANCE

In presenting a case for finance the normal high street or clearing banks should be your first point of call. They are your most likely lender and if you try other sources first without good cause, the other sources are likely to query why you have not tried the banks first.

Most of the major banks, especially in the UK, have small business centres and managers, whose job it is to look after their small business customers. These managers have targets which include getting new accounts. In presenting a case for finance to a bank, especially when you are starting, you do not have to stick with the bank where your personal account has been for years. By all means start there and see what is offered to you. You might find that you are offered a loan at anything from 3-7% over base rate whereas another branch of the same bank or another bank altogether will offer you the same loan but at a lower percentage over base rate. You can then decide whether or not to accept this better offer or go back to your original bank and ask them to match it if they want your business. You also may find that by talking to your accountant a different and cheaper source of finance is recommended.

You should bear in mind the fact that banks do not lend their own money. They lend money that has been invested in the bank and their job is to make as much money for the bank as they can as a return on this investment. Unfortunately the banks have been doing this for a long time and they are usually much better at this than the average small business person.

The banks also know how to charge for their services. If for example you need an overdraft of say £15,000 and the bank is willing to lend this to you at an agreed percentage over base rate, the interest is not your only cost. You are likely to be charged a massive fee of a few hundred pounds for setting up the overdraft in the first place, plus an annual renewal fee. Therefore in comparing quotations from different sources you have to make sure that all these 'hidden' extras are taken into account. If you do have an overdraft, the interest will be calculated on a daily basis on your debit balance and the interest charged to your account quarterly.

The banks are nowadays very aware of the opportunities they have with their small business customers. To assist in helping small businesses to start, all the banks have produced copious free literature outlining what you should do when starting in business and what financial information they would like to see from you in a business plan. Most even produce a floppy disk providing programs for use on your computer for such items as cashflow forecasts. It is strongly recommended that you obtain such packages from any banks you are thinking of approaching as this will give you a detailed indication of what they are looking for in your specific business plan.

In general it is highly likely that the bank will want to be satisfied on a number of points. The banks use different mnemonics as a guide to what they are looking for, e.g. SPARSE:

S = Suitability. i.e. Is the type of loan you are seeking suitable for the purpose stated? An overdraft for example is a loan facility to cover working capital for the day-to-day running costs of your business such as paying your suppliers, buying books for stock, giving credit terms to customers, and paying rent, rates and staff. It is not a loan as such but enables you to write cheques on your account up to a certain amount in the red. It is a short-term facility, is normally reviewed at least annually, and technically can be called in for repayment on demand by the bank. Interest charges could be of the order of say 3.5% to 7% over base rate. If however you exceed your overdraft limit without authorisation the bank is liable to either refuse to accept your cheques or to charge you a punitive rate over base for any excess, such as 15%. Be warned.

A capital or business loan is usually for the purchase of a tangible asset such as a vehicle, bookcases, a computer or possibly a building. This will be for a fixed amount, for a fixed term measured in years with regular monthly or quarterly repayments and it may have an option for a fixed rate of interest for the whole term or a floating one in accordance with changes in the base rate. If you are needing a vehicle then leasing is one option you should consider initially as this frees capital for you to use in your business, and leasing payments are tax-deductible

P = Purpose. You will be required to specify the purpose for which the loan is required and why.

A = Amount. Clearly you must say how much you want and justify this with appropriate figures in your plan.

R = Repayment. The bank will be very keen to know how the money will be repaid. For an overdraft a bank will not expect you to be permanently in the red. They like to see frequent swings well into the black. The best and really the only way to demonstrate your repayments here is through the use of a cashflow forecast as explained later. For a longer term capital loan your cashflow forecast should clearly show the regular repayments of both capital and interest. There is a certain amount of chicken and egg situation here as until you have the loan you won't necessarily have the exact figures to put into your plan. This just emphasises the reiterative and dynamic nature of a business plan.

S = Security. Banks tend to have a number of lending limits. You may be able to obtain an unsecured loan up to a certain amount which is within the discretion of the bank manager. Obviously if you are presenting a sound business plan and inspire confidence, you are more likely to obtain such a loan than would otherwise be the case. Over a certain amount the bank will require some security in the event that you are unable to repay the loan as agreed. This could take the form of a legal charge on any property you may own or other assets. They will not necessarily expect the full amount of the loan to be secured. If you do not have much security you should explore the Government Small Firms Loan Guarantee Scheme as outlined in the appendix. There are however severe limitations to this.

E = Eventuality. The bank will want to know what your plans are in the eventuality that things may not work out as you had outlined. You should be prepared for this and point out how easy it will be for you to re-work your business plan to take care of an adverse situation.

I well remember a bank manager presenting the above data at one of the small business conferences I had organised. Talking about the acronym SPARSE, he felt that Suitability and Purpose were particularly important, as if you took these away what was left was what you would fall on - your ARSE.

These are the main specifics. In general the bank manager will also wish to see that the business will be making sufficient profit both for the above repayments and to provide the cash for your living expenses. The bank will also need to be satisfied that you have sufficient money to put into the business yourself, i.e. that you are and are fully committed to it, and are a suitable person to run the business

Your business plan must therefore be divided into sections to provide the necessary information as shown in the following pages. The exact form it will take will depend on whether you are starting a business from scratch, are already running one, or intend to join or buy one.

If you are needing a loan then it is strongly recommended that you send or deliver personally, an advance copy of your business plan to your small business bank manager. This should be a few days before your presentation appointment, in order to give him an opportunity to read it thoroughly. He will appreciate your consideration and will have a greater

·opportunity of seeing the thought and effort that has gone into your plan.

You should be aware also that both the banks and the business support agencies have small business advisers who are there to help you. Contact one or more of these and go over your plan with them before presenting it to a bank manager, or using it to control your business.

Hint. Many people at work like to surround themselves with personal items such as family photographs, sporting trophies or certificates. When you first visit your bank manager quickly scan his desk and office walls to see if there is anything that will tell you something about him. e.g. If there is a golfing trophy there ask him what his handicap is and where he plays. This can often pay dividends in breaking the ice and in selling yourself, particularly if you play golf yourself.

This technique also applies in other situations, sometimes with exceptional results. In an earlier career I once had an appointment to visit the managing director of a large London firm concerned with buying UK products for a range of outlets in the USA. The staff warned me that he was a very busy man and that five minutes was the maximum time he usually allocated to representatives. On entering his office I noticed on his desk a large photograph of a former British prime minister. I mentioned quite spontaneously that I had met him during the war. He was immediately interested and asked how I had come to meet him. I explained that his sister lived in the same small Oxfordshire village as I did and that I had met him on one of his visits to her. 'Well' he said 'I'm married to his daughter.' I left **over two hours** later after one of the most fascinating and rewarding meetings I have ever had.

If you are unsuccessful in obtaining everything that you want from a bank, don't despair, there are other sources of finance. To find out about these either ask your accountant or contact your local Enterprise Agency, Business Link, Scottish Business Shop, or Business Connect in Wales - please see the appendix for details.

TAILPIECE

If you fail to watch your cashflow and your liquidity, the time may come when you have exceeded your overdraft limit and a letter arrives from your bank manager asking what steps you are going to take to reduce your overdraft. In this situation one bookdealer replied:

Starting at the old oak tree, take 10 steps north, 12 steps east, and dig.

CHAPTER 12

THE BUSINESS PLAN

A suggested sequence is given below, which should be followed.

TITLE PAGE

This should have your trading name, your name and the names of any others in business with you, and a date. If the nature of your business is not immediately apparent then this should be added e.g. Secondhand Bookdealer.

If you trade in your own name or those of yours and a partner then there is no need for these to be registered. If however you trade as a limited company or in any name other than yours e.g. Alpha Omega Books then such names must be registered. If you are male and trading in your own name DO NOT call yourself Mr. This is a courtesy title conferred on you by others and apart from surgeons, should not be used by anyone in referring to themselves unless it is on a form where you are asked for your title.

Hint. Try and select a name that does some marketing and communicating for you. If your name is say *John Brown* then this on its own does not convey much about your business. *Brown's Books* is both alliterative and more meaningful and at least says what you deal in. If you have a particular speciality such as history, then *Brown's History Books* gives much more data to the reader and can attract prospective history customers to you and those wishing to dispose of history books for sale. Changing my trading name from *Baldwin's Books* to *Baldwin's Scientific Books* some years ago has had an enormously beneficial effect on my business. This is also highly significant if you are proposing to market yourself by means of a website as outlined in part III.

NUMBERED LIST OF SECTIONS WITH PAGE NUMBERS

This is self evident and should follow the sequence given. The list of sections can be prepared early on but obviously the actual page numbering can be only carried out when the plan is complete. You do not need to start each section with a new page.

1. SUMMARY

This will be the first thing to be read though it will be the last part of your plan you write as it can't be done until the rest has been written. First

·impressions are important and you should therefore take particular care in preparing and polishing your summary.

It is important that it is succinct and well presented and normally should not fill more than two sides of an A4 sheet. In completing it you should cover at least the following points.

- Brief personal details of both you and anyone else who will be in the business with you, stressing experience and qualifications relevant to your particular business. What dependants you have.

- The type of business and what you are proposing to stock as indicated in chapter 1 on 'Business Options'. You should indicate whether you will be starting a business, joining one or buying one. If premises are involved then details should be given, e.g. freehold, leasehold, brick, half timber, etc., and your staff requirements if any.

- If you are starting a business then you should provide a summary, from your researches, of the evidence you have to indicate that there is a market or demand for the kind of books you will be stocking, and how you will be satisfying this demand.

- This should be backed up by an indication of your degree of commitment - have you signed a lease or already incurred expenditure? and your financial forecasts e.g. sales, profits, drawings, cashflow, break-even point, etc. (In sole traderships and partnerships, beginners are often confused over profit and drawings. Profit is basically your sales minus your costs and is taxable, whereas drawings are monies that you take out of the business for your personal use and are not taxable. Drawings represent a lowering of the capital you have invested in the business.

- The total cost of getting into business must be given. This should include both the necessary working capital for day-to-day running and capital expenditure on fixtures, fittings and equipment. e.g. book-shelving, computer, etc. The cost of stock must be indicated. If you need a loan, you must indicate what type e.g. overdraft, or long-term, how much, for how long and what security you can offer. The following layout is one that bank managers are used to and it is strongly recommended that you adhere to it.

The Applicant(s)

Name

Address, phone, etc.

Background

Include family and dependant details

The Business

    Business type. Include here details of what, where and how you will be operating and the kinds of stock as outlined in chapter 1.

    Premises   State whether home, shop, etc.

If buying a business then:

Present annual turnover	£xx,ooo
Staff	
Purchase price	£yy,ooo

The Market   Details of the market you are entering including your selling methods and publicity.

Outline Plan

Degree of commitment. e.g contract ready to sign subject to loan.
Expected take-over or start date.

Budgeted annual turnover	£aa,ooo
Budgeted net profit	£bb,ooo
Proposed staff	
Proposed annual drawings	£cc,ooo
Breakeven turnover	£dd,ooo

Financing

Total cost of getting into business including professional fees etc
    £ee,ooo

To be provided as follows:		
From own funds		£ff,ooo
Bank loans required:	Overdraft facility	£g,ooo
	Long-term loan	£hh,ooo

2. THE PROPOSED BUSINESS

Here you should describe in detail what business you are in or are proposing to be in. Describe the mix of methods of operation you have chosen as outlined in the chapters on 'Business Options', 'Book-fairs', 'Running a Book Catalogue Business', and part III, and why you have chosen these. Include a statement of the kinds of stock you will hold (chapter 1), and how you propose to obtain these. (chapter 3). You should specify how books will be despatched where relevant. Include a statement of the business you are in as indicated in chapter 2. i.e. Show that you are aware of the benefits that you will be providing. If on reading chapter 4 on 'Pricing' you have decided on a policy, then state it. The more you can add of this nature the more the reader of your plan will realise how thoroughly you have thought through your business and hence what a splendid person you are to lend money to.

If you are already running a business, or are proposing to buy one, or if you are planning to join an existing business, then give full details. You should include accounts for at least the last three years if the business has been going that long and you should summarise the history of the business. It is a sad fact that most small business that become extinct do so in their first three years. If you can survive this critical period then there is great hope for you.

3. PERSONAL DETAILS

In this section you need to demonstrate that you are a suitable person to run the business, and that you have the necessary skills needed in the business, or how you propose to acquire them. As shown in section 12 you should have at least a reasonable proportion of the money required, and you need to state what security you have to offer to cover any loan.

If you are forming a partnership, personal details of your partner will also be required as in that case the business plan will be a joint one.

Specifically the following additional points should be covered:
- Full name, address and age.
- Marital status and dependants (including ages of children)
- Education, qualifications and relevant experience. If you have been an avid book collector all you life, then this is relevant.
- Membership of professional and other bodies. e.g. ABA, PBFA, etc.
- Brief details of you career to date with an emphasis on anything that relates to your proposed business. You know your background better than anyone so try to avoid the temptation of writing a full scale biography of irrelevant detail.
- The date you started or are proposing to start your business.
- Any aspects of your health that could affect your business performance.
- Details of your driving licence including classes and endorsements.
- Details of any other business interests.
  Name and address of your present bank and account number.
- Any other personal details that are relevant and that may persuade a lender that you are a good risk to lend money to. e.g. you are an extravert, you can sell yourself and get on well with people and

have completed the bank's self assessment questionnaire with good results.

4. AIMS AND OBJECTIVES

You should state both your personal and business aims and objectives for the short term (1-2 years), medium term (2-5 years) and the long term (over 5 years). If you are not clear as to the distinction between aims and objectives, then please read the introduction to this book where they have been clearly exemplified.

In specifying your objectives avoid vague statements such as 'I want a good standard of living.' Quantify your objectives as far as possible e.g. I am looking to obtain a net income of £25,000 per year for the first two years. You will then have a yardstick for the future against which you will be able to judge your success. If an objective is to retire in say ten years and hand the control of you business to another member of the family, then say so. You might want to become the leading book dealer in the UK in a specialised field in which you are already an expert from your previous experience.

Objectives where possible should be expressed in financial terms such as turnover and profit. Whatever your objectives, there are two that are absolutely essential in any viable plan; these will really get the attention of your bank manager. They are **profitability** and **liquidity**. They are the life blood of any business and without achieving either of these your business is likely to fail. Whilst profit is an absolute measure, profitability is a relative measure e.g. profit measured against sales or capital employed and is one of the yardsticks used to measure the financial performance of a business. The free publications available from the banks provide plenty of examples of these terms.

Liquidity means in basic terms that you have ready cash or the ability to write cheques now to cover your expenses, purchases and other outgoings. Of these two, in the short term, liquidity is far and away the most important element for you to watch. In the long term, high profitability is a common aim but all too often business collapse because they fail to watch their liquidity (especially by neglecting cashflow forecasting and not carrying out budgetary control, i.e. by comparing actual cashflow with the forecast). In my time at the London Enterprise Agency I came in contact with many firms who had failed. All had potential profitability but most failed to realise their potential through lack of liquidity through lack of business planning.

Having specified your objectives, your business plan should indicate how you intend to achieve these objectives. A good starting point is to specify marketing objectives and forecasts. These later will be translated into financial terms which may result in a revision of your objectives.

5. MARKETING

This covers a wide range of subjects and is the key part of your business and your business plan, as, if you don't sell and don't get the cash in on time, you don't have a business. Marketing involves the right attitude of mind combined with the ability to spot a gap in the market and fill it profitably. What is meant by attitude of mind can be illustrated by the story of the shoe manufacturing company that sent two sales representatives at different times to a remote Pacific island where the natives all went barefoot. The first reported back that they did not wear shoes and that therefore there was no sales potential: the second reported that no-one had shoes and hence there was a fantastic sales potential.

The following topics should at least be covered. Market research, sources of stock, pricing, your method of selling or reaching your customers, a sales forecast, publicity and competition.

Market Research

It is vital to show evidence that there is a market for your books. The way that you do this is by carrying out some market research. There are two main kinds of research: desk and field. Desk research involves ploughing through existing publications such as directories of dealers and lists of specialist societies and noting down the size of the market and the geographical area of the market, e.g. if your market is the UK only, then give an idea of how many dealers there are already in the UK and what proportion cover the specialities that you are planning. You have to consider points such as - if there are a large number of dealers in a particular subject, is it because of big demand or is it over-populated; and vice versa, if there is no-one covering a subject that you are interested in, is it because there is very little other interest or is it because you have discovered a gap in the market, or is it just that there is no demand?

Field research involves physically going out and visiting shops and bookfairs, perhaps plotting on a map who is where and finding out in general what is going on. Having done this you should describe your market, i.e. what customers have you identified, are they other dealers, members of societies you belong to, and where they are. If it is going to be academic books then show how many universities throughout the world have the appropriate departments. Is there evidence that the market is expanding, static or contracting, and if so what are the trends?

Sources of stock

Precis from chapter 3 the mix of methods you will be using and try and give an indication of the planned contribution of each method to your total.

Pricing

Go through chapter 4 and abstract what you will actually be doing. You should also point out the unique nature of the secondhand book business in that there are no set margins or trade terms as in other businesses and hence things are far more flexible. The bank manager will like to see statements such as: For the first year or two, the emphasis will be on smaller margins to ensure adequate cashflow and liquidity, with a transition to higher margins and greater profitability, once the business has become established.

Selling

Here, from chapters 2, 5, 6, 16 and 17 you should show what methods you are proposing to use to reach your customers, e.g. is it going to be operating from home and just doing book-fairs or are you going to be issuing catalogues and putting your stock on to an internet database such as Antiquarian Book Exchange (ABE). This is one of the most important factors and you should give detail of your modus operandi.

If you are proposing to use an internet database, remember that the internet is still relatively new and bank managers will be most impressed if you include details of what a database such as ABE can do for you, e.g. put in your plan that it is the equivalent of having 25,000 visitors looking at your complete stock 24 hours a day for every day of the year. The bank manager will then be aware of your technological prowess and how up-to-date you are. If you are presenting your business plan to a bank manager, and you are already connected to the internet, ask him if there is any particular book that he has been trying to find for years. Go away and look for it on ABE or Bookfinder.com. If you can find what he is looking for, this could be a very practical demonstration of your business acumen.

Sales Forecast

If you have not yet started in business then you cannot be expected to make an accurate sales forecast at this stage. You must, however, do a sales forecast and make it as realistic as possible, as this is a vital input to your cashflow forecast which comes later. You should make a monthly forecast for at least the first year and at least quarterly forecasts for the next two years after that. Once you are started you will soon be able to update these figures and make them more realistic. Set it out properly in tabular form. e.g.

Year One Sales Forecast

	Jan	Feb	Mar	Apr	May	Jun	Jly	Aug	Sep	Oct	Nov	Dec	Total
Sales £													

The actual month you put first will obviously depend on when you are actually starting or on when your financial year starts - this is usually April or January and is something to be discussed with an accountant.

Publicity

Here you should outline how you are going to publicise yourself both by traditional methods as in chapter 7 and on the internet - chapters 16 and 17. It will be appropriate here to mention that you have included as appendices a draft printed brochure publicising your business, an outline press release with details of the proposed distribution list, a layout of your proposed website home page, and details of the size of web rings you are proposing to join.

Competition

All the textbooks and marketing literature emphasise that you should consider the effect on your customers of the competition and how they will react. You should indicate how many other dealers there are covering your specialities and where they are, and your best estimate of their likely reaction to your entry into the market. For many types of business there is cut and thrust and a limited market to share out. Bookdealing is somewhat different. It is a very friendly business and whilst, of course, there is competition, you should point out in your plan the mutually symbiotic nature of the whole book trade. You should point to the Charing Cross Road area in London and the famous book towns such as Hay-on-Wye, and more recently, Wigtown in Scotland, which welcome new dealers with open arms. The more there are the greater the attraction, which is the direct reverse of many other businesses. Moreover, you could use the exceptional popularity of the June book-fairs in London and the September one in York, to make a further point here and in your market research section.

6. PREMISES
Existing Premises.

If you already have business premises then describe them, saying whether they are freehold or leasehold, their location, and the type of area they are in. i.e. are they in an area designated for business use or are they in a residential area?. How old are the premises and what state of repair are they in? In the case of leasehold premises, details will be required of your liability for repairs and maintenance, the period of the lease, and the rent reviews. How secure is your tenancy?

The running costs in terms of rent, rates, repairs, etc., should be specified. Questions such as how well the premises match your requirements, and is there room for expansion?, should be addressed. A photograph or a plan would be helpful.

Finding Premises.

If you are proposing to find premises in which to start your business, outline your requirements. Say what steps you have taken to find suitable accommodation, whether you expect to buy or lease and what the costs are likely to be. Don't forget to take account of solicitor's and surveyor's fees, stamp duty, redecoration, heating and lighting equipment if this is not already present, the connection charge for services and of course bookshelving and office equipment. **Hint.** Local auctions are an excellent source of inexpensive equipment. New furniture is not necessary in an office. I have a splendid office desk that would have cost me some £250 new, but it only cost me £5 at a nearby auction some years ago, and the transport costs from there.

Make sure that all the services you require are there and before purchasing make sure you can afford it. Consult your solicitor, and your accountant as well as your business agency adviser.

Working from home.

If you propose to run your business from home, do you have or will you need planning permission? Obtain the free booklet *Planning Permission. A Guide for Business* from the planning department of your local authority and study it. In general, you will not need planning permission: if there is no change to the overall character of your home, or if it will still be used predominantly as a private residence, or there is no great increase in the number of vehicles or people visiting, or there is no unusual activity incompatible with a residential area, or if you cause no nuisance such as noise at unsocial hours.

If you have a mortgage then you should check with your lender as there may be restrictive covenants on the deeds of your house or there may be increases in the interest rate. The question of insurance has been covered elsewhere. You should discuss with a business adviser or an accountant what legitimate claims on your house you can make for tax purposes.

If you have made enquiries then specify the advice you have been given, particularly if you are proposing to employ staff at home.

Administration.

Full details of this should be in the appendix but summarise it in your main plan. You should indicate how you will be operating and controlling your business, e.g. an accounting package on your computer or simple sets of account books, and how you propose to pack and despatch books. Particular attention should be given to the financial aspects of getting money in on time. e.g. The Department of Trade and Industry, issue a free booklet *Better Payment Practice. Your guide to paying and being paid on time*. Reference URN98/965 and the associated wallchart URN98/964. Get copies of these and incorporate into your plan the major steps recommended, such as having an aged debt list and a chasing policy on overdue accounts. **Hint.** Though you need not put this is your plan, in practice you should try to keep up to date with your accounts on a daily basis. This avoids the chore of doing it all at the month end and you are much less likely to miss those minor petty cash purchases.

7. KEY ASSUMPTIONS AND SENSITIVITY ANALYSIS

In writing your business plan you will have to make many assumptions. Some of these will be relatively minor, but some are so important that the business plan rests on them and if they turn out to be wrong then this could seriously impair the outcome of your plan. It is important therefore that whilst you are putting your plan together you should gradually build up a list of key assumptions.

This list will obviously be unique to every individual and business but the following are some of the likely points that should be covered:

▸ Sales expected and how you arrived at the figures.
▸ Loans required, the repayment period and interest rate.
▸ Any grants, or capital injections, you expect to receive.
▸ Expected overall profit margin.
▸ Credit settlement terms for both customers and suppliers, and the proportion of credit and cash sales
▸ Stock levels in £s for each category of stock.
▸ Staff to be employed and rates of pay.
▸ Purchase, hire, or lease of capital equipment.

A bank manager looking at your plan will want to carry out a 'sensitivity analysis' on your plan by asking 'what if?' questions relating to your key assumptions to assess the consequences of anything going wrong. e.g. What if your sales are only two thirds of your estimates? You should anticipate questions that would arise in the mind of a banker or accountant reading your plan, and make sure that you have covered them.

You should draw attention to danger areas and the effect they could have, e.g. on cashflow, profits, etc., and say how you would deal with any situation that might arise. Whereas many assumptions may affect both profit and cashflow, some, e.g. time taken for debtors to pay, may barely affect your profits but could have a very serious effect on your cashflow.

If the business is going to rely heavily on one person such as yourself, what would happen if you had a long illness? Such dangers can be covered by 'key man' insurance and this should be looked into and details of the cover you intend to arrange given. If you can't give precise details at this stage then at least show that you have thought about it, and that it will be arranged, and ensure that you put a realistic figure for it in your forecast profit and loss account.

Small business will be interested to know that legislation has recently been introduced into the UK (1998), enabling them to claim interest on late payment debts incurred under contract. This should be a great help to cashflow and your awareness of this should be indicated in your plan to show how up-to-date you are and how much you appreciate the importance of cashflow. Further details are given in the appendix.

8. SETTING-UP COSTS OR START-UP BUDGET

If you are going into business there will be many costs to be met before you can actually start. What they are will depend on your individual circumstances. You should itemise these with the checklist shown in the appendix as a guide: You only include those items relevant to you and your business and add any not included in the checklist. When completed, this should appear as an appendix to your plan. Note that if you are renting premises as opposed to buying, then your first rent payment will go in the rent/rates row of your cashflow forecast.

9. THE CASHFLOW FORECAST

This is the key element in any business plan and in the financial running of your business. It is a simple month by month statement of what money you expect to come in and go out of your business, together with a calculation of what your bank balance will be at the end of each month. Where there is more going out than coming in during any month, this will tell you (and your bank manager) how much you need to borrow on overdraft to cover the difference. On a month by month basis over a 12 month period, your closing bank balance at the end of the month will be expected to show fluctuations - sometimes in the red and sometimes in the black. All the banks and the support agencies will be able to show you the details of a cashflow forecast and how it operates. The following should be read with a blank cashflow forecast sheet to hand. In principle it operates as follows: In the budget part of the receipts section, the main input will be your sales forecast as described earlier. To this you add any other income such as pensions, quarterly dividends on shares, or deposit account interest or any capital you are planning to introduce. For each month you produce a total. In the payments section you may have from 12 to 18 lines to complete covering all expenses ranging from annual accountant's fees, through quarterly phone bills, rates for ten months of the year, to monthly payments such as staff, your drawings, and payments to suppliers including capital items. With all receipts and payments you enter the details, inclusive of any VAT, in the month in which the money will be coming in or going out and not the date on the invoice.

For expenses you have a great deal of work to do initially, to estimate all the figures, but it must be done, and it will become much easier after you have been trading for a while. Business advisers at the banks and at help agencies will be able to help you - that's what they are there for. Note that depreciation appears in a profit and loss forecast and not in a cashflow, and conversely capital expenditure appears in a cashflow but not in a profit and loss account. The forms provided by the banks and help agencies are general ones and therefore you only need to complete those lines applicable to you and your business.

The term 'other' appears on the forms and needs a little explaining. First it means that if you have an expense not already itemised above then you write the figures and its description in here. Second, it is a fact of business life that there will always be some expenses that cannot be foreseen. Over a year these may be as much as 10% to 15% of your total expenditure. By putting a figure in here for each month it will be appreciated that you are aware of this and that it has been taken into account.

Budgetary Control or Using the Cashflow Forecast.

Having produced your forecast for the year, the major financial control of your business is carried out at the end of each month by entering the actual figures in the right hand column, and then comparing your budget and actual figures. This tells you what is going on and enables you to make management decisions based on current data, e.g. if there are any significant differences you can do something about it now, such as chasing debtors if payments are slow in arriving or pepping up your marketing campaign. Alternatively if sales were greater than anticipated you could decide whether to reduce your overdraft or to make those extra purchases. This way you are in control and are managing your business. Without this data you have far less idea of what is going on and cannot therefore make the right decisions.

10. PROFIT AND LOSS FORECAST

This is something that should be done in most cases. The banks and business agencies are very well qualified to help you with this and it is strongly recommended that you contact them for advice.

11. BREAKEVEN CHART

This is a simple statement in graphical form of your costs and the level of sales needed to equal these - called the breakeven point. Below this you are making a loss, and above it the magic word **profit** appears. Your costs will be twofold: fixed costs or overheads (those items of expenditure you will incur whether you are selling or not) and variable costs which will relate to your book purchases. This is something that should be of great interest to you, and your bank manager, i.e. how much do you have to sell, at what percentage mark up, before you start making a profit? As before, the advisers are there to help you with your chart.

12. STATEMENT OF YOUR FINANCIAL SITUATION

The purpose of this is to enable a lender to assess what funds you have or will have to put into the business, and what security you can offer on any loan and to see what liabilities you have. Your assets should be divided into current assets, e.g. money in the bank, building societies, value of any shares, or that redundancy payment or golden handshake just about to materialise and long term assets, e.g. the value of your house or any other property, the surrender value of any insurance policies, and the value of any other assets that could be used for security. A total figure for your net assets should be given. A similar list of what you owe, e.g. on credit cards, hire purchase, house mortgage, etc, should also be made.

Bank managers have often commented in the past that not enough emphasis has been placed on providing a detailed statement of living expenses when plans have been presented to them. If this is not provided it damages the credibility of your plan. To provide this information in your plan you should complete a statement on the lines of the schedule provided in the appendix. This provides the justification for your drawings needs and also reinforces your thoroughness in the bank manager's mind.

13. YOUR TOTAL CASH REQUIREMENT

You are now in the situation of being able to make a statement of what you need in the way of loans, (if any), whether overdraft or long term, for what purpose, for how long, and how and when they will be repaid.

14. AN ACTION PLAN AND TIME SCHEDULE

If you are still a little way off actually starting in business, then it is sensible to make out for your own use, a timetable of what has to be done, by whom, and when by and what tasks are dependent on other tasks being carried out first. This is often done in graphical form and if you have prepared one it can be attached as an appendix as further evidence of your commitment to the business.

15. APPENDICES

Include pages as necessary as indicated in other parts of the plan.

SWOT ANALYSIS

Finally in your plan, include a summary of the Strengths of your business, the Weaknesses, if any, as you see them, the Opportunities that you have seen, and any perceived Threats to the success of your enterprise. e.g. Strengths could include your specialist subject knowledge, and your previous business experience. Weaknesses could include being unknown at present, or your lack of knowledge of the trade. Opportunities could cover an expanding market, a large library on offer to you, or membership of a large society with common interests. Threats could mean a diminishing market, an economic downturn, or chronic illness. As with all parts of your plan, remember that help is out there just waiting for you to ask.

CHAPTER 13

A BUSINESS START-UP CHECK-LIST

A large amount of what is needed to start in business is already included in this book. There are however a number of topics not covered. These in general are very well explained in many other publications as listed in the appendix or alternatively, they can be learnt from the many sources of help available to you, e.g. Business Link. The following check-list of some of the more important ones is just given as a reminder.

Self Assessment

Are you the right person to go into business? Check yourself out by completing an assessment. The banks or support agencies will help you here. The Midland Bank two-page guide in their free *Starting a Business* booklet is particularly detailed, covering everything from health to family support.

Legal structure of your Business

Your business must have a legal structure. The possibilities are sole trader, partnership, limited liability company, a co-operative or franchise. The first three of these are far and away the most common and for further information on the pros and cons of each, you should contact a business agency adviser, or an accountant or solicitor for advice. Don't assume that a limited company will limit your liability, because if you borrow money, as a director you are likely to be asked to give a personal guarantee.

National Insurance, Income Tax, and Value Added Tax (VAT)

If you are going to be self-employed you should notify the Inland Revenue (details can be found in your local phone book), and ask them for two booklets: CWL1 *Starting Your own Business*, and CWL2 *National Insurance Contributions for Self-Employed People*. These give you details of the appropriate forms to complete. If your taxable annual turnover is expected to exceed £51,000 (April 1999 figures), then you must register for VAT - contact your local Customs and Excise Office (details are in the phone book). If your turnover is expected to be less than this, then you can voluntarily register to enable you to claim input VAT on your business purchases, e.g. vehicle fuel. A wide range of free booklets is available.

Employees

If you are considering employing anyone, many relevant booklets are available direct from the DTI or your local Job Centre.

Insurance

Check with your insurance company that you have the appropriate insurance on your vehicle(s) and premises for business use. If you expect customers or others to visit, you must have public liability insurance. If you are operating from home, it is vital that you notify your insurance company of this. If a claim is made and you have not notified them of your business activities, then they may well not pay out. Make sure your vehicle has in-transit insurance if you are carrying books at any time, e.g. to a book-fair.

Training

Have you checked with support agencies on the availability of small business training courses to help start you off, e.g the basics of business administration including record and book-keeping, computing, etc.

Services or Utilities

Agree a schedule, as required, with your electricity, phone, and water supplier and also check the rates situation with your local authority.

TAILPIECE

Adversity comes to all of us at times but the true entrepreneur is one who can turn an adverse situation to his or her own advantage. If things are looking black, try to be positive in your outlook or do some lateral thinking and you will be surprised at how often things can work out much better than you had anticipated. e.g. An American soldier serving in the regular army had an interest in genealogy and over a number of years had developed considerable professional skills in tracking down family trees both for himself and his colleagues. This enabled him to supplement his income and have a somewhat improved lifestyle.

He was called in to see his commanding officer the Colonel, one day, stood smartly to attention and saluted. 'Jones, is it correct that you have been tracing people's family trees for some time?' His heart sank as he thought he was about to be hauled over the coals. 'Yes sir.' 'Well Jones I'd like you to trace my family tree please.' (He was a very polite Colonel). Relief set in and a timetable and fee were negotiated and agreed.

The Colonel handed over recent family data and Jones set out on his search. Before long he discovered to his horror that the Colonel's great uncle Charles was a convicted murderer and had been executed in the electric chair at Sing Sing. However despite this setback the report was completed on time and duly presented to the Colonel. He read it with great interest including a short entry on great uncle Charles:

He held the Chair of Applied Electricity at a famous
American institution and died in harness.

Now that is what I call a true entrepreneur.

PART III

BOOKDEALING

AND

THE INTERNET

CHAPTER 14

INTRODUCTION TO THE INTERNET

A multiplicity of terms such as the internet, e-mail, the world wide web, websites, and book databases, have become common currency during the last few years.

- ▸ What do they all mean?
- ▸ How can they affect my book business?
- ▸ How do I get started?
- ▸ How do I use them?
- ▸ What equipment and computer software do I need?
- ▸ What benefits can I obtain from them?
- ▸ Where do I go for help and advice?
- ▸ Where can I learn about them?

The following pages and chapters are devoted to answering these and other questions as simply as possible.

What is the internet?

The internet is the system which allows owners of computers world-wide to link together to send information through the ordinary telephone network. Anyone with a desktop computer anywhere in the world can link into the internet, and thus link through to other users, by attaching their computer to their national telephone system.

The internet is currently the latest stage in the evolution of communication between humans, a process that has progressed over the last few million years through such stages as sign language, vocalisation, writing, printing, postal services, the telegraph, the telephone, radio, and faxes.

Most businesses, however small, need postal and telephone services. The advent of the fax machine greatly speeded up communications and has had a major beneficial effect on business. The concept of faxes is relatively easy to understand, the internet on the other hand is not quite so simple and as a result has been ignored by many.

The internet is here to stay, it is evolving and expanding rapidly and is already having a far greater impact than the fax and its predecessors both in private and business life. Its future rate of evolution and influence are likely to increase at an ever accelerating pace, and businesses who ignore it are likely to be left far behind those who use its facilities.

The ways in which information passes down the internet

Internet users pass each other information in, essentially, one of two ways: by one-to-one personal e-mails (= electronic mail), in simple text form, approximately analogous to everyday letters (known as snail mail), where somebody posts a letter to someone else to read at their leisure, or by connecting their computer to somebody else's web page or website - a part of the system where that person has set up information which is available 24 hours a day to be read by anybody who drops by to look at that information. Web pages usually have graphic elements as well as text and can display just about anything the owner of the web page wants.

Web pages are analogous to either static unchanging information-containing material such as printed brochures, catalogues and the like (although with fast-search facilities enabling you to home in on any required single piece of data in a matter of seconds) or, if appropriate, constantly, or regularly-updated information similar in operation to tv teletext but with high-level graphics. In either case, it's up to you as the user to access this information as the mood takes you. If you don't want the information then you don't bother going to look for it.

You should understand that - generally - this exchange of information is not taking place simultaneously with both parties being linked to each other at the same time and conversing together as in, say, a telephone conversation. Whether by e-mail or by web page, the information is put into the internet system by the author of the material and stored there electronically, to be retrieved later, or accessed when required by the ultimate recipient or end-user.

For example, although information retrieval from web pages is virtually instantaneous, e-mails can take several minutes, perhaps up to an hour or so, to be routed through the system and become available for the recipient by being 'delivered'.

How is each computer linked to the internet?

In order to attach your computer to the internet in the most usual way through the ordinary telephone system, you need a device called a modem (= **mo**dulator-**dem**odulator) attached to your computer which enables the computer signals to be transmitted and received down a telephone line. A modem, if not already part of your computer (most new computers these days have modems built in automatically) will cost somewhere between about £50 and £130. It is strongly advised that you obtain the fastest modem available, currently 56Kbps (= 56 thousand bits per second), as this can reduce the time you spend on the telephone system and hence your running costs. You also need to pay an Internet Service Provider (ISP), to provide the necessary link between your computer, the telephone system, and the internet system.

Internet Service Providers (ISPs)

ISPs are central to the whole operation of the internet and it is important to understand clearly their function in internet activity. ISPs are simply companies with big computers who perform the dual role of storing their subscribers' internet information and acting in the same way as a telephone switchboard to route internet connections worldwide. There are many different ISP companies in every country, e.g. in the UK there are some 300; the best known are perhaps AOL, Pipex, Btinternet, Globalnet, LineOne, Virgin, and Freeserve. However, if you are considering going on the internet, do NOT rush out to sign up with the first ISP you come across in a colour supplement advert or on a free computer disk. There really is an enormous choice of whom to use and there are advantages in learning a little more about the way in which the internet works before taking the plunge to use one rather than another, having been tempted by a free subscription offer.

Until recently, they mostly charged for their services; these charges differing from one ISP to another, depending on the range of services they offer, how efficient or large they are, and the usual other market forces. Up until the beginning of 1999, most ISPs in Britain charged a flat-rate fixed fee of between £7 and £12 per month for a full internet connection suitable for small businesses such as bookdealers. This charge covers providing an e-mail address, allowing anyone from around the world to send you e-mails which your ISP stores for you until you pick them up by dialling into your own private mailbox at your ISP; distributing all your own outgoing e-mails to the appropriate ISPs of others around the world; allowing you to access web page type information stored around the world on other ISPs, and providing you with free web storage space enabling you to display your own information on your own web pages.

Increasingly now, there are companies who provide a basic internet connection service at no charge. e.g. The internet ground rules have changed in that services are springing up such as Freeserve, which give their clients free internet access, in other words they do not raise any monthly charge whatsoever. Some, such as banks, do it to promote and retain customer loyalty; others will provide the service free but will raise substantial charges by the minute for telephone help if required.

162

Whatever your choice of ISP, they act as storage centres of computer information for their individual subscribers - you, and all the others who subscribe to the same ISP company as you do. Whenever you want to link into the internet, you dial up (via your computer's modem), your own ISP and the ISP automatically makes all the necessary connections for you. The vast majority of ISPs have made arrangements so that their customers (or subscribers), wherever they are, can dial into them on local British Telecommunications (BT) telephone call rates. For example, my ISP is Pipex, with a local office 50 miles away in Cambridge, and even though I am based at Witham in Essex, all my internet connections to the world through Pipex are charged to me by BT at local-call rates. As far as BT are concerned they are charging me for a phone line, and for local phone calls. They don't know or care that I'm using their phone line to access the internet rather than talking to friends down the road. My BT charges for being linked through to someone else's ISP in (say) New York for 5 minutes are exactly the same as if I'd been speaking to someone on the telephone in Witham for 5 minutes.

You can use your normal household or business telephone line if you want to, or have a separate telephone line solely for internet use; whichever suits you best. If you use only a single line, then your telephone or fax will not be available when you're attached to the internet, and vice versa. You can of course use services such as Call Minder, offered by BT in the UK, to take messages when you are online to the internet. Many businesses, including mine, have two separate phone lines and telephone numbers, one for the telephone, the other sharing duties between the internet and the fax machine. With the software provided by the ISP you will also find that it is easier, quicker and cheaper to send faxes via your PC rather than via your fax machine, though many use a fax machine for incoming faxes, even though fax modems can handle incoming faxes as well as outgoing ones. Having two lines also has the advantage that in emergency, if one of your lines is down, you can switch your phone, fax or computer to the other line.

When you sign up with an ISP, they provide you with free software enabling you to use their e-mail service and also to visit web pages. Different ISPs offer different types of software, and it's worth checking when choosing your ISP that the type of **Browser** software (i.e. the software you use on your computer to visit web pages) they provide is either *Netscape Navigator* or *Microsoft Internet Explorer*. Not using one or other of these from the outset could lead to problems somewhere along the line in the future for you.

In selecting an ISP there are a number of things you can do for yourself. First contact the British Internet Bookdealers Centre for advice (chapter 17), and second, see what comparative reports on British ISPs have been published. For independent reports the most useful I have found to date is in the internet article in the November 1998 edition of *What to Buy for Business*: contact details are in the appendix. You should at least check that you get a local call rate, the cost of unlimited access, what you get, e.g. is it one or five addresses, is your fast (56kbps) modem supported and what software and technical support do you get, and is the support helpline available 24 hours a day? For further advice on choosing an ISP look at some of the websites for beginners suggested in chapter 16.

As an internet user, you will have two main addresses through which other users contact you, your e-mail address and a separate website address which is also known as the Uniform Resource Locator or URL. Many when starting, use e-mail only and progress to a website later. These major topics are covered in the next two chapters.

CHAPTER 15

E-MAIL

E-mail is probably the most frequently employed and useful internet service. E-mail allows you to send private messages to any person or organisation with an internet connection. An e-mail message may be as simple as a single line of text, or it may include complex attached documents as large as printed books.

E-mail is usually delivered to the recipient's mail box at their ISP within minutes of being dispatched although it can take up to two or three hours. However, how soon the recipient actually receives the e-mail (and therefore reads it) really depends on how often the recipient downloads waiting e-mails from their ISP to their own desktop computer, rather than on the speed of the e-mail system itself. Downloading can be done manually, or your computer can be instructed to carry this out on a regular basis such as hourly.

One of the most immediately useful features of e-mail is how inexpensive it is. If you have to send the same message legitimately to 200 customers, you can do this for maybe 5p in total telephone charges plus the cost of your time to type the e-mail once. This compares well with the current UK £38 second-class postage costs and goodness knows how much extra in printing, addressing envelopes, and packing if you choose to do the same thing by mail. As an e-mail is usually much cheaper to send than making a long-distance phone call, this option should always be considered before phoning. Junk e-mail certainly exists but is more of a problem in the US than it is in the UK. However, 'spamming' (as the process of bulk-mailing unsolicited e-mails is called) is frowned upon heavily by the internet community. The speed of e-mail is so fast, and its convenience so great, that once you have had it for a while you wonder why you hadn't used it years before. e.g. a typical e-mail may come in overnight from abroad with a list of books wanted by a customer. A stock check, followed by weighing those available to determine the postage, and an e-mail quote to the customer can result in an almost immediate e-mail response ordering the books, which can then be in the post the same day.

E-mail addresses follow a fairly standard pattern on the lines of **ymg43@dial.pipex.com** which is the real address allocated to me by Pipex. The address comprises a unique identifier or name, e.g. **ymg43** is in effect my private mail-box within Pipex, all e-mail addresses have the at (@)

symbol somewhere in the middle, followed by details of the ISP site address with a dot separating the component parts of it: **dial.pipex**. The last item of the address may vary, e.g. **.org** indicates a non-commercial organisation, such as a charity, **.co.uk** means it is a business or company based in the United Kingdom, whilst **.com** originally meant it was a commercial organisation in the USA, but nowadays indicates an international business, thereby providing a higher cachet, i.e. in searching for and registering a personalised domain name as outlined below, go for the **.com** option rather than **.co.uk** if one is available, as these are far more highly prized. This is particularly important if you are planning to have a website and wish to publicise it world wide.

An e-mail address contains no punctuation other than the dot or period, does not contain any spaces, and by convention usually has no upper case letters. The . is always spoken as 'dot', e.g. you would say 'ymg43atdial<u>dot</u>pipex<u>dot</u>com' in giving my e-mail address over the phone in this form. Everything to the right of the @ symbol is known as the domain name, and there are a number of advantages in having your own personalised domain name or e-mail address.

Personalising your e-mail (and website).

If at some time in the future you decide to move to another ISP then your e-mail address will change, which means that all your business stationery will need to be altered, all your customers notified, and any of your adverts will be out of date. In addition your real e-mail address does no selling or marketing for you.

The best solution to this is to register a unique domain name that only you can use, rather like a company name or personal car number plate. Mine is **fossilbooks.co.uk** which I can move around from one ISP to another as required and also apply it to my website address. Instead of having **ymg43** in front of the @ I have a multiple e-mail address which means I can put anything I like and have put my name e.g. **sbaldwin**@fossilbooks.co.uk though it could equally be just **stuart**, or if my wife wants to e-mail her friends she uses **pam**@fossilbooks.co.uk - all on the same domain name. Not only does a personalised address do some marketing for you, it is also easier to remember and makes it much easier for people to find you, which is particularly important for publicising websites as you will see in the next chapter.

There are many thousands of domain names being registered daily, and currently there are well over 100,000 **.co.uk** ones in use with approaching 2,000,000 **.com** names. There is a database of world domain names which you can check on: http://www.i-search.net/ to see if a particular one is available. You just key in your proposed name, which should be highly relevant to your business, and within 30 seconds you will be told either that it is not available, (so think again), or that this domain does not currently exist - so act fast to register it before anyone else does. This is particularly important if you are planning to have a website. A number of firms are in the business of registering and/or selling domain names. There is of course a charge for doing this - in my case about £150 with a small annual service charge. An example of a particularly helpful and knowledgeable company who will carry out searches of available domain names and then register them for you, is given in the appendix, or you can check out http://www.netbenefit.co.uk. The *What to Buy for Business* internet article (see chapter 14) gives details of other companies who will register your domain name for you. In addition to registration you will also need a link to be established between your real address and your personalised one, which has to be done for you.

Sending e-mail.

Pipex is used here as an example. Other ISP software may differ in detail but will be similar in principle. Sending e-mail is very straightforward and once you have done it a few times it becomes as easy as using a phone or fax. At its simplest, on calling up your ISP Internet software on your monitor screen, a computer folder called *Inbox* will appear. You simply click on *Compose Message*, key in the e-mail address of the person you want to contact and a brief subject title, followed by your message in what is called a dialogue box. You can then click either on *Send* for immediate transmission or *Send Later* if you have more than one e-mail to go and only *Send* them when all have been keyed in. If you use *Send Later*, all your outgoing e-mails will be stored temporarily in another folder called *Outbox*.

You can also send copies at the same time to multiple other addresses, a carbon copy to someone else who might be interested, and blind carbon copies to others without them being aware that there are other recipients. It is a convention incidentally that you do not use all UPPER CASE in e-mails. In addition to keyed-in messages your e-mail can have attached files such as a document, a graphic illustration, a video or even sound. If you use the same addresses regularly they can be stored in an electronic *Address Book* which comes as part of the internet software. They can then be recalled as required rather than re-keying every time.

Messages should always be keyed in when you are offline, i.e. not connected to the internet, as otherwise you will be incurring unnecessary line charges. When you click on *Send* the software will automatically dial your ISP for you - you will know that this is happening as the modem makes characteristic noises when connecting. When you are connected, an indication that your e-mails are being transmitted will appear on your screen. If you are sending only one item this may happen so quickly that if you blink you may miss it. When you sign up with an ISP, you not only get given a real e-mail address, you also get a unique security code or password which must be used when sending and receiving e-mail. The ISP software can be set to insert this automatically so that in effect you can forget it.

Once e-mails have been sent, the full details will be stored in date order in a folder called *Sent Items* so they can be referred to at any time in the future. When e-mails are sent they will go initially to your ISP who will then forward them electronically to all the other ISPs concerned via the internet. At any time you have the facility to print out a hard copy from any of the folders.

Receiving and replying to e-mail.

When you dial up your ISP, either directly, or when you are sending an e-mail, your ISP will automatically check your mail-box where e-mails sent by others to you have been accumulated. These will be sent to the *Inbox* folder on your screen where you will be told how many new messages you have, how many you have in total, and how many of these have not yet been read. An index of all messages will appear giving the name of the sender, the subject, the date, and the time. Unread messages will appear in **bold** in this index. Once you have downloaded all your e-mails don't forget to disconnect from your ISP otherwise you will be wasting money on telephone line time.

To read an e-mail you just click on the item in the index and the e-mail will appear in the dialogue box, where you can look at it or print out a hard copy for action. If the message requires a reply you just click on *Reply to Author* and key in your reply in the space at the top of the received message. One of the enjoyable things about e-mail is that it is far more informal than normal correspondence, first names are much more commonly used and starting with 'Dear Sir' is almost unthinkable.

Once you have keyed in your reply, you follow the *Send* or *Send Later* procedure as outlined above. Having replied to an e-mail and sent it you have the option to delete it from your *Inbox*. Unless there are further actions to be taken with respect to any one e-mail it is recommended that you do delete it to avoid clutter. If you wish to look at the e-mail or your reply again you just look in the *Sent Items* or *Deleted Items* folder.

E-mail mailing lists

The term 'mailing list' on the internet is not the same as in the real world outside where it means just a list of names and addresses. Internet mailing lists or newsgroups, are worldwide or countrywide *groups* of people sharing similar interests and participating in an automatic system of round-robin e-mails. Each group's interests could be anything from research on Ostracoda, or wildlife conservation, to collecting modern first editions. Worldwide there are some 20,000 mailing lists with interests between them across the academic, commercial and social spectrum, to any of which you can 'subscribe'. Subscribers send e-mails whenever they want, to their own group's central address, which then automatically distributes those e-mails immediately to all the group's subscribers. Each subscriber ends up by getting between perhaps 2 and 50 e-mails a day, depending on how active or large the group is. For further general information on newsgroups you should contact http://www.dejanews.com

In the mailing lists for the booktrade, (there are some 15 booktrade lists worldwide of one sort or another) subscribers generally list small numbers of books for sale or wanted, or write in asking for quick help and advice from colleagues.

In the UK, the British Internet Bookdealers Centre (BIB), offers a friendly and informal e-mail sales, wants, information and publicity service for bookdealers, book collectors and librarians with a common interest in old, rare and collected books. BIB's other services are covered in chapter 17.

There are two groups, *Booktalk*, with an international circulation, and *Ukbooks*, a group for UK and Irish-based residents only. Each group enables members to send to each other, without charge and whenever they want, e-mails containing details of books for sale or wanted, news of web-sites, on-line services, printed catalogues, trade associations, societies, book-fairs, auctions or other services, or ask questions related to books or bookselling within the subject areas concerned.

Replies may be e-mailed to the original sender or to the whole group, and each group generates between about 10 and 20 e-mails per day. These may be received singly as normal or in 'Digest' form where the daily e-mails are amalgamated into a single e-mail which is sent every 24 hours.

Booktalk membership is £25 ($35) per year. Membership of *Ukbooks* is free and provides help and advice when required, to booksellers coming on-line for the first time. For further information and to subscribe, please contact http://www.clique.co.uk/groups.htm where you will be asked to e-mail your details.

E-mail is very widely used by people of all ages and walks of life from the Queen to primary school children. Youngsters have the advantage that they are being brought up on the new technology at school whereas most adults, especially oldies such as myself, have to learn the hard way. So much is happening and so quickly that it is difficult to keep pace. To communicate with youngsters, a whole new 'netspeak' vocabulary may need to be learned such as the cyberlinguistic abbreviations used in many e-mails.

There are hundreds of these in use BTW (By the way), but IMHO (In my humble opinion), and FYI (For your information) I just mention these in passing so that if you do get a message saying your last e-mail had me ROTFL (Rolling on the floor laughing) but I'll get back to you RSN (Real soon now) after I've been AFK (Away from the keyboard) having a BRB (Bathroom break), so TTFN (Ta-ta for now); you might get a glimmering of what is going on. Real oldies can take heart that they will at least know the last of these from the wartime radio show ITMA (Its that man again) starring Tommy Handley. These are more in use at a popular teenage chat level than in business e-mails, but no doubt they will appear before long as the younger generation grows up. Be prepared.

There is another group you may have come across called emoticons, a word derived from 'emotion' and 'icons', which are facial expressions and gestures represented by keyboard character combinations, e.g. :-) which has to be read on its side and indicates happy or smiling, as shown in the tailpiece to chapter 1 and at the head of the dust jacket spine. Many of the websites for beginners give long lists of these.

There is much more that e-mail can do for you but this covers most of the basics that you need to start.

For the future, the technology is already with us to enable mobile phones to be used for e-mails or for surfing the web, fast ISDN phone lines are likely to come down in price and speed things up generally, and the home television set incorporating the latest digital technology, is geared to become part of the world wide web within a relatively short time.

CHAPTER 16

WEBSITES

INTRODUCTION

The main reason for having a website is to use it as a marketing tool whereby millions of people around the world can have virtually instant access to any information you choose to put on it. Only you can decide on the content of your site but before you do this, you have to have some clearly-defined objectives so that your content can be tailored to realise these.

OBJECTIVES

One of the best ways of determining your objectives is to look at the websites of other bookdealers to give you an idea of what their implicit objectives are, from which you can select those relevant to you and your business. In working out the objectives for my own website I browsed some 20 other UK dealers' sites and the following checklist, though it does not claim to be definitive, does contain the 20 most commonly used ones.

▶ To sell books.
▶ To let the world know about you, and your background, your business, and specialities, your address, phone, fax and e-mail numbers, and details of your stock e.g. new, remainders, review copies, secondhand, and/or antiquarian: books, journals, manuscripts, ephemera, etc.
▶ To give details of your services for customers, e.g. shop, including opening hours, book-fairs, mail order, catalogue frequency, book searches.
▶ To provide news of purchases, e.g special libraries or collections, of catalogues just issued and past ones still available. This could be in the form of a news bulletin. e.g. *What's New*, or *Recent Acquisitions.*
▶ To enable easy access to your stock by author, subject. title, keyword, catalogue, etc. An online catalogue is great but is something to consider only after you have mastered the basics.
▶ To make it easy for customers and prospective customers to make enquiries or to order from you.
▶ To make it easy for customers to contact or respond to you (and vice versa), via e-mail, i.e. by providing an e-mail link on your site.
▶ To provide details of publications that you or your customers are looking for, e.g. permanent and specific wants lists and the type of

stock you are interested in purchasing.

- To provide a form for prospective customers to complete for you to obtain additions to your mailing list.
- To provide information enabling visitors to find your premises easily, e.g. location map and public transport timetables.
- To provide local tourist information to make their visit more interesting.
- To point enquirers in the direction of other dealers who may be able to help them.
- To advertise your presence at specific book-fairs or other events during the coming months or year. If you become well-known at certain book-fairs, customers will often place orders to be collected by them at the book-fair. One bookdealer has been exhibiting at a particular annual event for over 40 consecutive years and usually has a substantial turnover from this prior-ordering.
- To indicate your membership of one or more relevant professional bodies such as the Antiquarian Booksellers Association, and the Provincial Booksellers Fairs Association, by including their name, abbreviation and or logo. These associations have high minimum standards for membership and exhibiting at book-fairs which are well-known in the trade and to the book-buying public. Your membership should therefore indicate to a browser that you have high professional and ethical standards. This of course is not meant to imply in any way that non-members are not equally highly professional or ethical.
- To advertise for staff and publish job specifications. Computer literate job hunters may have their curriculum vitae on their own web-sites thereby making it easier for both parties.
- To inform potential customers of your terms of trade - how and when payment may be made and of any relevant bank charges. e.g. What credit cards you take, what should be added for cheques in a foreign currency, and the upper limits on Eurocheques - over a certain amount banks make extra charges. It should be stressed, as mentioned earlier, that customers should not send complete credit card details by any one e-mail, (to avoid misuse), unless by a secure line, but should be sent in two separate parts or phoned, faxed or posted. If you offer discounts then give details.
- To inform customers what despatch methods you use, the geographical areas you cover, and of any in-transit insurance cover you offer.

▸ To inform customers of your policy on returned books.

▸ To show browsers that you maintain your site and keep it up-to-date by including on relevant pages, especially those relating to stock, the wording: *This page last updated on dd.mm.yy.*

▸ To make the browser interested or amused and at least aware of **what you can do for them.** They are far more likely then to return to your site again.

WEBSITE NAMING AND STRUCTURE

Having outlined your objectives, you now have to decide on the content and structure of your site. Before getting to this, a little more internet jargon needs to be explained.

Any website will be one of millions forming the **world wide web** (www, or just the web), which is part of the **internet** - also known as **cyberspace**.

A website is unique to an individual or organisation or department and will be composed of one or more **web pages** linked to each other and to a home page. A **home page** is the most important page on a site, it is normally accessed first and usually provides links to the other pages forming the site. It may in some cases be the only page on a simple site.

Web pages are created, formatted, and linked using a special computer language called **HyperText Markup Language** (HTML). (You need to know that this exists but you don't need to know the details of this language or how to use it, as there are software packages available to do it for you, as you will see later). A web page containing text is consequently known as a **hypertext** document and will contain one or more **hyperlinks** which are usually images or highlighted text. By clicking on these hyperlinks with a mouse, (no you don't have to catch one first, a mouse is is a multi-function device attached to your computer that facilitates man-machine communication), you can be transferred to other web pages on a site or to other sites around the world.

There are two other bits of jargon which you need to know; both like HTML, were invented just ten years ago in 1989 by a physicist named Tim Berners-Lee working at CERN, the particle physics laboratory near Geneva.

The first is **HyperText Transfer Protocol** (HTTP) which is a standard format for computers to exchange messages between themselves. e.g. between web servers and their customers and other web servers. A **web server** is a computer connected to the internet that stores web pages and makes them available to others round the world. Companies running web servers are usually those who provide you with your e-mail services.

The second is **Uniform Resource Locator** (URL), which is a unique sequence of characters giving the address of your site on the web. Any site or page can be displayed on your PC if you know its URL. All web page URLs start with http:which tells you that they are hypertext documents. There are no spaces in a URL and where slashes are present they are always forward: / and not back: \ and most, but not all, have www following this, e.g. my main URL is: http://www.fossilbooks.co.uk, though for marketing reasons I have others, e.g.

http://www.secondhandsciencebooks.com

linked in to this, and if you access either of these you will (hopefully), find on your monitor, my home page occupying most of the screen and a contents page on the left giving hyperlinks to the other 15 pages on my site. The contents page is what is known as a 'static' frame and it will always stay on the screen where you will have the ability to scroll up or down it; the home page is called a 'live' frame and this will change whenever you click on the contents page index to bring up a fresh page. Other pages are linked to the home page in a hierarchical structure. Suppose you were a visitor wanting to visit my shop and wanted to know how to find me and my opening hours - you just click on <u>Visitors</u> and the hyperlink will instantly bring up the relevant page with all the information you need, and replace the home page on the screen. Having a static frame is a particularly useful way of navigating round a site and its use is recommended at the design stage of your site, though there is a disadvantage in that some search engines don't like frames. If you use a particular URL frequently then it can be saved in a menu which is either called bookmark or favourites depending on whether the web browser you are using is 'Netscape Navigator' or 'Microsoft Internet Explorer.' When you want to use it you just click on it in your menu. To understand the other jargon and acronyms related to computers and the internet; there are many sites with glossaries to help you, e.g. try http://www.newbie.net/ where you will find 9 pages of terms explained.

PUBLICITY FOR YOUR WEBSITE.

It is no use designing and creating a website, however good, and then expecting the world, (or the world wide web), to beat an electronic path to your door - even if you called it the new improved AcmeMicrochip-MouseTrap. You have to let the world know that you exist, and there are several ways of doing this:

▸ Use traditional publicity methods such as producing a brochure or press release or advertising, as discussed in chapter 7. Don't forget to include your URL on all your stationery, visiting cards, etc.

▸ Use the services of the British Internet Bookdealers Centre to publicise yourself in the UK, as outlined in the next chapter.

▸ Join a webring. This is certainly one of the more important ways of letting others who share your interests, know of your existence. A webring is a collection of websites sharing a common interest or subject matter and there are thousands of these. If you go to http://www.webring.com you can enter any keyword and search. I entered 'books' (in July 1999), and came up with 601 rings, many of which had well over 100 sites. On scanning these I found one devoted to palaeontology called Paleo Ring with 461 sites in its ring. Needless to say, as this is my main speciality, I applied to join immediately. Even if there were no other benefits, I have found in one swoop, a potential 461 additions to my mailing list. There were several other rings of immediate personal interest too. Search for yourself and join those related to your specialities or interests.

▸ Incorporate certain features into the design and content of your website to increase the chances of some of the many millions who use the web each day, of visiting your site.

▸ Let Search Engines know of your site.

To implement these last two you need to understand a little about how searches are made on the web.

Web Searches.

One of the main ways for users of the internet to find websites of interest to them, is to use search services which are generically called **Search Engines.** There are well over 400 of these and they are divided into Search Engines proper, e.g. AltaVista http://www.altavista.com/ and Directories or Index Sites, e.g.Yahoo: http://www.yahoo.com/ which differ in the way their web page listings are compiled. Search engines proper, use electronic robotic devices appropriately called crawlers or spiders, which will look at your web pages and automatically transfer copies back to the engine index. They may ultimately find your site but it speeds the process up if you send them details directly. Directories differ in that all the information has to be sent to them by humans. e.g. You may write a description of your site and submit it to the directory, or directory editors may look at or review your site and write it up themselves. If this is not done, then unlike search engines proper with spiders, the directory has no way of knowing you exist. Yahoo incidentally is the oldest, one of the largest and the most popular web search services with over a million sites in its index, and AltaVista is equally popular. In both cases software is used to look for matches against the key word(s) being sought, i.e. a search engine will look at all the millions of pages it knows about, looking for ones that match your search topic. These matches will be ranked so that you see them in order of relevancy.

With current technology, search engines are one of the weak links in the internet and there is very considerable room for improvement in this area. They are unable to understand the detailed context of a keyword, e.g. if you were looking for wood in the sense of forest, copse, or spinney, you are likely to get additional irrelevant references to golf clubs, timber, buildings, materials, etc, and in extreme cases you might not see the wood for the trees. Searches can be refined of course by adding other keywords and the use of Boolean logic in the form of and, or and not. The major problem however is caused by the explosive growth of the internet in the last few years and the sheer volume of data. A recent report in *Nature*, suggests that the search engines are currently only indexing up to about 16 per cent of the pages on the web, and the situation is likely to get worse in the short term. With approaching a billion pages on the web, and tens of thousands of additions daily, there is a huge backlog of search engine spidering and implementation of site registration submissions, which is likely to take a long time to improve. Though you should optimise your website design and search engine registration as far as possible to get publicity, there are growing numbers who feel that until significant improvements are made to search engines and to web management, the traditional publicity methods will be needed for many years to come.

Search Engine Ranking.

Search engines need to find out or to be told that your website exists and once your site has been vetted, it will be given a rank in a search engine listing for each set of keywords. The higher the ranking, the more likely you are to get users of any particular search engine to visit your site. The problem therefore resolves itself into two parts - how do you design the structure and content of your website to gain a high ranking, and how do you tell the search engines that you exist in the first place?

Obtaining a higher search engine ranking.

Search engines differ in the way they work and in the way they carry out rankings. There are however a number of steps you can take that should improve your ranking, provided of course the search engines ultimately find you, or are notified of your existence. In looking for a particular keyword or combination of keywords they will rate you on various characteristics:

▸   **Location** of a word or phrase on a web page. The higher up the page it is and the nearer it is to the start of a line of text, then the greater the ranking. i.e. give your home page a meaningful title at the top incorporating as many of your important speciality keywords as possible. e.g. Antiquarian Books on Art and Architecture. The words should be as relevant as possible to your site with the most important first. Some search engines may also prioritise alphabetically.

- **Frequency** of occurrence of a keyword on a page in relation to other words. It is fine to put Art Books, Etruscan Art, Art Deco or Arts and Crafts, etc, if art is your main subject, but do not just put Art, Art, Art, etc. This is known as spamming and most search engines are 'artful' enough to detect out-of-context words like this and may as a result give you a zero ranking or refuse to list your site.

- **Changes.** If you make frequent updates or changes to your site, this is detected by some search engines and can lead to a higher site ranking.

- **Popularity.** You should be aware that some search engines, e.g. Direct-Hit, use the popularity of a site to rank it. There is not much that you can do in this 'catch 22' situation other than using all other methods to improve your popularity as measured by the number of visitors.

- **Links.** Nearly all search engines, e.g. Excite, will rank a site in proportion to the number of incoming hyperlinks it has from other websites with important sites giving greater relevancy. One relatively easy thing that you can do for yourself, is to establish links to other dealers' sites and ask them to reciprocate.
  When I first set up my site at the end of 1998 I was not aware of any of these ranking elements, but fortuitously, as a service to my customers, I established a links page for their benefit giving details of 40 other UK bookdealers whose interests overlapped with mine, so that if I hadn't got what they wanted they could see where to go. Where other dealers had websites I set up hot hyperlinks to their sites and many reciprocated. I now find serendipitously that this helped my site. Needless to say this policy will be vigorously pursued and expanded at my next site update.

- **Site Review.** Search engines that review sites may also list them in a related directory. Such listings may give a site a ratings boost.

- There are a number of other hints and tips such as using TITLE and META tags. Details of these can be found on the web, for example on sites such as: http://www.builder.com, or http://www.search engine watch.com/, and http://www.bbc.co.uk/education/ webwise.

Telling search engines that you exist.

To do this yourself, all you do is to contact each of the main search engines, follow the procedure they give and submit your site. You should at least contact the following: Alta Vista, Yahoo, Lycos, Excite, Search.com, Snap, WebCrawler, Northern Light, HotBot, RealNames, Ask Jeeves, Go, Goggle, GoTo, Infoseek, and LookSmart. If you don't have their URLs you can find these and others on the web, e.g. at http://www.search engine watch. com/.

To get somebody to do it for you, there are a number of submission services which may be free or fee paying, e.g. try the BBC site for guidance on http://www.bbc.co.uk/education/webwise, or one of the many others such as http://www.submit-it.com, or http://www.submitit.com.

WEB PAGE AND SITE DESIGN
A few general recommendations.

Avoid the use of extensive multicoloured illustrations or maps with too much detail. These can take a long time to download to a screen and browsers may give up on your site in favour of quicker sites. Pictures can be switched off to speed things up, but then what's the point of having them. Access your own site occasionally and monitor the download time from entering your URL to the full appearance of your home page. If you get bored waiting what will others do? You should also bear in mind that you may be using a very fast modem and processor whilst others may have slower ones. There are no hard and fast rules here but you should expect your home page to be up fully in about 5 to 7 seconds. If you are proposing to put large files on your site such as catalogues containing 1,000 items or above, then break them down into smaller files first, otherwise you may find that some potential users do not have the capacity on their computer system to download them. One positive action that you can take is to include free data on your site that will be useful or valuable to a visitor.

Do not publish details of your website address until you are fully ready. There is nothing more annoying in visiting a site than finding the message *Site under construction, please try later,* or to follow a link to a page which says *This page is not yet ready.* Remember that there are many different computer systems on the market with different software, monitor sizes and screen resolutions and that what you see as a very readable page on your own website may appear less so on other systems. e.g. You may find that a whole screen on your system appears as one and a half screens elsewhere and does not provide the expected impact. A recommendation here is to check out your own website on friend's and colleague's systems and on different browsers, and make necessary alterations on a re-iterative basis. Try to avoid heavy background colours or designs. These can look attractive but can severely affect the legibility of text.

If you are starting from scratch in designing a website, there are several things you need to think about:

How many pages, their content, and how are they to be structured?

Having decided on your overall aims and objectives you now have to decide how many pages you want in your website, the individual aims, objectives and content for each page and to establish what connections or links you want between each page in a hierarchical structure. Only you can decide the precise wording you want for each page. For all practical purposes there is no upper limit on the number of pages you have, though many start with just a basic home page and add the trimmings later.

To help you to decide how many pages, their layout, content and structure, there is considerable help available to you. There is of course professional help available here for which you will have to pay but this is one stage that is best carried out by you as only you can decide what you want.

Initially, I would strongly recommend that you take a look at other bookdealers' websites to get an idea of what has been done and what is possible. Details of addresses of these can be found in various Directories of British Secondhand Bookdealers. From these you decide what features you like and print out a hard copy for reference. You don't of course have to restrict yourself to bookdealers' websites - there are millions to look at worldwide.

Secondly, it is well worth while looking at some of the many publications available, a few of which are listed at the end of this chapter. Most public libraries have large stocks of these They give excellent advice and enable you to understand the basics.

Thirdly, contact any friends or colleagues or members of your trade association who have a website and ask them for advice. I found this particularly useful as it enabled me to avoid many pitfalls.

Fourthly, look at some of the many sites on the web which are there to give you help and advice. Strongly recommended are : http://www.bbc.co.uk/education/webwise, http://www.newbie.net/, http://www.webmonkey.com, http://www.builder.com. These in turn will lead you to other sites and don't forget the tutorials on your browser software.

Before touching your keyboard, draft out in longhand the content and layout of each page unless you are one of those geniuses who can type it in directly onto a screen without thinking it through beforehand.

Producing and publishing a website.

Having thought about what you want on your website you now have to convert each page into a hypertext document, link them together and publish them on your ISP. This is done using HTML directly or an appropriate software package, and there are many ways of creating websites of which five are briefly mentioned below:

Use What You See Is What You Get Software. (WYSIWYG)

Many have created their own websites using a software design package. This is probably the cheapest and simplest method for beginners. Such packages enable you to see on your own monitor screen the layout as it will appear on the web. Some of the better-known packages are Microsoft *Frontpage 98*, Microsoft *Frontpage Express,* Adobe *PageMill 3.0*, and SoftQuad *HotMetal Pro 5.* These vary in price and in the features they provide. If you only need a simple home page, then there is no point in paying for a lot of features you never use. Look into them and at the plentiful advice available on the web. e.g. at http://home.cnet.com/ or http://www.hotwired.com/webmonkey/, or http://www.quik-free.com/tips.htm, and of course the BBC webwise site.

For a straightforward website which is perfectly adequate for most purposes, have a look at the PBFA's own site which can be found at http://dspace.dial.pipex.com/pbfa. This was created entirely from scratch by Gina Dolan the PBFA administrator using *PageMill 3.0*, and to quote Gina: 'If I can do it anyone can!'. **Hint.** Whatever package you use, check first with your ISP that they support it. *FrontPage* 98 for example has some advanced features that are not supported by all ISPs.

Learn HTML.

If you are the boffin type or enjoy an intellectual challenge then by all means learn HTML and create your pages from scratch. If you are having text only and no illustrations a simple text editor such as 'Windows - *Notepad*' will suffice or for more advanced work you will need a standard word processor such as Microsoft *'Word'* or Corel *'Wordperfect.'*. As usual there is plenty of help in the way of manuals and advice on the web.

Borrow some HTML.

Here you take a site that you like the look of, copy the details including the HTML code, and replace their text with your own. It is fairly straightforward, all you do is: Print out a copy of each page to help you decide offline, the wording that you will use to replace the existing text. For each page on your website of choice you then need to reveal the HTML codes and tags. This is done, e.g. in 'Windows 95 Internet Explorer', by clicking on **View** and then clicking on **Source**. Then save each page separately in your own word processor files. e.g. You may decide to call the home page **home**. (Great logical thinking here!). Each page however has to be saved as what is called a *text file* and to do this you add **.htm** to your file name so that you finish up with the file name **home.htm** in your word processor files. You then simply delete the original text using your word processor, being careful to leave all the HTML greater than and less than signs: <, >, (also called angled brackets) and the HTML **tags** e.g HEAD. You then replace the original text by keying in your wording. **Hint.** It is a good idea to print out each page as you save it and only delete text one line at a time and replace as you go using the hard copy as a guide. You now have a website all ready to publish on a web server.

Get professional help.

Pass your content and layout to a professional HTML programmer who will do all the work for you including inserting page links and placing it on the web with a web server. Their charges are likely to be from a few hundred pounds to well over a thousand pounds depending on the level of sophistication you aspire to. It is recommended that you keep it simple with as few illustrations as possible to start with. You can always add more later and you have to think: are you trying to make money or save on costs or are you in the business of employing programmers. **Hint.** Always ask to see sites that have been created by the professionals before deciding on one, and ask about their knowledge and experience of the secondhand book business. For advice on such professional help the following site may help you: http://www.hackney.gov.uk/library/hackbil/links891.htm#uk web design companies.

REFERENCE WORKS. (A small selection of the many in existence).
Durie, Bruce. *Creating a Web Site.* How To Books Ltd., 1998.
Jones, Graham. *Doing Business on the Internet.* How To Books Ltd., 1997
Creating Web Pages Simplified. IDG Books Worldwide Inc., 1996.
Internet and the World Wide Web Simplified. 2nd ed. IDG, 1997.
Schwartz, E.I. *Webonomics.* Penguin Books Ltd., 1997.
Smith, B. et al. *Creating Web Pages for Dummies.* 3rd ed. IDG, 1998.
Snell, Ned. Easy Web Pages. Que Corporation,1999. £18.49. Very strongly recommended if you are using Microsoft FrontPage Express.

Tittel, E. & James, S.N. *HTML 4 for Dummies.* IDG, 1998.

INTERNET BOOK AUCTIONS

During the writing of this book, notices have appeared in the trade press announcing that the major auction houses will be conducting auctions on the internet in future. Information to date has been hard to come by. In a press release issued on June 16th it was announced that Sotheby's and Amazon.com were forming a strategic auction alliance to form a joint online auction site hosted on http://www.sothebys.amazon.com with books being one of the collectibles featured. Sellers on this site will be able to market to Amazon.com's more than 10 million customers with the benefit of Sotheby's 255-year auction experience.

Sotheby's will continue with its http://www.sothebys.com site which will start offering books online this autumn, and Amazon.com will continue its auctions site Amazon.com Auctions. For further information and updates please contact the joint site or Sotheby's site.

For details of other auction house internet book auctions, please refer to their websites, details of which are in the appendix.

CHAPTER 17

THE BRITISH INTERNET BOOKDEALERS CENTRE (BIB) AND BOOK DATABASES

In the UK we are fortunate in having the experience and knowledge of Michael Cole who runs both the BIB and the Clique. The BIB was formed in April 1999 and provides the British and Irish book trade with a wide range of computer and internet-related services and publications. This chapter describes these, which are of great importance to bookdealers wishing to learn about using the internet.

British Bookdealers and the Internet.

This is an excellent 12 page A4 sized guide for British secondhand and antiquarian bookdealers considering whether or not to put their business on the internet. It is free but two first class stamps are requested to cover postage.

British Internet Bookdealers Register. **(BIB Register)**

This is an online, searchable database containing details of over 1,200 British bookdealers with an internet connection and their specialist subject areas, i.e. who deals in what and where. It is the major starting point for users around the world who are trying to find books in specialist topics in Britain. Entries are free and you can also set up a link from the register through to your own website for a small annual fee. If you have read chapter 16 you will see that there are some advantages for you in setting up such a link, with regard to search engine ranking. You can register online by accessing http://www.clique.co.uk/bibfind.htm (You will of course on this occasion 'clique' on your mouse, as they say in France!) Once you have registered, check you entry online and make sure that you update it if any of your details change in the future.

Internet Book News.

This is a quarterly, free A5 colour-printed newsletter giving brief details of new and developing book buying and selling opportunities online. Particular emphasis is placed on British bookselling websites and on booktrade and computer services.

It was first issued in July 1999, and has a circulation of approximately 5,000 within Britain including all UK bookdealers with an internet connection, book feature pages in national and local newspapers and magazines, and distribution at libraries and bookfairs. Please contact: http://www.clique.co.uk//ibnews.htm for details of how to receive your free copy.

Online Books-for-sale Databases.
There are several major online databases in the world on which individual booksellers can place books for sale and display them alongside books from fellow subscribers to the same database. Advanced Book Exchange (ABE), is an important one of these, offering a book buying and selling service on the internet. With 700,000 books for sale currently from 450 British and Irish bookdealers, and over 12 million books from over 5,000 dealers world wide, it is the most significant database for the British and Irish bookdealer as it enables the user to search the stock of either bookdealers in the British Isles alone, or bookdealers world wide. Databases such as ABE act as the booktrade's major central clearing houses for selling books online, attracting around 25,000 visitors from across the world each day searching for books for sale. A user wanting to search the database merely has to type in the database URL: http://clique.co.uk/abe.htm, the database opening page will then appear on the user's own screen. He then types in what he's looking for and within a few seconds a full catalogue description appears on screen of all copies available, from which booksellers in the world and at how much. The user then clicks on the bookseller's name to be linked by e-mail straight through to the bookseller concerned to order the book or get further details.

It's difficult to convey the power of these databases to someone who hasn't used one. However, for example, you might - as a non-internet bookdealer - be accustomed to going into a high street British bookshop and asking where the military history section is, to be directed towards maybe 8 or 9 titles. In contrast, within a couple of seconds of typing 'military' in the ABE search fork, the system has told me (July 1999) that it has found an estimated 16,994 (nearly 17 thousand) separate military entries in its records from booksellers in Britain alone and has started to list them on my screen in batches of 30. On looking on ABE world wide, over 186,000 matches were found. The search could have been refined to lessen the hit rate in just about any way required (author, title, Napoleonic, WWII, books published in the 1870s, or whatever.) Because of this, you'll appreciate that if an internet-equipped bookdealer needs military stock, or is looking for under-priced books in this field, it's probably a better use of his time to use ABE to search the world, or just Britain, from his own desk than travel on spec to a bookshop 20 miles away. Any transaction incidentally is entirely between the purchaser and the seller. ABE itself is merely the advertising medium - it takes no percentage or commission on any sales conducted through it.

You'll understand the potential of this for the booksellers who have their books on the system. Customers they've never met and otherwise wouldn't know existed now have access to details of their complete book stock 24 hours a day.

These databases also have inbuilt reporting systems where you can record your wants with the database, either specific titles or general subject areas, and the system will report to you automatically in the future by e-mail whenever any of your wants newly arrive for sale on the database from other bookdealers. Just cancel any individual want when you have no more need of it. Listing your wants on ABE costs nothing as it's a free service.

Putting your own books for sale onto ABE costs very little, somewhere between about £7 and £22 a month maximum. It's an easy process to transfer details of your own books to the main database if your books are already catalogued on database software on your own computer with built-in file compatibility. If you haven't yet started putting your books on a database then you really should start now as the advantages in all areas of bookselling are enormous. **Booklist**, an easy-to-use Books for Sale database programme with enough features for the day-to-day searching, sorting, quoting, catalogue and list printing needs of most bookdealers, and compatible with all other major booktrade services, is available from the Clique for £35. More complex databases, with built-in accounting and invoicing, are available from other suppliers for prices up to £500 or so. Alternatively, you could design your own database from proprietary database software such as Microsoft Works or Access although doing this demands considerable time and computer skills.

There are other major book databases, e.g. Bibliocity, Amazon.com, Bibliofind, etc., who work in similar ways and who will have a different range of users from ABE. It could be worthwhile later on, investigating the advantages of putting some of your stock on one or other of these. You can search all of these if you are looking to buy but you should be aware that not all searches are carried out in the same way by the different databases. Just to remind you, as mentioned in chapter 4, that there are meta search services that will look at all of these databases for you and report back, e.g. http://www.bookfinder.com will give you the results of a search for each of the major databases. You can vary the number of reports from 25 to 200 per database. This is particularly useful for buying and pricing.

Large-scale internet databases such as ABE represent a major part of bookdealing's future with far-reaching implications. In addition to the selling opportunities, they provide an enormous fund of information of what is actually taking place at any one time right across the world and which can be put to good use.

No longer need your bookdealing boundaries be constrained by the overheads of owning a retail shop or running a catalogue business where printing and distributing a couple of hundred copies of your book list or catalogue can cost you hundreds of pounds. These databases are virtually free to operate, use and access. They may not replace bookdealing in the traditional manner but they already have an enormous effect on the ways in which many bookdealers and other book buyers allocate their time and buying budget. It's also clear that they are introducing new book buyers and collectors into the book world.

Books always wanted. (BAW).

This is a recently opened site consisting of a searchable database for customers with long-term or permanent wants for authors or specific general subject areas as opposed to specific titles. If you have books for sale then you should check this site out. If you want to add your own wants to BAW then this is currently £10 for three months through to £25 for a 12 month period: http://www.clique.co.uk/bibwants.htm.

For details of other BIB and Clique services please refer to their website below.

Michael Cole
BIB: British Internet Bookdealers Centre
7 Pulleyn Drive, York, England, YO24 1DY
Tel: 01904 631 752   **Fax:** 01904 651325
E-mail: bib@clique.co.uk   **Website:** http://www.clique.co.uk/bib.htm

CHAPTER 18

LEARNING ABOUT COMPUTERS AND THE INTERNET

INTRODUCTION

Technology and advances are so rapid in this area that much that has been written or published, quickly becomes out of date, and if the history of computing, telecommunications and the internet is anything to go on, there is likely to be a great increase in the rate of acceleration of change in the future. If you are new to computing then you will need to learn at least the basics of PCs, word-processing, databases, spreadsheets, and preferably accounting/stock control packages. **Hint.** A PC with a Zip drive installed is strongly recommended to enable you to carry out daily back-ups of your data.

If you are new to the internet then you will at least need to know about electronic mail, websites, web browsers, web rings, search engines and newsgroups. You will also need to keep yourself informed so that you can take advantage of new developments, e.g. as I wrote this, an announcement appeared in the daily newspapers to the effect that BT telephone lines, as used by most people on the internet in the UK, may be upgraded shortly to be capable of much greater speeds. This will produce great savings on line time, but will your modem or other equipment be capable of taking advantage of this, and if not, what would be the cost of upgrading? How then do you go about learning in the first place, and after this, keeping yourself up-to-date?

SELF-TUITION

Most software packages are supplied ready for installation on your PC in the form of a CD-ROM. These usually have a built-in tutorial enabling you to learn how to use the package. Some also have a printed manual, usually of gradually-increasing complexity, providing guidance on most of the topics you are likely to need, and often much more. Many find it easier to work from a manual than from a CD-ROM tutorial and if the software does not come with a manual and you fall into this category, borrow one from your local library and if it suits you then buy one. To start with, it is strongly recommended that you learn about the latest Windows software, currently Windows 98, (Windows 2000 is imminent), followed by a word-processing package such as Microsoft Word 97 or Corel Wordperfect 8.

There is incidentally a vast publishing industry devoted solely to computers, software and the internet. Most public libraries have a very wide selection and I was in a major bookshop recently where they had 18 x 1m shelves devoted to websites and the internet alone and a similar amount of space devoted to other individual topics such as databases. The information is there, it is up to you to select according to your needs.

Much of what you need to learn about the web can be found on the web if you know where to look for it. Many internet sites contains tutorials on a wide range of subjects, e.g. try http://microsoft.com/insider/internet/ or http://www.learnthenet.com/english/index.html to get you started, or otherwise look at the excellent BBC Education site at http://bbc.co.uk/education/webwise/ which is probably the best available for beginners. This BBC site covers the basics of what the internet is, e-mail, choosing an ISP, website design, newsgroups, how to search the web, which search engines to use for what, and much more. A wide range of definitions is given, the answers to frequently asked questions (FAQs), and you are pointed towards many other useful URLs. You can easily spend an hour or more at this site so remember to stock up on printer paper before you start. **Hint.** If you are absolutely new to computing, it is so much easier if you can get a computer literate friend or colleague to start you off.

So much for teaching yourself, what about being taught on computing and internet courses?

COMPUTING COURSES

The UK is fortunately well endowed with educational establishments and many of these do provide a range of courses aimed at the beginner or improver in computing and the internet. Please check out your local colleges or technology centres, see what they have to offer, discuss course content with staff and enroll as required. If you already have your computer, then guess what, you can do it all on the web. Go to the BBC Education site again, click on 'net basics' followed by 'course finder' and 'map' which will bring up a UK map divided into regions. Click on your region on the map and you will get a list of all the colleges in your area offering relevant courses. Click on your college of choice and in most cases you will get a listing of all the courses on offer, their dates and fees. In general these courses tend to be specific, e.g. on PCs, Windows 95, keyboarding skills or on particular application software packages such as Access or Word. If you like what you see then follow it up. Many of these courses unfortunately do not always provide exactly what you are looking for or is needed, and there are alternatives in the form, appropriately enough, of online courses.

To find out about these, go back to 'course finder' at the BBC site again and click on 'online courses'. Currently you will be given a choice of four sites to visit. I looked at these and the Living IT range of courses looked quite interesting - http://www.living-it.org.uk/lvt/webwise.html, will give you further details. I then looked at the Open University site and found a new course they are offering on http://t171.open.ac.uk/pres. Note that their URL does not contain www.

Despite having worked for IBM for 17 years, learning how to program the 1401 in the early 1960s, (the 1401 was a computer occupying a space equivalent to the average domestic room, with a computing power several million times less than my current PC), and having had a succession of PCs during the last ten years, I feel I still have many basics to learn and need considerable updating in most areas. To quote the old chestnut - 'If you are looking for someone with a little knowledge, I have as little as anyone.' This new OU course is so exactly what is needed by many, that I forecast it will become one of their most popular courses of all time. I have already booked my place on it for next year and I would very strongly recommend it to anyone wanting to learn about computers and the internet, who should contact the OU immediately if they can't find anything locally or elsewhere online to suit them. Because of the importance of this course, and as you may not be in touch with the OU, I have obtained their permission to quote the following major extract from *The Open University Guide to Courses 1999/2000,* pages 32-33, so that you can see what is on offer:

T171 YOU, YOUR COMPUTER AND THE NET.
Description.

This is a new kind of course, designed to bring to the world wide web the supported open learning for which the Open University is famous. At the core of the course is a dynamic website to which only registered students have access. All the specially prepared teaching assessment and other material is published on the site, which grows and develops as the course progresses. The course also includes some specially written Open University booklets designed to get you started if you are new to computing, and a CD-ROM containing all the software you need to use the materials on the website. The course's aims are to:

▸ Give you an introduction to computers and the internet.
▸ Help you to develop the new skills of studying and communicating with online media.
▸ Help you to become a confident user of a personal computer both as

190

a tool in itself and as a communication device.

▶ Enable you to bridge the gap between the real world and the virtual world of cyberspace.

▶ Give you experience of working collaboratively at a distance using e-mail, conferencing and other online tools.

▶ Teach fundamental computer and internet principles.

▶ Give you a good understanding of the evolution of the personal computer and the internet.

▶ Encourage you to reflect on your learning processes in order to become a more effective learner.

Among the skills you will acquire from the course are:

▶ How to operate a personal computer and common types of software.

▶ How to communicate with electronic mail and online conferencing.

▶ How to search for material on the world wide web, and evaluate the reliability and quality of what you find.

▶ How to manage large quantities of information.

▶ How to write and publish web pages and manage a small website.

▶ How to work in a team on a collaborative project.

Behind the course is the desire to create a new generation of 'digital generalists' - people who understand the principles of the new communication and computer technologies and who feel confident about operating in cyberspace as well as in the real world. It is hoped to produce students who, because they don't suffer from fear of the unknown, are not intimidated by technology.

The course contains three modules. The first, *You: computing with confidence,* starts from the beginning and assumes that you may well be completely new to computing. It covers:

▶ Basic operating principles of a PC.

▶ The Windows 95/98 interface.

▶ Introduction to standard office-type programs for word-processing, database operations, spreadsheet calculations and simple charts and graphs.

▶ Modems, communications, using electronic mail and conferencing.

▶ Connecting to the internet.

▶ Using a web browser.

▶ Searching the world wide web for specified topics.

▶ Planning, designing and authoring web pages.

▶ 'Netiquette' and the principles of online behaviour.

Module 2 *Your Computer: the story of the PC* explains how the personal computer came to be one of the dominant technologies of our age.

It starts with the invention of the microprocessor and leads up to the present dominance of Microsoft. It is based on the book *Accidental Empires* and a website that presents a large amount of additional material, study guides, links, resources and assessment material. The module looks at the key technologies of the PC such as the microprocessor and the operating system and explains their importance and how they work. It also looks at the social implications of the IT revolution, the nature of the computer industry and the reasons behind the success and failure of computer products.

The treatment emphasizes three aspects of the story at each stage: key personalities - people such as Steve Jobs and Bill Gates who have shaped the industry; key companies, such as IBM, Apple, Microsoft and Intel, that led the revolution; and key technologies, such as the microprocessor and the graphical user interface, that determined the computers we use today.

Module 3 *The net: where it came from, what it is* describes the evolution of the internet from its origins in the inter-war years to the explosive growth of the world wide web in the 1990s. It is based on the book *Where Wizards Stay Up Late: the Origins of the Internet* and, again, a large amount of additional material is presented on the website. The module covers the history of the net in four stages:

- Prehistory: the evolution of ideas about computing from the 1930s to the 1960s.
- The ARPANET: the creation of the first packet-switched wide-area network.
- From ARPANET to internet: the metamorphosis of the original ARPANET concept into the 'global network of networks' that constitutes today's internet.
- The world wide web: the evolution of the web from its invention in 1989 to its present form.

Three aspects are again emphasized at each stage: key personalities - the people who made it happen; key institutions - the organizations in which they worked; and key ideas - the principles underlying the design at various stages.

Tuition and counselling.

The course is taught entirely online. You will have a personal tutor, available through electronic mail, and you will be a member of a tutorial group and of a team working on collaborative assignments. You will have intensive communications with your tutor, fellow-students and the course team at Walton Hall (where the OU is based) through e-mail and conferencing. Much of the technical material is taught through riveting stories about how the modern world was created.

Assessment.

There are four tutor-marked assignments and a consolidation exercise at the end of the course. All assignments are submitted and marked electronically. At each stage you will have the opportunity to work on your own or in a small group, and there are different assessment strategies for each option. There is no examination and no summer school.

Qualifications.

This is a Level 1 course, which makes intellectual demands appropriate to the first year of undergraduate study. It can count towards either a BA or BSc degree if required but can be taken as a one-off course. It is a half credit or 30 point course - six credits are needed for a degree.

You will need.

A personal computer with a minimum specification as described in the OU leaflet *Personal Computing for OU Study 1999/2000.* You will also need an account with an ISP to give you regular access to the internet. The Open University can act as your ISP for this course if you haven't already got an account. Because of the nature of the course you should be prepared to spend significant amounts of time online. (Several hours per week.) This will mean extra charges to your telephone bill.

Set books to buy (1999 prices)

R.X.Cringely *Accidental Empires*, reprinted with new material, Penguin, £8.99

K. Hafner, M. Lyon *Where Wizards Stay Up Late: the Origins of the Internet,* Simon and Schuster, £8.99

To Register.

You do not have to be an existing OU student or graduate and no prior qualifications are needed. You should contact:

Registration and Fees Centre, The Open University, PO Box 197, Walton Hall, Milton Keynes, MK7 6BJ **Tel:** 01908 653454 **Fax:** 01908 654914 **E-mail:** reg-fees@open.ac.uk

Most OU courses run from February to October each year and registration is usually in the spring or summer of the preceding year. Because of the unique nature of the OU and this course, anyone in the world with an appropriate PC and ISP can register. The OU expect to offer the course until at least 2006. After this there will hopefully be an updated replacement course. The current course fees (1999 for 2000) are: UK: £195, Eire: £385, other EC countries: £560, rest of the world: £765.

If at any time you would like some direct feedback on the course please feel free to contact me anytime from the summer of 2000 onwards.

For most, the course is likely to be a combination of both learning and refreshing. I have great expectations that the course will refresh parts that other courses haven't reached.

If you have an interest in the history of the internet, whether or not you take T171 or read the set books, there is of course plenty of information on the web ready for you to find. To start you off, try accessing http://www.microsoft.com/insider/internet/articles/history.htm This will give you a brief introduction. If you'd like more technical detail then go to the Internet Society site: http://isoc.org/internet-history/brief.html where you will find a 17 page history, or there are others on the BBC Education site.

KEEP UP TO DATE

Apart from courses or surfing the web, one of your best ways of keeping informed is to be in touch with the British Internet Bookdealers Centre as indicated in the previous chapter, and subscribe to their *Internet Book News*. Trade association newsletters should keep you posted on new developments. Read the book trade press, e.g. the *Bookdealer* and look at the computer and internet weekly and monthly periodicals from time to time. As a snapshot I picked up three at random in my local newsagents and came up with: *PC Computing,* July 1999 (£2.95) with an article on 'Search Engine Secrets.' *PC Direct*, August 1999 (£2.25) contains: 'Guide to Buying Web publishing software' with a comparison of 14 different packages; and *PC Advisor* August 1999 (£2.99), has an article on 'Windows 2000,' the Windows 98 replacement, and another on the '100 best websites' for finding information on the web. Finally don't forget the daily newspapers, e.g. *The Times* has a weekly Wednesday internet supplement - 'Inter//face'.

SUMMARY

Apart from the appendix this completes everything. If you have read this far, thank you for doing so, and may I wish you well in your business. If you have any comments, constructive, critical or otherwise, or on sins of omission, please feel free to let me know, so that future editions can benefit.

TAILPIECE TO PART III

There are many other aspects to life other than business, covering social activities, enjoyment and relaxation. The web is an inexhaustible source of information in these and many other areas. On the next page, is one such item which appeared on the web recently and is of great historical significance to bibliophiles.

Announcing the new **B**uilt-in **O**rderly **O**rganized **K**nowledge device: **BOOK**

BOOK is a revolutionary breakthrough in technology: no wires, no electric circuits or microchips, no batteries, nothing to be connected or switched on, and it is so easy to use that even a child can operate it. There is no warm-up time, just lift it and you have instant access. Compact and portable, it can be used anywhere - even sitting in an armchair or in the bathroom - yet it is powerful enough to hold as much information as a CD-ROM.

Here's how it works: each BOOK is constructed of sequentially numbered sheets or pages of paper (recyclable), each able to hold thousands of bits of information. These sheets are held together, forming a random-access file, by a custom-fitted device called *cover* which keeps sheets in the correct sequence. *Cover* is available in two versions of differing durability - *hardwear* and *softwear*. Whilst large issues of the latter are known as *macrosoft*, no name has yet been devised for small issues. By pre-formatting and recording on both sides of each sheet, i.e. in double density, manufacturers are able to keep costs to a minimum. Recording only takes place above a certain level on each page referred to as the *database*. Each sheet is scanned optically, (automatic scroll is standard), registering and transferring information directly into the brain. Recording can be at a larger scale for use where optical scanners are on the *blink*. For ease of scanning, adjacent pages are laid flat - a state known as *spreadsheet*. A built-in elementary digital device: *finger*, takes you to the next sheet without the need for a mouse.

The operating system enables BOOK to be taken up at any time and used with the simple command: *open*. Students, graduates, and staff of the Open University have been known to use the command *sesame* with equal success. The *browse* feature allows you to move instantly to any sheet, and move backwards or forwards as you wish. Most come with a *search engine* called *index*, which pinpoints the exact location of any selected information for instant retrieval. An optional BOOKmark accessory allows you to open BOOK at the exact place you left it in a previous session, without the need for a *save* command, even if BOOK had been closed in the meantime.

It is forecast that the future will see ever-increasing collections of BOOKs in the public domain, and that following on from this trend, **L**ending **I**nformation in **B**ooks giving **R**apid **A**ccess to **R**eaders of all **Y**ears, will catch on. The term **LIBRARY** is suggested for this.

Portable, durable and affordable, the BOOK is seen to be the entertainment technology of the future, and many new titles are expected soon, largely due to the user friendliness of its programming tool, the **P**ortable **E**rasable-**N**ib **C**ryptic **I**ntercommunication **L**anguage Stylus.

BOOK can truly open *gates* for you and let *windows* into your life.

Anon. but attributed to a William Caxton c.1476.

APPENDIX

PHONE AND FAX. NUMBERS
(Overseas callers should use the code: +44 to replace the initial 0)
NB A number of UK phone area codes changed in 1999.
e.g. Old London area code 0171 is now 0207 and 0181 is now 0208.

BOOK AUCTION HOUSES
Bloomsbury Book Auctions, 3 & 4 Hardwick Street, off Rosebery Avenue, London, EC1R 4RY
Tel: 0207 833 2636/7 & 0207 636 1945 **Fax:** 0207 833 3854
E-mail: info@bloomsbury-book-auct.com
Website: http://www.bloomsbury-book-auct.com
Bonhams, Montpelier Street, London, SW7 1HH.
Tel: 0207 393 3900 **Fax:** 0207 393 3905
Website: http://www.Bonhams.com/
Christie's, 8 King Street, St. James's, London, SW1Y 6QT
Tel: 0207 839 9060, **Fax:** 0207 976 2832
Website: http://www.christies.com
Christie's South Kensington, 85 Old Brompton Road, London, SW7 3LD
Tel: 0207 581 7611 **Fax:** 02071 321 3321
Website: http://www.christies.com
Dominic Winter Book Auctions, The Old School, Maxwell Street, Swindon, Wiltshire, SN1 5DR **Tel:** 01793 611340 **Fax:** 01793 491727
E-mail: info@dominic-winter.co.uk
Website: http://www.dominic-winter.co
Sotheby's, 34-35 New Bond Street, London, W1A 2AA
Tel: 0207 293 5000 **Fax:** 0207 293 5989
Website: http://www.sothebys.com
Phillips, 101 New Bond Street, London, W1Y 0AS
Tel: 0207 629 6602 **Fax:** 0207 629 8876
Website: http://www.phillips-auction.com/
Y Gelli Auctions, Y Gelli Chambers, Broad Street, Hay-on-Wye, via Hereford, HR3 5DB
Tel: 01497 821179 **Fax:** 01497 820978

BUSINESS AGENCIES: GENERAL HELP FOR SMALL FIRMS
Before starting in business you should be aware that there is a great deal of help, much of it free, to help you with your enterprise. This ranges

from advice on working from home or the legal structure of your business, help with business planning or sources of finance, information technology, to training for yourself, and a multiplicity of other topics such as marketing. **Business Link.**

This is a national network of organisations providing partnerships between the local business community and the Government. Organisations involved include Local Authorities, Chambers of Commerce, Training and Enterprise Councils (TECs), or Local Enterprise Councils (LECs in Scotland) and most importantly Enterprise Agencies. The Enterprise Agencies offer advice and training for business start-ups and running.

To contact your local Business Link please look at the directory on their website: http://www.businesslink.co.uk or call 0345 567765. You will be put in touch with other organisations as appropriate and a Personal Business Adviser. For Enterprise Agencies please phone: 01234 354055.

Business Connect.

This is the Welsh equivalent of Business Link, operating from 30 centres across Wales. Advice is obtainable on **Tel:** 0345 969798

Scottish Business Shop Network.

A network of 38 locations offering help and information to new and existing businesses. **Tel:** 0800 787878

Department of Trade and Industry. Tel: 0207 215 5000

Website: http://www.dti.gov.uk

Please phone to obtain copies of the following booklets:

A Guide to Help for Small Firms   Ref. URN 95/569

Make the Cash Flow   Ref. URN 94/553

Small and Medium Enterprise Policy Unit. Tel: 0114 259 7535

FINANCE

For advice on sources of finance and finance management please contact your nearest Business Link or equivalent.

Small Firms Loan Guarantee Scheme (SFLGS)

This unfortunately it does not apply to retail businesses or to any business where sales are direct to the ultimate end user. This rules out book-fairs, catalogue bookselling and shops; however if you are proposing to set up a wholesale bookselling operation then it does apply. It operates as follows: If you prepare a business plan as outlined in part **II** and present it to a bank as your first choice as a source of finance, the bank may say that it is viable but that because of your lack of security they are not prepared to lend you the money. In such cases, under the SFLGS the Government may guarantee most of the loan. e.g. for new businesses you may borrow up to

£100,000 with the Government guaranteeing 70% of this. The average loan is of the order of £33,000 and most repayments are spread over a period of 2 to 7 years. There may also be a capital repayment delay or holiday for up to two years. Interest charges start the moment the loan is approved.

The Late Payment of Commercial Debts (Interest) Act 1998: A User's Guide. This guide (reference URN98/823), explains how and when the Act works and it can be obtained free from the DTI. An important Act for small businesses as at last they can legally charge interest on overdue accounts. This is a significant help to improving cashflow. In conjunction with this another free guide is also strongly recommended: ***Better Payment Practice. Your guide to paying and being paid on time.*** Ref. URN98/965

LEGAL HELP

Contact **Lawyers for Small Business. Tel:** 0207 405 9075, or the Law Society **website:** http://www.lfyb.lawsociety.org.uk

MAILING LABELS

If you are going to carry out a direct mail campaign as mentioned briefly in chapter 7 on 'Publicity', then you will need mailing lists. The Post Office will provide details of commercial list suppliers. The following two are just given as examples.

Library Association Publishing, 7 Ridgmount Street, London, WC1E 7AE **Tel:** 0207 636 7543 **Fax:** 0207 636 3627
E-mail: lapublishing@la-hq.org.uk
Website: http://www.la-hq.org.uk/lapublishing

Details are available of Libraries in the UK ranging from a full set of 2670 labels addresses to a named Chief Librarian, currently at £320 plus VAT, to 297 named Schools Officers at £65 plus VAT.

Mardev, Quadrant House, The Quadrant, Sutton, Surrey, SM2 5AS **Tel:** 0208 643 0955 **Fax:** 0208 652 4580
E-mail: mardevlists@rbi.co.uk **Website:** http://www.mardevlists.com

Mardev have over 30 million names spread across more than 300 lists covering business, academia and science including book buyers. I used *IBIS*, one of their divisions, for many years in marketing my former manufacturing business and found them highly professional and up-to-date. To see what they have to offer they will supply you with a floppy disk called *ListSearch* for your computer. This is an interactive guide to their portfolio of lists and databases.

N.B. The UK postal authorities specify that the Postcode should be the **last** item of your address, and that the town or area should appear on the envelope in capitals. If you are planning to export or to have a website then the postcode should appear after say, England or U K on your stationery or website. e.g. A.R.F. Calf, 7 Bookdale, LIBTOWN, England, LB2 4GJ. Many businesses are either not aware of this or choose to ignore it. As it can help to speed the mail, its use is commended to improve your efficiency.

REFERENCE PUBLICATIONS

These are in addition to those given in chapters 8 and 16.

Croner Publications Limited, Croner House, London Road, Kingston upon Thames, Surrey, KT2 6SR **Tel:** 0208 547 3333 Publishers of:

Croner's Reference Book for the Self Employed and Smaller Businesses. An excellent reference work covering the important legislation affecting small business in a readily digestible form. e.g. Taxation, National Insurance, Employment, Health and Safety, Consumer Law, and Company Law. It also has a very useful section on sources of finance. It comes in a loose-leaf ring binder, and is available on annual subscription which includes frequent updates during the year. It is strongly recommended that you at least look at a copy in the reference section of your local public lending library while you are at the planning stage of your business.

Business Start-up Guide. A Guide to Businesses in Scotland. Obtainable free through the Scottish Business Shop Network for those in Scotland.

What to Buy for Business, Room L316, Quadrant House, The Quadrant, Sutton Surrey, SM2 5AS **Tel:** 0208 652 8700 **Fax:** 0208 770 1284 **Website:** http://www.whattobuyforbusiness.co.uk

This is a monthly publication containing independent reports of equipment and services likely to be of interest to any small business. It is like the consumer magazine *Which* but covers business products only, such as recommendations on the best buys for PCs, phone systems, health insurance, mobile phones, computer software, fax machines, office furniture, etc. It is well worth subscribing for a year as discounts are available and one-off back issues can also be purchased. The current annual subscription is £130 and by following their advice you can easily save this on one purchase. If after 60 days you are not satisfied, a full refund is available, and a partial refund after this time. Special introductory offers are available from time to time. Details of subjects covered and information on key markets are available on their website.

SUPPLIES

Book-Cloth Cleaner.

Edgar Backus, 22 Fairefield Crescent, Glenfield, Leicester, LE3 8EH **Tel:**

0116 287 1095 Half litre canister: £9.50 including postage and VAT. Leather Binding Polish is also available at the same price and size.

Label , Glue, and Foxing Removers, Page and Jacket Repairs.
PaperSafe, 2 Green Bank, Adderley, Market Drayton, Shropshire, TF9 3TH **Tel:** 01630 652217 **Fax:** 0870 0548747
E-mail: philip@papersafe.demon.co.uk

Leather Cream.
Liberon Waxes Ltd., Mountfield Industrial Estate, Learoyd Road, New Romsey, Kent, TN28 8XU **Tel:** 01797 367555.

Suppliers of neutral leather cream in 250ml dispenser containers. It can be purchased direct but is cheaper to phone them to ask for your local stockist as they have a minimum order value postal charge.

Printed Plastic and other Bags.

Trade Associations will provide these free to their members at book-fairs for customers to take purchases away in. They may be purchased at standard prices for use at other times. If you would like personalised bags for your own business, there are a number of manufacturers who specialise in this work. Your trade organisation or local reference library, will be able to put you in touch with these. One such firm had the initiative and good timing to send me a sample just as I was writing this so their details have been included here:

Templecoombe Limited, The Old Maltings, High Street, Olney, Bucks, MK46 4BE Tel: 01234 712121/241777 Fax: 01234 241888

A number of bookdealers provide their customers with very substantial carrier bags made of a heavy duty cloth with their details printed on. These are most useful, are works of art in their own right, are unlikely ever to be thrown away, and form a permanent reminder of and advertisement for the dealers concerned.

MISCELLANEOUS
Computer Supplier and Website Design
CMX Computers Limited, BWP House, Dedham Road, Ardleigh, Colchester, Essex, CO7 7LD. **Tel:** 01206 231789 or 01473 231800
Fax: 01206 231802 **E-mail:** cmx @dial.pipex.com
A firm I can recommend through personal contact, as having excellent technical competence and a superb service, with many years of experience.

The Data Protection Registrar.
The Office of the Data Protection Registrar, Wycliffe House, Water Lane, Wilmslow, Cheshire, SK9 5AF **Tel:** (Information) 01625 545 745; (To register) 01625 545 740

Fax: 01625 524 510 **E-mail:** data@wycliffe.demon.co.uk
Website: http://www.open.gov.uk/dpr/dprhome/htm

Under the terms of the 1984 and 1988 *Data Protection Acts* in the UK, you are required to register if you keep records of individuals (customers, suppliers etc.), either on your computer or in any other form such as record cards or written notes. The data need only include a name and address for the *Acts* to apply. A standard fee for registration (£75 currently), covers three years and failure to register can involve you in a penalty of up to £5,000 or more.

Domain Name Registration, Website Design and Implementation
Allan Edwards, Oxygen Limited, Tel: 01268 459396 **Fax:** 0870 0882384
E-mail: info@02.co.uk   **Website:** http://www.o2.co.uk

Oxygen are a young consultancy specialising in working with small and medium sized businesses to use technology for marketing and profitability. The Oxygen team will work with you to get the technology right for your needs, from PC and Printer upgrades, to office automation, custom databases and internet sites.

If you are developing an internet site, Oxygen will work with you, from defining your plans, registering your site name, choosing an ISP, to setting up your software, and designing, building and promoting your site.

This a firm that I can recommend, having had excellent personal experience of their services and knowledge.

Savings on Phone Calls.

There are a multiplicity of offers at any one time from many different firms e.g. BT, Mercury, etc. An example of one recent one that could be worth looking into is:

Telecom Plus plc, Dryden House, The Edge Business Centre, Humber Road, London, NW2 6EW **Tel:** 0208 955 5555
Website: http://www.telecomplus.co.uk

Video Arts Ltd., Dumbarton House, 68 Oxford Street, London, W1N 0LH
Tel: 0171 637 7288   Fax: 0171 580 8103
Video: *How Not To Exhibit Yourself.*
Booklet: *What every exhibitor ought to know*.

Year 2000 Compliance (The Millennium Bug).

If you have an older computer or other equipment with a microchip, then you need to take immediate action to avoid potential problems which could severely impact your business.

Contact your local business agency for advice, or phone the Millennium bug hotline on **Tel:** 0845 601 2000 or visit their **Website:** http://www.bug2000.co.uk

Press Release Example

One

Baldwin's Scientific Books

9th July 1999   **PRESS RELEASE**

UNIQUE NEW BOOK FOR SECONDHAND
BOOKDEALERS AND BUSINESS START-UPS

Stuart Baldwin has written **'A Beginner's Guide to Secondhand Bookdealing'**, giving for the first time a unique, detailed description of what is needed to start and run a successful secondhand book business. It is being published by the author on Friday September 17th at the 1999 Provincial Booksellers Fairs Association (PBFA) National Book-fair at the Barbican Centre, York - Britain's largest book-fair - where he is also an exhibitor. Over the centuries there have been many books written for booklovers and collectors, but there has never been an in-depth study for bookdealers or beginners giving the practical details of the trade. Stuart's book fills this large gap.

It is aimed at four main groups: those wanting to start in business; those who would like to convert a book collecting hobby into a full or part-time enterprise; those recently made redundant or retired early who would like to put their nest-egg to profitable use; and existing bookdealers who would like to know more about using the internet profitably, training staff or expanding their businesses.

Topics in Part I include the various options available (including chapters on book-fairs and catalogue bookselling), where to obtain stock, pricing and pricing policy, how to publicise yourself and your business, trade organisations, publications and reference works, and simple repairs. Part II provides detailed guidance on business planning for both starting and running a small business with the emphasis on cashflow and profit, and how to present a case for finance to a bank manager. Part III gives an introduction to the internet, covering e-mails, designing, using, and publicising your own website, and the importance of online book databases in bookdealing on the world wide web. An appendix gives many sources of further information and help, e.g. Business Link. Tailpieces to chapters provide a little light relief.

More follows

Two

The author, who runs a large secondhand bookshop specialising in the sciences with over 350,000 items in stock, built his business from a hobby. He issues catalogues and has a background in electrical engineering, pharmacy, computing, manufacturing and palaeontology. He is also a specialist in helping business start-ups, having spent two years with the London Enterprise Agency as their first small firms adviser, and 16 years as visiting university lecturer, during which time he helped well over a thousand individuals to start their own businesses. This is the fifth book he has written (or co-authored), and published, and it incorporates over 50 years business experience with some 30 in bookdealing.

Hardback with dust jacket, coloured frontispiece, illustrated, about 220 pages.
ISBN   0   9508063   5   8   September   1999   **£24**

End

For further information, please contact Stuart Baldwin:

Phone day:	01376 583502
Phone evening:	01621 891526
Fax:	01376 585960
E-mail:	sbaldwin@fossilbooks.co.uk

Stuart A. Baldwin, BSc (Open), FGS, FLS

Baldwin's Scientific Books (P.B.F.A.),   VAT No. 219 1793 51
Fossil Hall, Boars Tye Road, Silver End, Witham, Essex, England, CM8 3QA
Telephone: (01376) 583502   Facsimile: (01376) 585960
E-mail: sbaldwin@fossilbooks.co.uk   Website: http://www.fossilbooks.co.uk

New, secondhand & antiquarian books, journals, maps & offprints on Geology, Earth Sciences, Palaeontology, Natural History, Science, Mathematics, Archaeology, Anthropology, Biography, Evolution, Botany, Zoology, etc.

Start-up budget check-list.

Items	Cost excl. VAT	Month ordered	Month delivered (VAT input)	VAT	Price incl. VAT	Month for payment	Cashflow forecast entry line
Premises							Capital item
Solicitor fees							Legal fees
Lighting equipment							Capital item
Heating equipment							Capital item
Water heating/toilets							Capital item
Ventilation equip.							Capital item
Gas installation							Heat/light/power
Electricity supply							Heat/Light/Power
Telephone/fax m/c							Capital item
Redecoration							Repairs/Renewals
Repairs/alterations							Repairs/Renewals
Office Equipment etc.							Capital item
Desks/tables etc							Capital item
Bookshelving etc							Capital item
Floor coverings							Capital item
Typewriter							Capital item
Tel. answering m/c							Capital item
Mobile phone							Capital item
Cash box/register							Capital item
Weighing m/c - letters							Capital item
Weighing m/c - parcels							Capital item
Fire extinguishers							Capital item
Packaging equipment							Capital item
Photocopier							Capital item
First aid case							Capital item
Reference books							Capital item
Account books							Printing/stationery
Computer/software							Capital item
Stationery							Printing/stationery
Vehicles							Capital item
Book Stock							Trade creditors
Other							

·Annual Personal Living Expenses.

	Qtr 1	Qtr 2	Qtr 3	Qtr 4	Year
Electricity					
Gas					
Telephone					
Rates					
Water Rates					
Food, drink, etc.					
Clothes					
House maintenance					
Recreation/hobbies					
Motoring expenses including tax and insurance					
Fares					
Holidays					
Mortgage Payments or rent					
House insurance					
Other insurances					
Spending money/presents					
Health care, prescriptions, dental charges, vet fees					
School fees, night school fees, etc.					
TV & video licence/servicing/hire					
Other					
TOTAL EXPENSES (A)					**£xx,xxx**

Other income (Annual)

Spouse's earnings after deductions	
Any pensions after deductions	
Any other net income, e.g. shares, etc.	
TOTAL OTHER INCOME (B)	**£yy,yyy**

NET DRAWINGS NEEDED FROM BUSINESS (A - B)	**£zz,zzz**

INDEX

Publisher's Advertisement

Publisher's Advertisement

NEW REMAINDERS

Postage, packing and insurance is extra at cost. **J = with dustjacket; P = Paperback.**

A. ROYAL SOCIETY PUBLICATIONS

1. Proceedings of Discussion Meetings.

All mint 4to hardbacks except where otherwise described.

No.	1st Author/Ed.	Description	Original Price	Our Price
R1	Potter, W.G.	Biotechnology: Spinks Eight Years On. Pages 173, 1989.	£55	£8
R2	Turner, G..	Diffuse Matter in the Solar System... 199, J, 1987.	£55	£8
R3	Laughton, A.S.	Disposal of Highly Radioactive Waste. 187, J, 1986	£50	£8
R4	Holliday, R.	DNA Methylation & Gene Regulation. 160, 1990.	£45	£8
R5	Cadogan, J.I.G.	Environmental Effects of North Sea Oil and Gas Developments. 217, J, 1987.	£55	£8
R6	Fersht, A.R.	Enzymic Catalysis. 78, J, 1991.	£40	£5
R7	Cox, D.R.	Epidemiological & Statistical Aspects of the Aids Epidemic. 149, P, 1989.	£37.50	£7
R8	Hirsch, P,	The Fast-Neutron Breeder Fission Reactor. 163, J, 1990.	£40	£8
R9	Clarke, B.C.	Frequency-Dependent Selection. 182, J, 1988.	£45	£8
R10	Chengfa, C.	The Geological Evolution of Tibet. 413, J, 1988.	£110	£20
R11	Harper, J.L.	The Growth & Form of Modular Organisms. 250, J, 1986.	£65	£8
R12	Green, M.H.L.	The Influence of Organometallic Chemistry on Organic Synthesis... 151, 1988.	£35	£7
R13	Berridge, M.J.	Inisitol Lipids & Transmembrane Signalling. 199, 1988.	£55	£8
R14	Pease, R.S.	The JET Project and the prospects for controlled nuclear fusion. 211, 1987.	£55	£10
R15	Laws, R.M.	Life at Low Temperatures. 176, J, 1990.	£50	£8
R16	Beynon, G..	The magnetosphere, the high-latitude ionosphere, and their interactions. 251, 1989.	£65	£10
R17	Kornberg, H.	Microbial Membrane Transport Systems. 173, 1990.	£45	£8
R18	Leaver, C.J.	Mitochondrial Biogenesis. 124, J, 1988.	£35	£10
R19	Midwinter, J.E.	Optical Technology and Wideband Local Networks.152, J, 1989.	£40	£8
R20	Litherland, A.E.	Ultra-High-Sensitivity Mass Spectrometry with Accelerators. 172, J, 1987.	£40	£8
R21	Battarbee, R.W.	Palaeolimnology and Lake Acidification. 219, J, 1990	£50	£8
R22	Edwards, J.H.	The Prevention & Avoidance of Genetic Disease. 157, 1988.	£40	£8
R23	Cox, D.R.	Complex Stochastic Systems. 307-428, 8vo, P, 1991	£22.95	£5
R24	O'Nions, R.K.	Seismic Tomography & Mantle Circulation. 152, J, 1989.	£45	£8
R25	McLaren, A.	Sex Determination in Mouse & Man. 157, 1988.	£45	£8
R26	Runcorn, S.K.	The Solar System: Chemistry as a Key to its Origin. 251, 1988.	£65	£15

R27	Carrington, A.	The Spectroscopy of Molecular Ions. 220, J, 1988.	£60	£8
R28	Mansfield, P.	NMR Imaging. 170, 8vo, J, 1990.	£37.50	£5
R29	Dewey, J.F.	Allochthonous Terranes. 199, 4to, 1991.	£35	£5
R30	Pyle, J.A.	Studies of the Middle Atmosphere. 185, J, 1987.	£45	£7

2. The Correspondence of Isaac Newton edited by J.F.Scott, A. Rupert Hall & Laura Tilling.
R31   Volumes 4-7, (1694-1727) Roy. 8vo, mint with J. 1967-1977. Published at £295.   £75

3. Philosophical Transactions of the Royal Society.
We have recently purchased the complete back stock of the Royal Society from 1914 back to 1803. There are no complete runs but in many cases complete volumes and part volumes. Specific enquiries are invited. A complete stock list will be available in due course. Volumes from 1880 are mostly hardbound. Prices range from £15 to £100+ each. We will also quote for disbinding individual articles on request and also have many offprints. Some of these are in catalogues 12 (Vertebrates) & 13 (Mining, mineralogy etc).

4. Proceedings of the Royal Society Series B: Biological Sciences.
We have also recently purchased the back stock for the first half of this century. (About 2 tonnes) Specific enquiries are invited. Multiple copies are available. A list will be available in due course. Prices range from about £2 - £10 per issue.

B. OTHER PUBLICATIONS. All mint hardbacks and **8vo** except where otherwise described.

R32	Mitchell, M	History of the British Optical Association 1895-1978. pp 308, [nd] but 1982.	£20	£4
R33	Hawksworth.C.J.	Continental Basalts & Mantle Zenoliths. 272, 1983	£18	£4
R34	Hawksworth, C.J.	Continental Basalts & Mantle Zenoliths. P. 1983.	£12	£2
R35	Stace, H.B.	Natural Science Collections in Scotland. 373, 4to, P, 1987.	£25	£6
R36	Open University	S365 Evolution A Biological and Palaeontological Approach. Book 1. Ch 1-4. 195, P, 1992	£14	£2
R37	Open University	S365 Evolution Book 5. Ch 12-13. 112, P, 1992	£12	£3
R38	Open University	S365 Evolution Book 7. Ch. 16-17. 159, P, 1992	£14	£3
R39	Oldroyd, D.R.	The Highlands Controversy. (19C Geology) 438, P, 1990.	£24	£5
R40	Cleevely, R.J.	World Palaeontological Collections. 365, 4to, 1983.	£50	£18
R41	Ager, D.V.	The Geology of Europe. 535, 1980.	£30	£15

R42   THOMAS, J.M. & PHILLIPS, D. (eds.) Selections and Reflections: The Legacy of Sir Lawrence Bragg. Frontis., [viii], 308, illustrated, 8vo, hardback with dust jacket, Royal Institution, London, 1990. **Mint.** [£18.50]   Our price **£8**
Lawrence Bragg, the youngest ever Nobel Laureate, was one of the most successful scientists of all time and is remembered in this work by those who knew him, particularly by ten Nobel Laureates who were influenced by him. In Earth Sciences he is revered at the founder of X-ray Crystallography.

Substantial trade discounts are available on multiple copies of any one item.

A selection of the remainders stocked by Baldwin's Scientific Books

PROVINCIAL BY NAME

For 25 years the Provincial Booksellers Fairs Association has been organising book fairs - large fairs, small fairs, fairs in the North and fairs in the South. But large or small and wherever located a PBFA book fair stands out by its quality - quality of presentation, quality of organisation and quality of stock offered.

All PBFA members are established bookdealers who abide by a code of practice and trading details are readily available in the Directory of Members available at £3.00 (p + p extra). Nor is our membership restricted to UK dealers. We have a number of North American members and have been encouraged by the number of European booksellers who have joined us and regularly exhibit at our fairs. All are very welcome.

Our fairs in the Hotel Russell have a well-deserved reputation as **the** place to buy books in London, and in recent years we have added to our events for the specialist dealer and collector. Our Natural History & Gardening Book Fair at the London Zoo attracts buyers from all over the world and the latest venture, the Travel Book Fair at the Royal Geographical Society, is fast becoming similarly well-established and our Performing Arts fair continues at the National Theatre twice a year. In late 1999 we hold our first fair devoted to the flourishing Private Presses and the Art of the Book and in 2000 we introduce a Sporting Book Fair, specialising in all kinds of sports.

WORLDWIDE BY REPUTATION

PBFA Members have

The support of a national association

Recognition and respect within the trade and the bookbuying public

The chance to exhibit at book fairs throughout the country

Free advertising through our national directory and on our website

Discount schemes on essential services - postal, insurance, credit card processing

Discounts on essential equipment - bookshelves, software

Access to up-to-date information on the trade via a regular newsletter

If you are serious about bookselling
you should seriously consider the PBFA

Further details of all our book fairs or membership of the Provincial Booksellers Fairs Association is available on request from: PBFA, The Old Coach House, 16 Melbourn Street, Royston SG8 7BZ. Tel: 01763 248400; Fax: 01763 248921. e-mail: pbfa@dial.pipex.com Web site: http://dspace.dial.pipex.com/pbfa